JOURNEY INTO THE MIRACULOUS

Todd Bentley: An Ordinary Man
Touched By A Supernatural God

Todd Bentley
with Jackie Macgirvin

Foreword by Wesley and Stacey Campbell

Edited by Kevin Paterson

Printed by Hemlock Printers Ltd.
Suite 320
1070 Douglas Street
Victoria, BC, Canada V8W 2C4

Published by Sound of Fire Productions Ltd.

Cover design by Dan Brennan
Text layout by Aquarius Design; revisions by Dan Brennan

Printed in Canada

For order information contact:
Sound of Fire Productions Ltd.
Box 1163, Ladysmith, BC, Canada
soundoffire@shaw.ca

To order on line go to:
www.freshfire.ca

ISBN 0-9733874-0-8
Spiritual Life/Christian Living/Autobiography

The New King James Version of the bible has been used for all scripture references.

Individual testimonies and revival reports may have been edited for space or language. However, the content or message has not been changed.

Dedication

I dedicate this book to my wife, Shonnah, and my three wonderful children—Lauralee, Esther and Elijah—who lovingly sacrifice me to the world. This is their story too. My family helps Jesus to shine through me.

Acknowledgements

I want to thank the following people for sowing into my life:

The Holy Spirit for incredible seasons of visitation.

My mom and dad — what a joy that God has turned the heart of the father to the heart of his son.

Henry and Erica Schmidt — you were my first real pastors. You looked beyond my biker exterior.

Cliff Robertson, who helped lay Fresh Fire's foundation. Thanks for your love too, bro.

My prophetic mentors — Bobby Connor, Patricia King, Bob Jones, Wesley and Stacey Campbell and Paul Keith Davis. How could I avoid success with input from such godly, anointed friends?

Thank goodness for Bonnie Jaggard, the intercessors and their prayer. They are the true secret of my success.

My hard working, awesome office staff that keep things functioning when I'm on the road.

The many anointed speakers I've had the privilege of working with.

The body of Christ, God's wonderful people.

The following people who contributed reports or photos to this book: Greg Babish, Daniel Brennan, Greg Dennison, Ken Greter, Brian Hill, Dave Mercer, Clif Pash, BB Rail, Ivan Roman, Steve Schultz, Jeff Vosgien and Claudia Wintoch.

Finally, Jackie Macgirvin who assembled this book for me, Kevin Paterson for the hours of editing and proofreading and Darcia Bentley who took care of all the many publishing details.

Endorsements

"Todd Bentley's life story will inspire faith and courage. What an amazing story of God's mercy and power. Read it and then give it to a friend. Todd has ministered in several of our conferences in Kansas City. I have seen the Holy Spirit move powerfully through him as we have witnessed a number of dramatic healings. The Lord has graciously released an unusual anointing for healing in his ministry. I enjoy Todd and support his ministry. I know you will be blessed by his story and ministry."

Mike Bickle, Best selling author, Director of The International House of Prayer, Kansas City, MO

"I love Todd Bentley's ministry and everything about it. Rarely have I seen such a gift of faith in operation almost all the time. His faith is so contagious. When you're under Todd's ministry, you feel like you can go anywhere and do anything. No problem or obstacle is too big. He's so inclusive. He wants everyone to go with him all the time. To me, that's how Jesus would be. I encourage you to read this book, be inspired, laugh, cry, and then go out and do something about it!"

Stacey Campbell, Cofounder of New Life Church, Praying the Bible International and Revival Now Ministries, Kelowna, B.C. , Canada

"There are few people who believe you can live in the supernatural on the daily level. We have this earthly life – there are bills to pay, people to contend with and thorns in the flesh. The thing I love about Todd is that he talks about living in the supernatural on a daily basis. That's what I love and live for too – the

supernatural every day – and I think God has clearly identified that in Todd. He has the revelation, that, since we are great in God's eyes already, we don't need to prove it to man... just walk simply in the revelation of the greater One in us, as so few have ever done. Then let's go and preach the Gospel."

Kevin Prosch, Worship leader,
Christian recording artist, Amarillo, TX

"It has been my delight to serve on the board of Todd Bentley's ministry advisors. I've been able to watch this young man from the early days of his ministry. God has placed an awesome anointing upon Todd's life. I believe he is a forerunner of a new breed that God is now raising up – part of a breed of believers with great grace and anointing. Your faith will be expanded as you read about how God is moving through this outstanding young man."

Bobby Conner, Founder of Demonstration of
God's Power Ministries, Moravian Falls, NC

"I love this book. 'Journey Into the Miraculous' is a moving story about the extravagant grace of God. While Todd Bentley is a wonderful man with an unusual gift, this book is more than a story about his life. It's a prophetic declaration of God's intent for an entire generation. It invites those who are hungry and desperate for God, to abandon themselves for the treasure of His presence. This book will ignite a holy passion for a holy God!"

Bill Johnson, , Author of*When Heaven Invades Earth*,
Senior Pastor Bethel Church, Redding, CA

"Todd Bentley is a prophetic signpost of how, in this end-time hour, God is supernaturally raising up men and women who will literally change the course of history. Todd is not only a sovereign vessel, but he lives in a sovereign time. The supernatural grace and the amazing acceleration that mark his life are not only available to him, but also to you – if only you will grab hold of all that God desires to give you!

This book is a must – it is an insider's guide into how God can give us beauty for ashes, take the 'Saul' in us and make us into a Paul, and defy all logic through His transforming love. Todd pulls back the curtains and lets us peer into the personal molding and making of one who lives with eternity set in his heart.

His story disproves old paradigms, obliterates old wineskins, and is nothing less than one miracle after another. How amazing God's grace is in the life of this modern day hero of the faith. Absolutely nothing is impossible when we ask for 100% of God and give Him nothing less than 100% in return."

Jill Austin, Author of *Master Potter* and Master Potter Ministries, Kansas City, Missouri

Todd Bentley is a genuine Ephesians 4 gift to the church and the nations. He carries a powerful anointing for healing and miracles that's touching the globe. Todd shares this gift in a unique manner with compassion and humor. I know Todd personally. His own story is a powerful testimony of the awesome transforming power of the risen Christ. This book is for all those hungry to see more of God's power in their lives. Get this book; digest it. You will be refreshed and inspired.

Dr. Mahesh Chavda, Evangelist, Author, Founder of the Watch of the Lord and All Nation's Church, Ft. Mill, SC

CONTENTS

FORWARD

We need to realize that God is moving on the earth today like never before. More people have been saved in the last decade of the second millennium than at any other time in history. In just ten years, over one-third of all conversions since the days of Jesus have taken place. At this present rate of salvation, soon there will be more Christians on planet earth than there are in heaven! But we need workers for the harvest field. So you must read Todd Bentley's book, not as theory or as an entertaining story about one person, but read it as a manual that will teach you how you also can do what Todd is doing.

In the late 1980's, we experienced a mini-revival that was to change us forever. God moved unexpectedly and within months, scores of conservative Evangelicals and Baptists were propelled by the word of the Lord to prayer, the poor and the next generation. God prophesied to us over and over again about *"The Children."* He told us about a coming generation that would do greater signs and wonders than anything we had ever seen. During the same time period that God was speaking to us at our church, He was also revealing the coming revival to many others in different locations. Ironically, at the very time we were receiving promises regarding "the children," Todd Bentley was only 12-years-old and well on his way to becoming a criminal, an alcoholic and a drug addict. In this book, you will read about what the blood of Christ can do in a life like that. We believe that Todd is a "first fruits" of what God has been planning for decades, and that an unprecedented wave of the power of God is about to hit the Church. We believe that Todd is a proto-type of young revivalists–male and female– who are being called out of the depths of darkness to move in a power that hitherto we had only hoped to see.

However, more than anything, Todd's story is a story about God. It is a story of the faith of God, who chooses a wild, broken, young man— one whom no one would have believed in—to become a vessel of healing for the multitudes. It is the story of the mercy of God that transcends all social, economic, racial, and religious barriers, and heals even the most incurable of diseases. It is the story of an invisible God who makes Himself visible through miraculous signs and wonders.

But it is also a story about a man co-laboring together with God. In fact, Todd's life provides us with a graphic example of what happens when a man pushes in for the revival experience that many in history have received. His testimony vividly shows the co-operation between God and man. Where would Todd be if he hadn't exercised tenacious faith? Even with sovereign callings (see Ephesians 2:10), many people don't walk them out. All the just live by *faith* and Todd looked at what others had done in God and determined that, if God had done it for someone else, then God could do it for him.

From our close friendship with Todd, we have seen the uniqueness of how God touches a man. God literally imparted to him supernatural intelligence, extra dimensions of personality and business acumen. In other words, God equipped Todd to do the job He gave him to do. No one today could imagine Todd Bentley as an introvert, but that is what he used to be. He cooperated with God to receive what most people never receive. And now the world is a better place for it. I would that we had millions more like him – millions who activated *their* faith and touched the power of God.

What most people don't realize is that Todd also has a passion for the poor. He is preaching an apostolic gospel, complete with signs, wonders, and care for the poor. As we near the end of the age and the billion-soul harvest, we know conclusively that it will not take place without reaching the poor of the earth – especially women and children. The masses of humanity that are being exploited throughout the earth will have to be reached with a holistic message that gives them salvation, counteracts the powers of darkness, and elevates their physical well-being through healing, mercy, social justice, and micro-enterprise. In effect, this powerful message will have to totally transform communities. Todd is a new breed of revivalist who carries this transforming message. We encourage you to read this book, be inspired, laugh, cry, and then go out and do something about it!

Read this story for two reasons. First, although Jesus said, "Blessed are those who have not seen and yet believed," this book will give you the benefit of "seeing and believing." Beyond a shadow of a doubt, you will increase in faith as you read about real miracle after real miracle. In addition, you will learn that what God has done through Todd Bentley, He is also doing through many others around Todd. This young revivalist freely gives away what God has given to him and, as a result, there is a multiplication of the anointing. When you see what is possible in God *today*, you will gain faith to pray for a whole generation of believers to do the greater works that Jesus said His followers would do. As you read, cry out that the wave of power that has begun will turn into a *tsunami* and turn the hearts of people in every nation back to God. Pray for Todd Bentley to continue to minister in, and multiply, the miraculous anointing that God has given him. And pray for yourself, that you too will see miracles in your own sphere of influence. Then God will receive even more of the glory He deserves.

Wesley and Stacey Campbell,
Founders of New Life Church, Praying the Bible International
and Revival Now Ministries, Kelowna, BC, Canada
September, 2003

Chapter 1

THE END TIME HEALING REVIVAL

I was born on January 10, 1976 and born again between Christmas 1993 and the first week of January 1994. Looking back, it's amazing to me how much sin I packed into those first 18 years. But what's even more amazing is that God sovereignly plucked me from the kingdom of darkness and translated me into the kingdom of His wonderful Son. And He did it while I was His enemy. "While we were yet sinners, Christ died for us" (Rom. 5:8). Praise the Lord!

Forerunner of Fire

For 20 years the prophets have been talking about a youthful generation that will rise up, do holy exploits and usher in a healing revival. In 1973 the Lord showed Bob Jones this coming anointing that would fall on God's people. Bob told me that I'm part of the "first fruits" wave of a billion people that are going to be lit on fire. My life is a message, a prophetic signpost of what God wants to do with millions of others. I am a forerunner and one of many who will carry the healing anointing to the nations. God has led me to put this book together not just to tell about my personal journey into the miraculous. I also believe this book will help many people understand what God is doing in our time and will encourage readers to take steps of faith in areas where they may have been holding back.

If not you, who? If not now, when? We have an awesome, powerful God and we are living in amazing times. It's time to walk into the miraculous.

Joel's Army: a Vision by Paul Cain

For the past 30 years Paul Cain has had recurring visions concerning the end times that many Christians believe are rapidly approaching. One particular last-days revelation, which has come to be known as the "Joel's Army vision," has appeared to him more than 100 times and still recurs to this day.

In this vision the sports stadiums all over the United States are filled.

1

Thousands of people are being healed and miracles are happening in Jesus' name. People are turning to the Lord in droves and the whole nation is burning with revival fires. It seems like all the nations of the earth are turning to Christ.

Television news reporters, in the vision, are broadcasting stories of resurrections and miracle healings. A TV anchorman is saying, "There are no sporting events to report tonight because all the stadiums, ball parks and arenas are being used for large revival meetings and are filled with people shouting, 'Jesus is Lord, Jesus is Lord.'"

None of the secular reporters can get near the men and women on the platform and they don't know who they are. Paul describes them as "almost faceless". In the vision, Paul sees these men and women minister for three days and nights without food, water or change of clothing. Supernatural strength enables them to continue for these long periods.

In the vision, Paul is standing at the crossroads of life and sees a billboard that says, "Joel's army now in training." People are being trained to walk in obedience to Jesus. They have learned patient endurance, know how to demonstrate the power of God and having done all, they know how to stand against the enemy. These Christian soldiers will have the mind of Christ, says Paul: "They will partake of the heavenly calling and be a new breed, God's dread champions." As heaven's champions, these believers will be filled with such passion for Jesus and power of the Spirit that the host of darkness will dread their assault.

God is preparing such an army in hiddenness today, says Paul, even in the midst of a Laodicean church age of lethargy and apathy. This fearful host is being trained to pull down enemy strongholds and to go out, in the power of God, with pure and undefiled religion. He's going to do this with a people who have stripped and separated themselves from the world, the flesh and the devil.

"They will realize the end time is here and that things are in a mess," says Paul. "Just as it required total sacrifice on the part of the disciples to begin this thing, it will require an equal commitment from us to complete the task in the end times… Joel's mighty army, as described in Joel chapter two, is the army of God – not a wicked army, as some have thought. They are the ones with 'feet of iron not mixed with clay', with the wisdom of God alone, not imitators of other men of God. Some of the superstars of the Church will fall. The Lord will have an army of holy anointed vessels to usher in His kingdom so that no one man can take credit for it. It will be to the glory of God alone." (*Grace City Report Special Prophetic Edition*, Fall 1989)

Here is what Paul and other leaders have said about this time:

- "No prophet or apostle who ever lived, equaled the power of these individuals in this great army of the Lord in these last days. No one ever had it, not even Elijah or Peter or Paul. No-one else enjoyed the power that is going to rest on this great army." (Bob Jones and Paul Cain. Selections from the *Kansas City Prophets*, audiotape tape: 155C).

- "The Lord said this, 'This is where my people will rise up as an army and bring millions into the kingdom of God.'" (Benny Hinn, Honolulu, Blaisdale, January 21, 1999).

- "This army is unique," says Jack Deere. "When this army comes, it's large and mighty. It's so mighty that there has never been anything like it before. What's going to happen now will transcend what Paul did, what David did and what Moses did…."

- According to Rick Joyner, "What is about to come upon the earth is not just a revival, or another awakening; it is a veritable revolution. The vision was given in order to begin to awaken those who are destined to radically change the course, and even the very definition, of Christianity. The dismantling of organizations and disbanding of some works will be a positive and exhilarating experience for the Lord's faithful servants...the Lord will raise up a great company of prophets, teachers, pastors and apostles that will be of the spirit of Phinehas... this 'ministry of Phinehas' will save congregations, and at times, even whole nations… nations will tremble at the mention of their name..."(*The Harvest*, Rick Joyner)

- Paul Cain says, "I believe one day soon Joel's Army will be in training ... until it graduates into the stadium... But a right understanding of the plan of God for this generation brings this tremendous inclusion.... God's offering to you, this present generation, a greater privilege than was ever offered any generation at any time from Adam clear down through the millennium."

- "God's raising up a new standard, a new banner, if you will, that's going to radically change the expression, the understanding of Christianity in our generation...God has invited us to have a role in establishing a new order of Christianity...God is offering to this generation something He has never offered to any other generation...beware lest old-order brethren rob you and steal this hope from you." (Paul Cain, *You Can Become the Word!* 1989, Vineyard Prophetic Conference)

- Benny Hinn agrees: "The day is coming, I tell you this, I know it like I know my name, the day is coming when there will not be one sick saint in the body of Christ. No one will be raptured out of a hospital bed. You're all gonna be healed before the rapture." (Benny Hinn, *Praise the Lord*, 7/8/96).

- "You better be ready, church," Benny Hinn says about a last days revival. "They're going to walk up to you at K-Mart and Albertson's. They're going to walk up in the mall and say, 'Hey, I know you're a Christian. There's something funny about you. I'm not sure I understand it.' And they're going to say to you, … I've seen something in you and I got to have it right now. I don't know whether it's called God or Jesus, but I've got to have it right now.'" (Blaisdale Arena, Honolulu January 21, 1999)

- As Paul Cain says, these days will be marked by miracles: "All the sick are gonna be healed, the dead are gonna be raised and nations are gonna turn to God in a day." (Bob Jones and Paul Cain, *Selections from the Kansas City Prophets*, audiotape from discernment newsletter).

- "In the near future we will not be looking back at the early church with envy because of the great exploits of those days, but all will be saying that He certainly did save the best wine for last. The most glorious times in all of history have not come upon us. You, who have dreamed of one day being able to talk with Peter, John and Paul, are going to be surprised to find that they have all been waiting to talk to you." (Rick Joyner, *The Harvest*, Morning Star Publishing, 9, 1990).

Marks of this Healing Revival

I want to share briefly four aspects of what I believe will happen in this healing revival.

Last Days Anointing of Power – I have seen a glimpse of the anointing that will be on the last days church. We think the book of Acts was glorious but, as scripture tells us, "the glory of this latter house shall be greater than of the former." We are going out with a bigger bang than we came in with.

Massive Healings – There will be a renewed focus on the message of repentance because sickness and disease started with sin. As a revival of repentance and righteousness sweeps through the church, we will see a mighty healing revival. During times of repentance, healings will take place supernaturally without the laying on of hands.

Saints' Revival – God is going to do away with a clergy/layman mentality and raise up the body of Christ to do the work of the ministry. It has always been God's plan that every believer gets involved in the ministry of Jesus.

"He who believes in Me, the works that I do he will do also; and greater works than these he will do, because I go to My Father" (John 14:12).

Children's Ministry – We know that the kingdom isn't in word only but in power. I have seen a great move of healings and miracles at the hands of children as young as 11 and 12 years old. Today children are being used to grow limbs and work creative miracles as they speak words of faith. Increasingly, children are going to move in the power of the kingdom, driving out spirits and healing the sick because the kingdom truly is theirs.

Jesus said, "…let the little children come to Me, and do not forbid them; for of such is the kingdom of heaven" (Matt. 19:14).

I'll examine these four characteristics of the healing revival in more detail at the end of the book.

The Warrior King Rallies His Troops

Just prior to being launched into the ministry, the Holy Spirit took me into a vision. I was on the face of a mountain that I knew to be Mount Zion. It was an interactive trance because all my senses were fully operating. I could feel the chill of the wind as it blew through my hair.

I looked off the mountain and saw one small stream that flowed from its base to the desert below. I saw groups of two or three men clad in shining, brilliant armor riding white horses; they were coming from four different directions to follow the stream to the base of the mountain. I knew in my spirit they were being called to a secret council of the Lord.

One fascinating aspect of the vision was that each individual thought he was the only one called. However, there were actually thousands of these warriors coming to the council. Yet they were hidden from each other and from the enemy. As I climbed to the mountaintop I encountered Jesus as King of Kings and Lord of Lords.

His face was stern and set like chiseled stone. There was fire in His eyes. His grizzly beard and hair was silver-white like wool. I saw His breastplate with the imprint of a golden eagle on the front. He was so muscular; the breastplate took on the ripples of his mighty chest. His biceps were huge, like the size of my head; He had massive forearms and huge hands. Jesus was the mighty warrior God. He towered over me, three to four times my height – He was so tall that He had to bend down on one knee to communicate. Jesus' sword and shield lay beside Him and without actual words being spoken I suddenly received this revelation: "This is the council of the Lord. I have called you as one of many to be part of a last days army and a last days generation. My trumpet call has gone forth. There will be men and women who will be driving to work one day and the next day I will call them into the harvest."

Around the mountain there was a canopy of dark clouds spewing thunder and lightning. I remembered how God would come down and visit Moses in the stormy tempest (Ex. 19:16-25). In the vision I saw other men and women on the mountain resting and refreshing themselves around campfires. They anointed their shields and swords for battle.

The Lord said, "I have a hidden, secret army around the earth that I will enlist and uncover at My time. They are hidden away in the secret prayer closets, a generation of nameless, faceless nobodies. In My time, even in a day, I will uncover a new breed of apostles, pastors, prophets and teachers—a new breed of ministry. You are one of many first fruits of an entire army that I am equipping in these days."

The Last Days Elijah-Anointing

I have seen a glimpse of the anointing that will be on the last days church. That end time anointing is the Elijah-anointing! Scripture indicates that John the Baptist walked in that same Elijah-anointing. John was the forerunner, the one who prepared the nation for the first coming of Jesus. The Elijah-anointing is described in the gospel of Luke.

> He will also go before Him in the spirit and power of Elijah, 'to turn the hearts of the fathers to the children,' and the disobedient to the wisdom of the just, to make ready a people prepared for the Lord (Luke 1:17).

The bible promises through the prophet Malachi that Elijah the prophet is coming again before the great and dreadful day of the Lord. So the spirit and power of Elijah will be the forerunner anointing for the second coming of Christ.

> Behold, I will send you Elijah the prophet before the coming of the great and dreadful day of the Lord. And he will turn the hearts of the fathers to the children, And the hearts of the children to their fathers, lest I come and strike the earth with a curse (Mal. 4:5-6).

The Elijah anointing turns the hearts of children and nations to God like it did when the whole nation of Israel turned back to God in 1 Kings 18. This passage describes the story of how the 450 prophets of Baal were defeated on Mt. Carmel after Elijah called down fire from heaven. Hundreds of years later, when John the Baptist entered his ministry, many thought he was Elijah the man. However, they were actually seeing the Elijah-anointing which rested on him. When Jesus proclaimed Himself as Messiah, the Jews knew the promise that Elijah must come first. In Matthew 17 the disciples asked Jesus why, if he was the Messiah, the scribes said Elijah must come first. Jesus answered in verse 11: "Indeed Elijah is coming first and will restore all things." When He tells His disciples that Elijah has already come, the passage tells us, they understood that Jesus spoke of John the Baptist.

In the end it won't be one man with the Elijah-anointing but the spirit and anointing of Elijah on the church operating in miracles and signs like Elijah did. In Matthew 17 on the Mount of Transfiguration the Father sent Moses and Elijah as a prophetic fulfillment and sign of the law and the prophets, and to show that Jesus was who He said He was. It was here that the Father announced: "This is My beloved Son, in whom I am well pleased. Hear Him!"

In this mountaintop experience, Moses represented the old covenant to the Jews while Elijah represented the ushering in of the new covenant and the coming power, which would rest on John the Baptist. The book of Revelation makes reference to the two witnesses who clearly demonstrate the same miracles that Moses and Elijah demonstrated when they were on earth:

> Then I was given a reed like a measuring rod. And the angel stood, saying, 'Rise and measure the temple of God, the altar, and those who worship there. But leave out the court, which is outside the temple, and do not measure it, for it has been given to the Gentiles. And they will tread the holy city underfoot for forty-two months. And I will give power to my two witnesses, and they will prophesy one thousand two hundred and sixty days, clothed in sackcloth'. These are the two olive trees and the two lampstands standing before the God of the earth. And if anyone wants to harm them, fire proceeds from their mouth and devours their enemies. And if anyone wants to harm them, he must be killed in this manner. These have power to shut heaven, so that no rain falls in the days of their prophecy; and they have power over waters to turn them to blood, and to strike the earth with all plagues, as often as they desire (Rev. 11:1-6).

This is a picture of the last-days anointing; God will give power to His two witnesses (messianic Jews and gentile believers). This passage describes the last-days anointing of power, signs and wonders as in the days of Moses and Elijah.

Powerful miracles and healings will be released to bring in the great harvest. I believe that this passage describes, not just two people anointed as "super evangelists", but the end time church, messianic Jewish and Gentile believers operating in the spirit and power of Elijah and Moses. I believe Moses represents authority and Elijah represents power. Moses also speaks of the old covenant and Elijah speaks of both old and new covenants. How does Elijah represent the new? John the Baptist was the promised forerunner of the first coming. His came to prepare the way of the Lord and tell God's people to get ready for his coming! John was born in the anointing of Elijah (Luke 1:17). God has promised the spirit and power of Elijah in these last days we live in, before the coming of the great and dreadful day of the Lord (the second coming).

With the coming of the Spirit and power of Elijah, we also have a promised healing revival (Mal. 4:2). I believe that the key to the release of Elijah-power and the great healing revival will be the great prayer movement. Remember in Revelation 11, before the power is given to the church (vs. 3), John is given a measuring rod. The angel instructs John to measure three things: the temple of God, the altar, and those who worship there. The temple can represent the believer's life or the church— local, city wide or national. When worship, prayer and intercession in the church rise to a certain level, God will release his end time power and the promise of the spirit of Elijah. God is checking the levels of intercession, worship and prayer in the life of believers, cities and nations. Only when the bowls of Revelation 8 are full can God release his power to the two witnesses, the church both Jewish and Gentile. These two groups are called to represent the old and new covenants, to demonstrate a level of authority and power Moses and Elijah walked in. The power in Revelation 11 was given to the two lampstands. Jesus walked in Revelation Chapter one in the midst of the seven lampstands (which represent the church). So in these last days, it will be the church that will do the same miracles, signs and wonders that Moses and Elijah did.

As on that mountain, I believe as we near the second coming of Christ, God will again confirm the church as His beloved and His voice in the land. The Father will speak to the nations by bringing the Spirit and power of Moses and Elijah upon His end-time army. Then He will release the forerunners to prepare the way of the Lord and get a nation ready for God. It will be a movement of prophetic revelation, power evangelism and healing that will turn nations to God, some in only a day!

The Cost of the Anointing

God said to me once, "I can give you any anointing that I have ever given anyone else if you can do what they did to get it." The anointing will cost you everything.

Someone once shared the following vision with me: He said a man looked across a big open plain – rolled up mantles lay all over the ground. (A mantle is the anointing, the authority, the power and ministry from someone else's life.) As the vision continued, he said, "I saw the mantle of Smith Wigglesworth, Kathryn Kuhlman and Aimee Semple McPherson. I saw the mantle of Elisha, of Elijah, and all the greats that had gone on before us. Then the Holy Spirit spoke to me and said, 'Take any mantle you want. What do you want? Pick it up, take it; any one of them.'" The man said: "Oh, I want Elijah's! Oh! I want to be like Smith Wigglesworth and have great faith. The mantle of John G. Lake! Oh, my! The mantle of Elisha, think of that anointing! I could pick Kathryn Kuhlman's mantle and move in great miracles... or Martin Luther's and be a part of a great reformation." Then suddenly he saw a bright glow come up from the ground. As he looked down, he saw another mantle, which spoke to him: "Enoch walked with God so intimately that he was not." After seeing the life and the anointing of Enoch, he made his decision. "Before all the power mantles, I'd rather have the presence of the Lord." Then he picked up Enoch's mantle.

I believe that God is re-digging the ancient well and that He will use a last-days army usher in Isaiah 61:4: "And they shall rebuild the old ruins, they shall raise up the former desolations, and they shall repair the ruined cities." God is going to restore the desolations of many generations. He's going to take what's been lost in past revivals, the destinies that men and women didn't fulfill. God is going to take those mantles and put them on people. God is not going to give just one Kathryn Kuhlman or one Aimee Semple McPherson. As the Father pours out His Spirit in power again, He will restore those mantles to the church all at once. It won't be 40 years between moves of God.

I believe that every man or woman God has used is an example. In

Hebrews 11 the bible lists great heroes of faith and their exploits. Those examples, I believe, are just the foundation, or the floor of God's kingdom for us to build upon. God is offering the opportunity for *you* and me to dare to believe God to do in us what He did in their lives. Their experiences shouldn't be the ceiling, but rather the starting point for our upward journey of faith.

The Hall of Faith

The Lord once took me by the Spirit to a place where I saw a hallway that went further than my eye could see. I call it the Hall of Faith. The walls were golden and shimmering with the light of His glory. I felt like I was in a museum, a place in the Spirit where history had taken place. There was a red carpet leading down the hall.

I walked this long corridor and on each side were portraits, faces of men and women that God has used—Elijah, Elisha, Peter, Paul, Martin Luther, John G. Lake, Alexander Dowie, Aimee Semple McPherson, Jack Coe, A.A. Allen—people used throughout history to shake nations and turn cities upside down.

Each portrait chronicled the achievement of a man or woman, how the Lord used them, and the mantles that were on their lives. The corridor was like a memorial to great history makers. I've decided that I also want to do all the works that God has preordained for me and I want a huge portrait in the hall of faith!

In the vision, I knew this hall of faith was a place in the Spirit called the great cloud of witnesses. I knew I was in the hall of faith referred to in Hebrews 11, but the cloud of great witnesses mentioned in the next chapter surrounded me. "Therefore we also, since we are surrounded by so great a cloud of witnesses, let us lay aside every weight, and the sin which so easily ensnares us, and let us run with endurance the race that is set before us, looking unto Jesus, the author and finisher of our faith, who for the joy that was set before Him endured the cross, despising the shame, and has sat down at the right hand of the throne of God" (Hebrews 12:1-2).

During the experience I said, "God you're re-digging the ancient wells. It's time for a last-days army to receive Your power, apostolic authority and healing. Bring it to the church again—revival, reckless faith and the anointing of authority that was on great men and women. It's time for the church to see Your power. God, You're releasing the mantles of old. Bring the mighty anointing of the great women and men. Release new mantles and anointings, promises and commissions—an anointing that will come upon a generation like we've never seen before. Oh Lord, release the purposes that were never fulfilled."

When I came to the end of the hall, I stood in behind the throne. I was ushered before King Jesus and He commissioned me before His throne. In the same way, God wants to commission all of us. I believe that we are living in God's end-time chosen generation. Who is going to be the Charles Finney, Mary Woodworth Etter, Smith Wigglesworth or Jonathon Edwards of today? These great men and women, these saints of old are gone. As we read the history of God's past moves, we need to lift our standard of expectation so we can receive the great commissions He wants to give today. If God can do it for them, he can do it for us. Remember, the bible says, "Elijah was a man just like us...." (James 5:17).

God wants to do it again and in even greater measure. He promises, "The glory of the latter house will be greater than the glory of the former house," (Haggai 2:9). The church will go out with a bigger bang than it came in with. The example of normal Christian living in the book of Acts is the blueprint of what the church will look like, but the new dimension will be greater.

Have faith in the God who does miracles. I pray that this book will be an encouragement for new Christians and those who were Christians long before I was even born. This book is a testimony of what God has done with one man, a forerunner. I pray that God will use my testimony to lift the bar of expectancy of how much of God we can receive and manifest now.

I want to challenge you to go hard after God. I pray, like David did, that God would "teach us to number our days, that we may gain a heart of wisdom" (Psalm 90:12). Then when our brief lives are over, when I'm dog paddling around the celestial sea in front of the throne, you can come and find me and say, "Todd, they just put my picture up in the hall of faith and it's even bigger than yours!"

Chapter 2

MY CHILDHOOD

My dad said it wouldn't be proper to have a child out of wedlock, so he married my mother. They moved from Ontario to the Sunshine Coast on a peninsula near Vancouver, British Columbia, Canada. They lived in a small apartment in the same building as my uncle. He had found my dad a job working in a mill. I was born when my dad was 19; my mom was nine years older.

Dad, Mom and me!

Within a year of my birth Mom went totally deaf. She worked in a factory on an assembly line making washers and dryers and damaged her hearing due to loud machinery. I can't remember a time when my mom wasn't deaf. Dad was very frustrated over Mom's hearing loss. It made it very difficult for them to communicate.

Satan's Plans to Kill Me

Satan had plans to take me out early in life. After my birth, my dad was driving a small Spider car when he brought me home from the hospital. He backed out on the road in a hurry and didn't see the dumpster truck coming toward us. We actually went between the front and back wheels of the truck and it tore the roof off our car. I was in my car seat in the back. I believe the devil tried to take my life but God preserved me. The devil always tries to kill a move of God in its infancy. Moses and Jesus are examples of that. We also see the illustration in Mark 4 of the sower sowing the seed and the birds of the air coming immediately to snatch it away. I believe the enemy knew that God had a plan and purpose for me even when I was a newborn. I think that he and God were the only ones who knew. I certainly never thought God would use me.

Five years later, I almost died in another bizarre accident. Dad and I

13

were hanging out with one of his friends. I don't know why, but Dad's friend, Joe, threw me off a pier into the water and I almost drowned. My dad fished me out just in time to save my life. Looking back, I now believe that a spirit of death pursued me throughout my growing up years. Even though that spirit didn't get me, it did sometimes succeed in killing those I loved.

My earliest memory, during the time my parents were still together, was of my dog Goldie, a golden retriever—I loved this dog. She was my best friend. Dad came home one night and said the dog was killing the neighbor's sheep and it was important that we keep him in the pen or on a leash. I didn't really understand what that meant. The dog continued killing sheep and eventually had to be put down.

I had another close call one day when accompanying my dad and his best friend on a bear hunting expedition. We were stalking a bear that had been coming onto a neighbor's property, attacking the sheep and rummaging through the garbage. They knew the bear was close by but when I told Dad I needed to go to the bathroom, he sent me around the corner of a shed by myself. All of a sudden, about 14 feet away, there was the bear. It looked at me and rose up on its hind legs. You have no idea how big a bear on its hind legs looks to a little boy! My dad shot it. Later he joked that I had been "bear bait". That night he skinned the bear and cooked it on an open fire. I can still remember the smell and gamey taste of that meat. Not everything tastes like chicken. That incident left me terrified of bears. I loved nature and camping but every time I was in the woods I would get scared.

Divorce and Broken Promises

I was about four when Dad left. Really, my mom kicked him out because they were fighting and arguing all the time. He was also struggling with drug and alcohol problems having grown up with the hippie generation in the late 60's and early 70's—the era of free love, peace and sex. Dad lived in a hotel for a couple of weeks and then moved into a basement suite where he lived below a woman by the name of Darcia. Her boyfriend used to buy drugs from Dad. Within a few short months Dad was involved with Darcia and filed for divorce from my mom.

As a young boy, I struggled with the huge loss of my father, with the pain of rejection because of the divorce and with the frustration of not being able to communicate with my mom. I felt that Darcia was the wicked stepmother of the East. I always hoped and dreamed that Mom and Dad would get back together and I saw Darcia as the only thing preventing that. I felt that she never accepted me as her son because she had her own two daughters. Technically they were my stepsisters, but I never felt we were a family even though we did things together. I felt like her children were more important to her than I was and that Dad had put Darcia before me, treating her as if he cared for her more than me. I felt a lot of anger over all this; I guess that's a part of the pain of divorce.

I was constantly subjected to Mom and her family bad-mouthing Dad. To them, he was always a dead beat, a bum, and a drug addict who was never going to go anywhere. He had a grade 6 education and had left home at 16 to start working. They weren't too fond of him.

Growing up I had to wear second-hand clothes; we also went to the food pantry and used food stamps. Mom got a small check once a month for her disability and then we could eat out. For a few days there would be good food in the fridge and the kind of cereal I liked. .

Kindergarten Graduation, age five

Memories of my younger years are filled with broken promises and betrayal from my dad. Money and gifts that he promised often seemed to get "lost in the mail". I remember the tremendous disappointment when these eagerly anticipated gifts didn't show up. My birthday was January 10, not long after Christmas. Most years during that holiday season, I was disappointed twice. I was always devastated when I talked to Dad on the phone and would say, "I didn't get the Christmas present or the money you said you sent me." It seemed to me that year after year he said, "Son I sent it, the post office must have lost it. I'm going to phone the post office and see what happened because I really sent it."

I was so frustrated hearing my Mom talk about how Dad was supposed to send child support that hadn't come in years. Mom would say, "I'm not surprised that the parcel didn't show up in the mail, he doesn't even send support for your food, clothing and allowance." I wondered why Dad didn't take care of me and I blamed it on Darcia. I would think, "He must want to, but she won't let him."

I felt rejection on top of rejection. No matter how many times I felt betrayed, when Dad said, "Son, believe me," and then blamed the post office year after year, I always believed he was the good guy. I refused to believe what people said about him; I still idolized him. I wanted all the bad stuff to be a lie— in some ways it was and in some ways it wasn't, as I later realized.

I would see my dad for summer vacation and he would come and visit me once or twice a year. He usually wouldn't call me unless it was Christmas or my birthday. I always had to initiate. I wondered what was wrong with me and why my father didn't want to be with me. So I eventually closed my heart to him because I thought he had closed his to me.

Adventures on the Farm

When I was about six, Dad and Darcia married and moved to a farm in Alberta. One summer I got to visit him for five or six weeks. I really enjoyed

Getting ready to feed the pigs, age six

it; it was so different. I fed pigs and climbed in the hayloft. I loved the farm, except for those dumb chickens. For some reason I was scared to death of them. In an effort to help me over my fears, Dad took me to the chicken coop and told me to gather the eggs. "How do I get them, they're all sitting on them?" He said, "Just reach under their tails." I was too afraid so I shooed them away. I was totally disgusted–the eggs were still warm and we were going to eat them. That wasn't how they came from the store.

One day that same summer, Dad stopped to see one of his friends. He left me in the back seat

16

of the car with instructions to stay put. His friend's son came out and while we were playing in the car I decided to show him how I could drive. I put the car in neutral—it rolled forward, hitting the house and causing some damage to both.

Besides some of the more pleasant adventures at the farm that summer, I didn't have much of a childhood and I don't have many fond childhood memories. I had to grow up quickly after Dad left. I was forced to take on adult responsibilities. I soon became a very mixed up, angry kid.

I didn't know much about God or religion while I was growing up. Mom had been raised in the Salvation Army Church in Newfoundland but backslid at age 18. She didn't want anything to do with God anymore because of her strict religious upbringing; that religious spirit had ruined her. She made me attend Sunday School for a few weeks. That experience was enough to teach me that there was a God we should serve, but I wasn't really interested in spiritual things at the time.

Descent into Darkness

By the time I was eight, I remember having an interest in the occult. The devil was pulling me into his kingdom using heavy metal music as bait. I was filled with a deepening anger and growing rage and I took comfort in the music of AC/DC, Iron Maiden, Motley Crue and Metallica. Some of my favorite songs were 'Highway to Hell' by AC/DC, '666 The Number of the Beast' by Iron Maiden and 'Howl at the Moon' by Ozzy Osbourne. Then I began to be fascinated by death-metal and bands that I knew were Satanists. I began to idolize certain bands and singers.

The anger I felt drove me to violence against my own body. As I listened to this music I would cut my arm with a knife until I was bleeding and then lick the blood off. Once on a bus I broke out a window by ramming it with my head. I would throw tantrums, punching holes in walls and slamming doors—random acts of anger. The music started the whole process; it fed the hatred in me. I remember the music of these heavy metal, satanic and death-metal bands would make me feel strong and immortal. The music seemed to calm my fears, insecurities and feelings of rejection—it gave me a false sense of security. I felt untouchable, like I could take on the world.

17

I got involved in pornography around age nine. Dad had a huge trunk filled with pornography and I'd steal his movies and magazines when I'd visit. Soon it became an unmanageable addiction that I continued to feed through one of my friends who had access to pornographic materials. Before I was twelve, I had several sexual encounters.

My downward spiral continued—I started smoking and drinking at around the same age and soon became addicted to both. I remember my first cigarette; I took it from my mom and smoked it outside in the bush. The

At age ten I was headed for big trouble

experience left me so dizzy I could barely stand. I was sick to my stomach and wondered, "How can anyone smoke this stuff?" Later, when I felt better, I thought, "I kind of liked that dizzy feeling." First I smoked because of the head rush but then I wanted to look cool and be like the other high school kids. I soon became addicted.

The first time I took a drink of alcohol, it was out of curiosity. I wondered, "Why do Mom and her family and my friends drink?" My first alcohol was rum mixed with Coke. I remember the taste. I liked the warm feeling, the buzz I got, when I drank. Mom stored her alcohol under the cupboard where I could often be found sipping gin, rum a nd vodka. Christmas Eve was a highlight

for me. Mom invited family and friends and the bar was always well stocked. They all had a drink or two and I'd get eggnog with a little rum. When the friends left and Mom went to bed, I'd raid the cupboard. You can guess how I'd usher in Christmas morning.

At about 11 I started stealing money from mom to spend at the arcade. Once I went to a music store and stole a bunch of heavy metal music cassettes. My uncle, who lived in the upstairs apartment, discovered my "crime" and made me return them and tell the manager what I had done. However, this humbling experience wasn't enough to make me "go straight" and my behavior just got worse.

The Descent Continues

I longed to be with my father and I enjoyed the times we were together, but these times were usually destructive. We usually drank a lot. One of my earliest remembrances of drinking with my father was playing darts with him while drunk. I was 11 years old. Impaired coordination and sharp objects—not a good combination. I threw a dart wildly off course and it veered into the birdcage. Fortunately, it was a narrow miss and I didn't 'shish kebob' Dad's pet canary.

I remember vividly when I was about 12, Dad told me, "If you ever want to do drugs, don't do drugs with your friends. If you ever want to smoke a joint, smoke one with me." I thought, "Wow, Dad does dope and it's OK. He's inviting me to do dope with him." That was a seed. It birthed a desire in my heart. I started with marijuana—one here, one there. I did it with my friends to be sociable, but I quickly became addicted to the high. Soon I lived from one high to the next. Moderation was a foreign concept because I tend to be a very extreme person—no matter what I do, I do it with everything that is in me, or not at all. As a Christian this trait has been

Age twelve

redeemed. I still do everything all or nothing. Today, I want to be a radical, totally abandoned disciple who will take up the cross, deny myself and follow him. (Luke 9:23)

However, back in those dark days, the last high was never enough. Before long, one joint turned to several joints, then to joints laced with opium, cocaine and, eventually, PCP. Next, my addictive behavior led me to hash and hot knifing, then mushrooms, acid and speed. Never satisfied, I was always looking for more. It didn't matter what the drugs were, whether pills, Codeine, Tylenol or even sniffing gas. In my desperation for a high I would do almost anything. I wasn't a Satanist but I dabbled in many areas of the occult. I had a spiritual hunger but was filling it with the dark side. Because of my drugs and growing communication with evil spirits there was a high level of demonic activity in my home. Once when Mom was getting a glass of water, even though no one was there, something shook her violently. Remember my dad's friend who threw me off the pier? A relative of his named George used to have a garage sale every Sunday in this big old house. When he died, a spirit posing as his ghost grabbed me and woke me up at night. Unfortunately, Mom continued to have weird demonic encounters even after I left home because I had opened the door to that realm.

I loved to communicate with spirits from the grave. I would ask different spirits to visit and empower me. When I did drugs, a familiar spirit, that I believed to be the presence of Jim Morrison, would visit me when I was high. I never saw it but I could feel the presence. This spirit would fill me with mystical feelings; I believed that when I died I would spend eternity in bliss with Jim. How's that for screwed-up theology? There was a period of time when I would get high on acid or speed and I'd listen to the Doors for six hours a day and watch his movie over and over. I loved Jim Morrison; I worshipped him. That's not a figure of speech—I literally felt that way toward him.

I met a girl who also liked the Doors. Together we got high on acid. During one of our trips, we started acting out one of the scenes from the movie but we were unaware that we were doing this. We weren't even talking in our own voices. The people with us were freaked out so badly that they didn't want us around anymore.

I was involved in the occult and I would make deals in my heart with the Devil in order to achieve better drug highs and sexual ecstasy. I thought about giving myself to him if he could increase my pleasure. Although I never did make an actual covenant, I did make that deal in my heart by calling on different sexual demons.

I was so hungry for the spirit world and fascinated by demons, ghosts and horror movies that I used to go to cemeteries to do drugs and get drunk. I was really hungry for God but I didn't know Him or how to find Him. Today, people ask me if my involvement in the occult and my hunger for the dark side had anything to do with how quickly I eventually grew in the anointing. I believe that those demonic experiences did help me to be more sensitive to the spirit realm. God is amazing; He can redeem anything.

20

Chapter 3

ADOLESCENT CHOICES

I grew up with few restraints and little discipline. My mom always warned that my uncle would spank me when he got home... but he never did. By age 13, I was smoking in my own home in front of Mom. She complained a little but really had no control over me. I was hate-filled and very violent to the point of physically abusing her. Once she chased me down the hallway with the belt when, to my shame, I grabbed it and slapped it across her face instead. I used violence to intimidate her to get my way. A simple gesture with my hand or a single glance of my eye struck fear in her.

I also liked to light fires as a teen. Once a friend and I broke into an excavator and stole a lighter and matches. I lit some grass on fire in the ditch outside of a home and it nearly spread to the neighbor's garage. You can imagine how my mom felt when the fire department arrived. After the fire incident I got a small spanking and was grounded for a day or so. I found out that, since I was a juvenile, the police couldn't charge me. "Are you kidding?" I exclaimed, "What a great law!" From then on I really took advantage of that loophole, constantly lighting fires in the bush outside our house.

I used to have fantasies about blowing up a grenade at school or random acts of violence. I actually talked about how many people I thought I could kill in one day, how many murders I could get away with and how I would commit them. If somebody hurt me, I would dream about revenge.

I went to school through grade 8 before dropping out due to conflicts with other students as well as my own battles with criminal activity and court appearances. I'll come back to these events a little later. When I did attend school, I struggled with being able to apply myself and even grasp some of the simplest concepts. I remember being the class clown, and being picked last for sports teams.

In most classes I usually got F's and D's but once I got a B—in French class. No, it wasn't my great love for the beauty of the French language; it was because I sat beside a student more gifted in French and made a deal with her. I wouldn't snap her bra strap as long as she gave me the answers. What can I say?

A scholar I'm not. If the teacher wanted us to read a book I would ask if it was available as a movie.

My best school memories are of my grade 8 year when we would arrive at school an hour early every day just to have a slurpee at the nearby gas station.

Small-Town Life, Parties and Gangs

Gibsons, the town where I lived growing up, boasted a population of about 5,000 people. It was in the boonies—the middle of nowhere. You had to take a forty-minute ferry ride just to get to the small peninsula we lived on. I got to know some people who lived in the same apartment building as Mom and I. At times I would play Crib with a 60-year-old woman who lived below us. As a kid, the rest of my social circle consisted of my aunt and uncle who lived upstairs as well as a few of the neighborhood kids I would play kick the can or hide 'n seek with.

Through my teen years, there wasn't much for us to do on Fridays except go to the cinema (which showed one movie for several weeks) or hang out on the street or the skate board park. Sometimes 100-200 young people would congregate in front of the grocery store or in a small mall. The cool thing to do was to cut classes and smoke cigarettes behind the mall or go to the local swimming pool.

Life in Gibsons was similar to what was portrayed in the movie Footloose. The school dance was the big thing. There were two high schools that always competed with each other. In those days we had small-town gangs, with a membership of what I call "wanna-be gangsters." I was never in a gang but had relationships with a few people who were affiliated with the Los Diablo's. Most of these "gangsters" were more like your local thug, small-town trouble-makers who hung out in front of the local pizzeria.

I always wanted to be a member of the Hell's Angels when I grew up. (Who says I didn't have goals and ambition?) I knew my father rode sometimes as a friend of different biker gang members and I always enjoyed the parties Dad took me to at a place called Angel's Acres. There was a certain terror that spread over the town when they rode through. It was three days of drugs, heavy metal music, women and whatever else they could find to amuse themselves.

I always hung out with people older than I was. I didn't associate entirely with one gang because I wanted everybody to like me and because I wanted peace with everyone. I was the go-between guy; sometimes that position got me into trouble because I was never initiated into any one group. However, gang involvement wasn't good to many of my old friends; today some of them are dead, in prison, still in gangs or have even committed suicide. Not long ago one of my childhood best friends, hooked on cocaine and other drugs, shot himself with a shotgun and died. Considering where I could have ended up, I am so thankful that God kept me through it all.

I could get anyone to do what I wanted just because I knew how to "talk the talk" and make deals I could never deliver. I used gang connections and threw around names to protect me in the street. If it was time for a fight, everyone would fight for me… until they realized what was happening. "Hey wait a minute, why are we fighting your battles?" they would say, "You started this mess." I was a loud mouth, talk-bigger-than-I-was kind of guy. When my mess would finally catch up with me, (bad relationships, drug debt, theft or just to much "heat") I would just sneak away, tell no one and head for the next town, sometimes after just a few months of living where I was. I burned many bridges, made countless enemies, ended up on the wrong side of gang members, received death threats and just hurt and lied to many people. I always lived with a false identity because I never wanted anyone to know who I really was. I was afraid of rejection. Since I never changed my behavior from town to town, it usually took me about 6 months before I had to flee again. That scenario repeated itself at least three times in my life in about a two-year time span from 16 to 18 years of age.

A New Creation in Christ

At times when I've shared my testimony I've said, "There are events and activities in my past I don't speak about because I'm ashamed of them. My testimony is about who I am and what I am doing now, not who I was."

I know that the testimony is a powerful tool. "And they overcame him by the blood of the Lamb and by the word of their testimony" (Revelation

12:11). I have shared my story hundreds of times, quickly generalizing the highlights of my past without going into any specific detail about what actually put me in prison. I've always felt that the story of who I am today and what God is doing is powerful enough testimony of His transforming power.

However, in recent years, several stories have appeared about me in a political magazine that focused on critiquing religious and political issues and on digging up dirt about frontline leaders. Yes, there were many inaccuracies in the articles; however, I must admit that my naivety and lack of wisdom in dealing with the press also fed the fire of controversy. Today, I want to be sure that in the future no one can say I hid things or mislead people about my past.

I am going to share some things here that you won't hear from the pulpit. In recent months God has been giving us favor with Christian and secular media, TV, radio, magazines and more. With increased positive publicity we can expect that the accuser of the brethren will be right there to stir up controversy.

They say old news is no news but I want to be sure that I don't conceal any past details that could damage my ministry in the future. As I've recounted so far in this chapter, as a hate-filled, messed up youth, my life-style continued its descent into darkness until, eventually, I found myself involved in criminal activity and charged with sexual assault. Before I was saved, and as a minor, I hurt a lot of people and spent time in prison because of it.

I haven't spoken in detail about many areas of my childhood—many of those early events were very painful. I was sexually abused at 8-years-old and my childhood friend was abused by his step-father. I watched my friend abuse his step-sister and continue the destructive cycle. He became a drug addict, reached a place of despair and committed suicide with a shotgun after years of drug addiction.

I was forced into my first sexual encounter with a woman at age eleven. I thank God for the blood of Jesus! The world system says once an alcoholic always an alcoholic, once an addict always an addict, but I know that "if the Son makes you free, you shall indeed be free!" (John 8:36). God can restore purity to the prostitute, set the rapist and sex offender free and save the worst murderer, like Saul, and make him into Paul, the greatest apostle. There is hope for everyone lost in sin. The bible says that "if anyone is in Christ, he is a new creation; old things have passed away; behold, all things have become new" (2 Corinthians 5:17).

Although these areas of my past are very ugly, the blood of Jesus has washed away every stain. "If we confess our sins, He is faithful and just to forgive us our sins and to cleanse us from all unrighteousness" (I John 1:9).

For centuries people have asked this one question—"Is the blood of Jesus enough?" In my own ministry, this issue has been raised repeatedly... especially by the media. I have been challenged by the mistakes of my past and I've wrestled with whether the blood is enough. In the future, the accuser of the brethren will continue to challenge the wonder-working power of the blood of Jesus and the salvation experience of the cross. Yet, no assault of the enemy can overcome Christ's power, in my life and in others, to save and transform.

The devil has many in the church today living under guilt, condemnation and shame. His plan is to keep us in a prison of regret, constantly challenging the authenticity of the blood. When the devil keeps bringing up our past he is saying you are forever guilty of your past actions and sin even though your repentance is genuine. Yet we know the devil is a liar!

For years I knew God's love and forgiveness but still felt the sting of shame and guilt. When man, circumstances, media or the devil would bring up my past, I would relive the pain, defeat, regret and hopelessness of sin. Remembrance of sin separates us from God's love and creates a feeling of unworthiness before God.

Even though I knew God's forgiveness and unconditional love, I was challenged with this thought: "Does forgiveness mean forgetting?" The cross, the message of grace and the power of the blood of Jesus has been, and will be, challenged in my life and the life of all believers. I felt it necessary to exalt the Blood of the Lamb in this part of my testimony and to revel in its power to cleanse the conscience, forgive the sinner and overcome the accuser. The Blood of the Lamb is our greatest weapon of spiritual warfare! When I got saved I did a lot of repenting and reconciling, trying to make relationships right. I'll talk later about the process that God took me through so I could get out from under the constant condemnation of the devil.

Destination—Prison

After the courts sentenced me to prison, I remember being escorted, with my hands and feet shackled, to a small aircraft which I was convinced would crash. Although I was going to a juvenile facility, I definitely didn't find myself at a country club or a minimum-security institution. I was incarcerated, at times, with murderers and sex offenders. Inmates were raped and stabbed. What an environment for a young teen. I spent time in five different prisons, but for just one sentence. It was typical to be moved around a lot in those days because each facility emphasized different rehabilitation programs.

First I went to a mental evaluation facility for 14 days. Most young people came there for assessment and placement. I wasn't crazy or anything, at least not then (that didn't happen until I got into the ministry, ha ha!). I was in "lock down" most days when they weren't conducting stress and other psychological testing on me.

The first night in youth prison I was afraid because I had heard a lot of stories of what happens to the new guy. One story described a "blanket party" initiation. Four or five guys would wrap a person in a blanket and hold him down. Then they would place a bar of soap in a sock. A bar of soap in a sweat sock is a dangerous weapon—it can do a lot of damage. I was really scared. I lay awake worrying almost all night. However, the initiation never happened to me... but it sure did to the other guys.

My first day in another facility, one of the inmates wanted to test me. He walked up out of nowhere, shook my hand and greeted me. Then he punched me in the face and took off running. I didn't follow. It was a "what-will-this-guy-do-and-who-is-he?" moment of testing. He wanted to know if I would rat him out or run in fear. I eventually started to become friends with this young man. In all the times I was incarcerated, this was the only time that I got hit. Some of the older guys protected me because I was a first-rate manipulator and could get people on my side.

While I was in the 3rd prison, several Christians tried to share with me about Jesus. Every Wednesday I went to the Bible study because the woman who led it was pretty and because I always had a God hunger down deep inside. I just wanted to do what I wanted to do and worry about God later. Those meetings also helped fill time and answered many of my questions. I would stay behind after the session, asking all about God and the universe and about what I thought were contradictions in the bible. Once the leader showed a video on the discovery of Noah's ark from an archaeological dig. The documentary showed physical and scientific evidence that the ark rested on Mount Ararat. I was really gripped by that.

Sometimes I went to church on Sunday morning with the chaplain because it was the only time I could get out of the prison. I thought it was tough and cool to walk into church in my prison clothes and have everyone staring at me. I thought the women would admire me because I was a macho, bad boy from prison. I figured that most of the girls were probably forced by their parents to attend and really didn't want to be there. I knew that I needed God, but always thought I would get serious about Him when I was older.

Several times in the correctional facility or on the street, a preacher would come up to me, give me his business card and say, "If you ever want to have a coffee, give me a call." I remembered that. There was a man in the youth detention center who took an interest in me and in the music I liked. He was going through the lyrics asking why I listened to that kind of music. He said that I could get music with the same kind of beat but with different words and a different spirit. He was trying to explain to me why there was power in music.

He bought me a Christian metal tape by a group called Holy Soldier. They were a screaming, metal-head band. I was really interested and impressed that he went out of his way to pick out a Christian metal cassette. When I got out of prison I carried my ghetto blaster on my shoulder and I blasted *Virtue and Vice,* my favorite song then. It was Christian music but nobody knew. (Years later when I became a Christian I found this man and told him what happened and it really blessed him.) In prison I also met a young man who would always want to walk with me; he took time to ask me about my life and my dad, about growing up and what that was like. I was greatly touched by his friendship. I knew that both he and the other young man that bought me the metal music were Christians and were praying for me.

I was released a little early for good behavior, serving 14 months of an 18-month sentence. I was a ward of the court and so was placed in the foster care system. The town where my mother lived prohibited me from returning because of my criminal background and because my mother and I couldn't get along. On numerous occasions, the manager of our apartment building had complained about our screaming, swearing arguments.

The First of Many Foster Homes

The first foster home was temporary until they could find a permanent place for me. It was in Cloverdale, BC. I was there for only a few weeks, but that was where the Lord started working on my heart for what was to come. At this home, I met Shane, another foster kid who had lived there for a couple of years. His past was similar to mine—gangs, prison, drugs and so on. He invited me to come to church to see him get baptized. He was a Christian now. Two other foster kids who lived there were also Christians and attended an on-fire youth group at Christian Life Assembly in Langley, BC. The foster parents were also Christians. I believe God appointed them to help prepare my heart.

Although they never shared the gospel with me outright, they took me to church to watch Shane's water baptism. It happened to be the same church that the correctional facility had taken me to once for a Christmas play. I watched him and about 30 other young people as they shared brief testimonies and got baptized. I wondered, "could this happen to me?" I was amazed at the sense of family and nearly cried when others shared how the love of Jesus changed them. I nearly accepted Christ at the altar that night but didn't. I remember thinking to myself, "God have you been trying to speak to me over these last eight months? First the ministry in prison and now my first foster care home."

I really wanted to stay in that family and to know what it was like to belong. What I really was looking for was my heavenly Father's love. I was soon shipped to another foster home in Maple Ridge, British Columbia. I still remember the two tiny, white, Maltese, dogs I playfully and endlessly tormented for fun; I loved those little dogs, especially Jeepers. I used to wrestle with them, body slamming them until they'd get so wound up they would want to eat the couch. Then they just wouldn't calm down. My foster parents made me a part of their family and went out of their way to father and mother me. We would even have meals together. I felt like they truly cared about me and my future. While I lived there, an 18-year-old foster sister and two other foster kids came and went.

In this home, I continued to use drugs with some of my younger foster brothers. Once I was doing drugs, when someone drove by, rolled down his window and yelled, "Jesus loves you!" It was a "drive by" evangelistic effort. I went home that night thinking, "Did he say that because God told him to or did he say that because he's weird? Maybe God's thinking about me. Did He tell him to say that?" I really started thinking about God. I remembered instances when people took time to demonstrate the love of Christ to me, starting in prison and continuing in Cloverdale at the foster care house. It softened my heart knowing people were praying for me.

Yet, my sinful lifestyle continued. When I was 16 I started breaking into vehicles to find drugs or to sell what I stole to get drugs. One night I broke into 24 cars. Another time, when a friend got drunk with me, he said, "It would be great if we stole a car." I asked, "How are we going to do that?" He told me about a car in a underground garage where he babysat. I asked, "Where are we going to get the keys?" He pulled an "extra set" of keys out of his pocket and said, "I took them while I was babysitting. It will be easy—you get the car in the parking garage, then I'll drive us to downtown Vancouver for a joy ride." I remember thinking, "I can't even drive!"

I got in the car and realized that it was a stick shift. "Just my luck," I thought. I didn't know how to drive an automatic, let alone a stick. The last time I'd tried to drive was when I put the car in gear and ran through the wall of my Dad's friend's house. This time I was also drunk. I started the car and it jerked and stalled every time I tried to drive. I finally pulled it out about 10 feet. My friend was yelling at me, "Hurry up. Hurry up!" I said, "I can't, I can't." The car was in the middle of the underground parking garage at 2:00 a.m. and that's where I left it. I took off running. I was so embarrassed that I couldn't steal the car. But my friend and I laughed about it later.

It was in Maple Ridge where I really became addicted to drugs and got in trouble with gangs because of my bad temper. Numerous times in six months I found myself in dangerous situations and fights. I always talked bigger than I was and if I was involved in a fight I was going to fight dirty. One time a guy was talking badly about a girl I liked. I was hoping that she and I would have a relationship that was more than just sexual. He was saying different things that he wanted to do to her and we argued about whose girl she really was. It was evening and I was walking back to my foster home on a dark street when he came up from behind me and tried to give me a butterfly kick to the back of my head. I got so angry with him that I stuck my switchblade to his throat. I would have killed him but he called out to some people in nearby houses.

About half way through my stay with the family in Maple Ridge, things really began to go down hill for me because of my growing drug addiction. A girl I liked broke up with me. It shouldn't have been that big of a deal… but because I was an emotional wreck and delusional because of the drugs, I was deeply affected. I couldn't decide if I wanted to live or die. I decided to scare the group that I was hanging with, especially the girl. I was at the mall when I decided that dying was better than living. I stole a bottle of Extra Strength Tylenol and took 40 pills. Then I got scared and realized my life was slipping away and I was wandering around the mall by myself. (That experience gave new meaning to the phrase, "Shop 'til you drop.")

One of my drug friends found me and I was able to tell him what I did. The mall had a leisure center outside with a pool; my friend ran to the lifeguards and they sent me to the hospital. The doctor pumped my stomach and hooked up IV's. Unfortunately I was allergic to the drug overdose treatments so I broke out in red hives and thrashed around uncontrollably doing the "funky chicken". I really thought I was dying and it terrified me. My foster mom came into the room and when I saw her I screamed, "I don't want to die. I don't want to die." She began to cry too, then stayed with me in the hospital, as they pumped my stomach. This was the first of three drug overdoses in 18 months.

Even though many other foster kids had come and gone, my family really wanted to keep me. But my out of control lifestyle prohibited that. I pretty much violated all the rules; the anger and hurt inside and dark forces from outside seemed to compel me to continue pursuing my destructive lifestyle. More than once I was hauled home drunk after the police found me in a ditch. The drug overdose wasn't enough to stop me using drugs or alcohol. On one occasion a drug dealer even knocked on the door looking for me and saying that I owed him money. I also snuck women into the foster home where we did drugs and partied together. Sometimes I even broke into different rooms in the house that were off limits. Just imagine—for all those "minor" infractions—I got kicked out! This foster family truly wanted me to be a part of their family but I wouldn't receive their love; I didn't know how. They finally said, "We can't keep you." I realize now that I still need to let them know what happened to me.

I was moved to another foster home (the third one) which was more like a holding tank while they looked for a drug rehab program for me. I saw a drug counselor weekly, yet didn't really want to be free of my addiction; I still was doing drugs and drinking regularly. Before I was accepted into the rehab program, ironically called "Exodus", I was kicked out of the whole foster care system because of my continued late night drinking and drug use. Many times I never knew how I got home or what happened the night before. I was 17.

I Need Help, Dad

I had nowhere to go so I phoned Dad, hoping to go back to school and get a job. He hadn't heard from me for over two years. I had assumed that because we only talked once when I was in prison, that I had shamed him so much he just went on with his own life. In all my rejection and fear, I never kept up contact with family. According to my dad, I shut him off and didn't want a relationship with him.

But when I called I said, "I need help Dad; I've got no place to live. I'm a drug addict and I can't go back to Mom's." He said, "Come to Qualicum Beach (a town on Vancouver Island, BC). You can't stay with me and Darcia but I'll find a place for you." Qualicum Beach is a popular tourist destination and retirement town which is, believe it or not, smaller than the town I grew up in. In the off-season the hotels rented their spare rooms at very low rates. Dad rented me a furnished apartment on the beach and I stayed there. I really liked that small hotel called the Captain's Inn. I was less than two blocks from Dad and I'd go over for dinner four times a week or so. Dad and I were the same size so he gave me some of his clothes and my favorite pair of boots—black Dayton's—a kind of biker boot. Dad and Darcia tried their best

Age 16, after leaving foster care

31

to help me rebuild my life.

He got me a job as a dishwasher at a hotel. I was also still receiving monthly assistance from the government, which I squandered away on addictions and parties. (I do want to say here, though, that I eventually payed back to the government, over a period of several years, all the money I had obtained fraudulently). I got fired from my job after 6 months because I stole my employer's booze, dropped acid an hour before work, was late and sometimes didn't show up at all. I also started back to school; they started me in grade 10 because I was 17 but within the first month I was expelled because I missed so many days, dropped out of classes, and did no home work. When I did attend I was usually high.

Dad got me another job at a gas station working the night shift but I soon quit because I wanted to party instead. In spite of Dad's best efforts to help me, nothing was working. I couldn't stay away from the drugs or alcohol. Almost every day I'd go to Dad's and he'd give me beer; we would drink together just like when I was 11. Then we went outside and smoked pot and hash together. I was like a cat at the sound of a can opener. If I couldn't find drugs, Dad would "sell" me some or I'd clean out the garage, walk the dogs or wash his car to get a hit. Then some days he just gave them to me.

When peak season came, I had to leave the Captain's Inn. I moved to a large room in a single mother's house. I would have to go into her part of the home to use the bathroom. I came home drunk several times and was nearly kicked out of her home after barging into her private room at about 2:00 am and using her bathroom to get sick. I never remembered how I got there or back to my own bed.

Overdose Again

It was here that I overdosed a second time, this time on LSD, which, unbeknownst to me, was laced with strychnine (rat poison). I was on a bad trip and ran to her screaming, "I'm dead. I've died and the demons are coming to get me right now." I was crying and truly believed I had died and would go to Hell. I went out on her lawn, ran all around the yard, looked around and ran back and forth, convinced I was dead.

32

When the ambulance arrived, I yelled at the paramedics, "I don't want to die, I don't want to die." They put me into a straight jacket and sent me off to the hospital. Then I really started hallucinating. I was in a tropical jungle and there were big, colorful birds, like the Fruit Loops toucan. Everything was colorful and I could feel the heat from the Amazon. I was asking the nurses, "Do you know that we're on a safari?"

The next day I woke up not remembering anything. The nurses told me about the strychnine and the "safari." I asked, "Where's my shoes?" They said, "You didn't have any on when you came in." I was over 30 minutes from home and didn't know how I was going to get back. There and then I made a decision, "I'm never going to do drugs again. I'm done with them." However, I still knew that I had another hit back home.

Moments later I was in the hospital lobby trying to figure out how to get home with no shoes or money. I didn't want my Dad to know what happened but by now the whole small town did. I saw a Hispanic man sitting in the lobby of the hospital. He looked at me and I looked at him. He came over and said, "I'll give you a ride, Where you going?" I said, "Back to Qualicum Beach." I'd been in his car for about ten minutes and was still thinking that I was swearing off drugs forever when he said, "Hey buddy, open up the glove box." I popped open the glove box and there was a bag of dope. I don't know how, but I attracted drug dealers like manure draws flies. It was like the devil himself was there to meet me. He said, "Roll one up." I asked, "How big?" He said, "Make it as big as you want." Free dope! This had to be Satan! So I rolled one up the size of a cigar and got high in the car.. Five minutes after I arrived home, I popped the rest of the acid. It was after this incident that I was evicted again. Fortunately the off-season had come again and I moved back into the Captain's Inn.

Sex, drugs and rock and roll were my life. I got high every day for years. I smoked a bag of marijuana every day just to keep a buzz; it was like cigarettes for me. I regularly used LSD, speed and whiskey.

My Third Overdose

Then I had my third drug overdose. A friend and I went out picking mushrooms. We went to the farms and dug through the dung and each got a full bag. He wanted to sell his and I just wanted to eat mine. I went back to the apartment. I knew what the mushrooms were because I had done them before with Dad. He had baked marijuana brownies and put the magic mushrooms in cookies.

I didn't have any idea what quantity I should use. After careful consideration I decided to use them all. I ended up eating nearly a whole bread bag full and then stuffed the teapot full and drank mushroom tea. In a couple of hours the room started to spin. I vomited several times and the walls closed in. Sick and hallucinating at the same time, I became so paranoid that I kept looking out my window thinking that every car was actually stopping and hundreds of people were meeting to conspire against me. Imagine those old movies where the villagers storm the castle carrying torches and pitchforks, shouting, "Let's skin him alive." I thought the whole town was in on the plot. I ran out to the street— it was dark and behind every headlight was a driver that was coming to get me. I stayed sick for days, vomiting in the bathroom, and it took me months to overcome my paranoia.

I continued to get in trouble with the police but never changed my ways. Once I hid a 17-year-old escapee from a woman's juvenile prison. We got high together in my hotel for days. I didn't pay rent, choosing instead to spend my money on drugs and parties. Eventually, I was evicted from the Captain's Inn hotel for good. It wasn't till some time later that Dad found out about the eviction and the two jobs that I had already lost.

Sometimes he would come by and wake me up in the mornings so I'd make it to work on time. One day I didn't answer the door, so he used his key to get in. Unbelievably, the apartment Dad had furnished for me was empty and the trunk was gone. When I first moved to the Island, Dad had even brought me a 70-year-old antique trunk filled with clothes. The trunk had belonged to my grandfather. I had sold everything for drugs and money, including this family heirloom. The rest was taken by drug friends or traded for money. I was gone.

Chapter 4

THE HOUND OF HEAVEN ON MY TRAIL

I woke up that last morning and realized I was on the street with no place to go. I had lost everything and had no sense of direction. I was afraid to turn to my Dad again after failing so many times. I finally broke into a trailer and slept there one night. The next morning I admitted to myself that I had hit rock bottom. I decided to hitchhike back to Mom's. I called my Aunt Bell and asked her if Mom would have me back home and I knew by the excitement in her voice somebody would be glad to see me.

It would be good to have some familiar family and old friends around me again. I had lost lots of weight and I was not in good health. This was just before I turned 18. I hadn't lived with Mom since I was 14 and had rarely contacted her. Keeping in touch was difficult because she was deaf and I did not like to write. Also, I moved around so much she did not know where I was at times. She was still afraid of me, and for good reason. I was angry, out of control, violent, under the influence of demons, and addicted to drugs and alcoholic. Many times she just never knew what I would do next. But, other than those minor flaws, I was a model son.

My Old Friend Aaron

When I arrived home I found that Aaron, one of my best friends from grade school, was now a drug dealer with access to everything. I remember growing up and sleeping over at his house and phoning girls I had a crush on. He would pretend I was not there and ask them questions about me while I listened in on the other phone.

Now that Aaron was a drug addict and dealer, it seemed like a golden opportunity to get my drugs for the next few months. Our relationship became that of supply and demand—he supplied me and I demanded everything that he could get his hands on. Because he was such a good friend I could pay him later, or sometimes not at all.

Aaron had had frequent demonic visitations since he was a young child. Apparently, a demon named Raven who would ride around on the back of his bicycle. We would sit at Mom's apartment and talk about ghosts and demons, Ouiji boards and more. Aaron and I would "hot box" my small room. We'd close the door and smoke so much marijuana that the room would be filled with smoke. When Mom went to bed I would hot-knife hash on her stove, drink her alcohol till 4:00 am and then sleep until noon everyday.

My drug habits escalated until I did a little coke and used LSD and speed three to four times a week. I laced my joints with PCP (angel dust), opium or met amphetamines (speed or crank). Sometimes I was so desperate for a high just to function, I'd resort to sniffing gas and popping pills. When I rolled out of bed, I'd reach for a joint or a beer. I couldn't function, talk to people or even meet new friends without being high! I was living in a fantasy world rooted in anger, fear, rejection, self-hatred and more. But that was all about to change.

Aaron, Born Again?

One day I went looking for Aaron to get a fix. Instead, I got a big shock. He wouldn't sell me anything. He said that a few days ago he was in his trailer walking from the living room to the kitchen and the heavens opened up. God Himself came down. Aaron cried, fell to the floor, had a revelation of Jesus and was born again. "Born Again"—I was beginning to hate that phrase.

A few weeks later I was having coffee in a restaurant with about six of my friends when this boisterous guy named Wally came in. He was about 6'4", 240 pounds and had a big beard. Wally had a reputation in our community; no one messed with him. He'd been to prison and was an alcoholic. At one time, he made his living as an enforcer for the mob—they had a loan shark operation and if anyone was behind in his payment Wally found him, roughed him up and broke his legs. (Ironically, Wally, who was instrumental in bringing me to the Lord, used to work with Doug, the man who first discipled me. Together they used to break legs for the Mafia.)

Wally was carrying a large, white, Catholic family bible. He slammed the bible down on our table and said, "Do you know where I got this bible?" I was thinking, "No, and I don't really care." He told us he had gotten saved and needed a bible so he went to the Catholic bookstore saying, "I'm going to buy me a bible." He continued with his story: "I saw this bible and looked at the price tag written on the shelf below. It was more money than I had in my pocket, so I just asked God for the money I needed, put the bible on the shelf and turned to go. I heard a thud and turned around. The bible had fallen off the shelf and opened up. In red ink in the corner was the sale price and it was the exact amount of money I had. So I got me a bible."

That was the second supernatural testimony I had heard. I was thinking, "Oh no, another one like Aaron?" I was starting to have questions. "What is going on?" I'd always believed in God and figured I would come to Him "sometime, but not now." Along the way, lots of people had made their time available to share about the Lord but I turned them all down. God was setting up divine encounters, yet I didn't want anything to do with Him. The seeds were planted, though, and I did have a grandmother and grandfather who were regularly watering those seeds in prayer.

Evangelism—Wally Style

A few weeks later, I was sitting in Aaron's trailer. I had badgered and begged him to get me one more "doobie". He finally caved in. I was getting high in his bathroom when someone outside the trailer started banging on the door. "This is the police with a search warrant," yelled the intruder. I said, "Oh no." We really thought it was either the police or someone out to get us.

Aaron and I were so paranoid. That's the way we lived. Because of our lifestyle and involvement in the drug world, we "lived scared," thinking that everything was a conspiracy against us. He kept guns, baseball bats and crowbars all over the trailer. If someone knocked on the door, we could quickly pull a knife out from under the sofa.

Aaron grabbed a baseball bat and peeked behind the curtain. It was Wally and his big white bible. He wasn't knocking normally; he was almost kicking the door down. He came in, grabbed a chair, sat down right in front of me and started preaching. He didn't take the kind approach; he didn't even use the Four Spiritual Laws. He was in my face with "hell fire and brimstone."

He crammed that big white bible down my throat. I'm talking about Bible thumping. He said, "Todd, you're going to have to get saved." I said, "I don't want to listen to you, stop preaching at me." He just kept on. "You better repent or you're going to burn." I said, "Stop preaching at me. I don't want to listen." He wouldn't quit. I got irate and again yelled, "Stop preaching at me—I don't want to listen!" He said, "If you'll do one thing, I won't talk to you about Jesus any more." Relieved, I asked, "What do you want me to do?" He replied, "Take this bible and put it on your lap. Close your eyes, open it up any place you want to and put your finger on the page and look down and read out loud the first words that you see."

I wanted to get this guy off my back, even though I knew what he was saying was true. I only wanted to give my life to Christ "later". Yet, I also wondered if God would really speak to me. He put the bible on my lap—I opened it, raised my finger in the air and brought it down on the page. I looked smack dab above my finger, not in the general area, but directly above my finger. I read these words, "Listen now". They rolled out of my mouth like thunder and lightning. In that moment, the fear of God, accompanied with great urgency, came pouring into that trailer. I cried out for Jesus to save me. I wasn't playing around any more. I prayed the sinner's prayer and I gave Him my heart and life. I'd prayed this prayer before, but that night I really meant it.

(By the way, I don't recommend Bible roulette as a good way to get direction, but God was gracious and used it on that occasion.)

A Jesus High

I was born again in that trailer and for the first time in my life I felt free. The paranoia and burdens fell off. I felt as light as a feather. I thought that if I jumped in the air I would float away. I was on a super high. There's no high like the Most High… believe me, I've experienced them all. I was immediately delivered from drugs and alcohol. I never had a craving or withdrawal symptom. Three weeks later I quit cigarettes. What drug and alcohol programs couldn't do, Jesus did.

I ran out of the trailer; I wanted to tell everyone. I found a phone booth and called my aunt. She was a good Catholic and I thought she would be excited. I was jumping up and down in the phone booth. Her first response was to laugh. "Maybe someone else, but not Todd Bentley." I hung up the phone and turned around; several elderly women had observed my ranting and raving while waiting for the phone. From that day forward I was as bold for God as I was for unrighteousness. I started witnessing right away and I haven't stopped. I've never been ashamed of the gospel. I had an experience with the living God; He's as real as any person I know and He's my Friend.

The Last Bad Trip

Two days later I was at Mom's house and I saw a joint there... the last one. I knew that I was free from my addiction but I wondered what would happen if I smoked it. I had two small puffs and immediately I was higher than I'd ever been; my senses were dramatically heightened.

I knew that it was a bad supernatural trip. I was used to constant paranoia but this was paranoia times ten. I ran around the apartment from one window to the next to see who was coming for me. I collapsed on the couch, my mind racing. Darkness invaded the room and evil beings gnashed out at me. They were inches away from my face; in the spirit I heard shrieks. I could almost feel their breath.

God let me feel separation from Him; it was a taste of Hell. The minute I realized what was happening, I cried out and immediately joy and the Spirit of the fear of the Lord came. This experience contributed greatly to my desire to see people snatched out of the fire as spoken of in Jude 1:23.

Satanic Attacks

The enemy didn't give up easily. The number 999 (666 upside down) appeared on my cupboard within two hours of my being in Mom's house and leaving. It looked like the paint had been removed in that one area and all the rest was untouched. When I saw that number on my cupboard I felt a demonic presence. I knew that something had been in the house and left a mark just to say, "Todd, we know you. We know where you live." It was an attack from the enemy to plant fear in me. I didn't know what to do except pray and rebuke it.

That was the beginning of a renewed satanic assault on my life as a recently born-again believer. I would hear demons growling and scraping on the walls of my home. It got so bad that for several nights in a row, at 1:00 or 2:00 in the morning, I heard voices, banging, crashing and clanging, as well as the sounds of people fighting and hitting each other in my mom's bedroom. When I ran into the room, nothing would be going on—Mom would be sleeping. However, her body would be turned 90 degrees so she was lying horizontally along the headboard with her legs on the bedside table and the rest of her body lying across the pillows. She'd be startled when I woke her up but would have no idea of what had gone on.

Once I found Mom on the middle of the floor with a broken wrist. I took her to the hospital and as they were putting the cast on they asked what had happened. She said it was a bad dream. Later she told me she thought I had done it because of my past history of abusing her. She protected me by saying it was a dream.

After those experiences, over the course of many months, the Lord orchestrated three or four deliverances sessions for me. Although I was radically saved and serving Jesus, the Lord needed to set me free from demonic influences I had allowed into my life through my past ungodly lifestyle. During the deliverance sessions, I spoke in difference voices and demonstrated supernatural strength. It would take four or five men to hold me down. On one occasion, 25 demons were cast out. No pigs were safe that day. Praise God for His cleansing, healing and delivering power!

The reason I'm spending a lot of time recounting my past is certainly not to glorify sin; I'm ashamed of the lifestyle I lived. The reason I retell these parts of my story is to emphasize the fact that I'm ordinary. God didn't choose to use me because my mother dedicated me to the Lord and sent me off to live my early life cloistered away in a monastery studying "the disciplines" each day.

In the rest of the book I'm going to talk about some extraordinary encounters with God, but I wanted to lay a foundation first by letting you know how real and common I am. God can take ordinary people and do extraordinary things through them. We see this from Genesis to Revelation. As God said to the apostle Paul: "My grace is sufficient for you, for My strength is made perfect in weakness" (II Corinthians 12:9).

Chapter 5

FIRST VISITATION—THE OUTPOURING

Immediately after my salvation I got into the bible. I was so hungry I would read the four Gospels in one setting. As I read, I could feel wind blowing up and down my arms. The windows weren't open, so I knew God was near. I remember the excitement of those first months and the hunger that I could never satisfy for His presence and Word.

I'd stay up all night Saturday reading the bible and praying and watching Christian broadcasts. I was so hungry for God there was not enough time in a day and I was afraid I'd oversleep and miss church on Sunday. Remember, it was my habit to sleep in until 1:00 in the afternoon.

Come Holy Spirit

As a new Christian, I hung out with men who were part of the Full Gospel Business Men's Fellowship; these men taught me about the baptism of the Holy Spirit. They discipled me and let me give a 10-minute testimony at their retreats. On Mondays, I would also hang out with the charismatic Catholics. Their meetings had a really laid-back atmosphere where people learned to move in the gifts.

I began to learn about the kingdom of Heaven and Jesus through the Holy Spirit. My second real encounter with the Holy Spirit started out of hunger to know Him. I did word studies on the Holy Spirit in a Catholic concordance I bought. I didn't know there was a difference between a Catholic and Protestant concordance. (Wally and I were, apparently, the Catholic bookstore's best customers.)

The first two months after I was saved, I had an overwhelming desire for the Holy Spirit. I was never satisfied. I kept thinking that there must be more. In my search, I read and wrote down numerous biblical references to the Holy Spirit.

I told the Full Gospel Business Men, "I want more. I'm a new Christian reading the scriptures 4-5 hours each day. I have a hunger burning in my soul."

They said, "We've got to get you filled with the Spirit." They prayed over me for the baptism in the Holy Spirit. They tried to jump start me, but I didn't like repeating, "Abba, Abba, Abba." They told me that I had gotten tongues even though I wasn't able to speak in another language. "This is ridiculous," I thought, "I don't feel a spring springing up. I don't feel living water flowing from my belly. I was seeking a baptism in fire, like in the book of Acts. I wanted something supernatural like a spontaneous burst of uncontrollable joy and tongues, so that I knew I was filled with the Spirit and not just making something up.

As God would have it, I came to the city of Kelowna, a great eagle's nest today for many prophets and prophetic people. This is where I would receive my wonderful prayer language. Even though I felt like I was speaking in tongues, my mind wouldn't believe it.

It was about midnight, three days into my stay and I was overwhelmed by the presence of God. As I stepped out to the shore of Okanagan Lake, my heart felt like it was bursting. My heart said, "Yes, this is tongues." My mind said, "No." My mind was trying to figure out what was taking place in the deeper parts of my Spirit.

Dove from Heaven

I said, "Holy Spirit, give me a sign." Then in an instant, the dark midnight sky was illuminated with heavenly glory. The heavens opened with a bright flash and a white dove materialized out of thin air and flew across the lake to a nearby tree. It was one dove but it sounded like the flapping wings of ten thousand doves. The noise filled the sky and rumbled in my spirit, the sound of a ripping, rushing, mighty wind filled my ears. I knew in my spirit heaven had opened. When I turned toward the tree, the dove was gone. I thought, "OK, that works."

I had received not only tongues, but an enduement of power from on high for miracles, signs and wonders. I continued speaking in my new language until the wee hours of the morning. I still don't know if I really saw the dove in the natural or if it was a vision. However, that was my first real experience with seeing in the Spirit. To this day I spend a lot of time speaking in tongues. It's how I stir up the Spirit of wisdom, empty myself, receive revelation and get into the mind of Christ. I consistently and constantly pray in tongues.

More of the Holy Spirit

After that experience I got hungrier for God and the word. The words jumped off the page; it was like taking a drink every time I read the bible. I asked, "What's next?" They said, "That's it. You're baptized in the Holy Ghost, speaking in tongues; you have the gift of prophecy."

One of the men from Full Gospel Business Men gave me a book by Benny Hinn called *Good Morning Holy Spirit*. I thought, "That's what I want, more of the Holy Spirit." When I got saved in 1994 I didn't know anything about Benny Hinn, Toronto or revival. After I finished the book, I realized that I also needed what Benny had—intimacy with God's Spirit. I now understood that God wanted me to have a deeper relationship with His Spirit. God is not partial but He favors those who diligently seek Him; He favors those who hunger and thirst after Him.

I didn't know what to do except pray simple prayers, so I said, "I want to know you, Holy Spirit, just like Benny knows you and just like this woman, Kathryn that he talks about. I'm asking You to come into my bedroom as a person in the same way you did for Benny. I want to have a conversation with You wonderful, Holy Spirit. I want to feel electricity and weep uncontrollably. I want so much of Your presence I can't get up off my bed. I want you to be more real to me."

He answered my cry; I had a visitation of the person of the Holy Spirit. My body began to shake and I felt electricity. Once while I was under a heavy anointing my friend stopped by and yelled to me, "Come on let's go." It was all I could do to shout, "I'm in my room." He opened up the door and asked,

"Why are you shaking?"

"I don't know. I think it's the Holy Spirit."

"Why would the Holy Spirit make you shake?"

"I don't know but He's been doing it for about three hours."

"Get up off your bed."

"I can't. I can't move. My whole body is numb and I'm sinking into the mattress."

"This is a demon that's possessing you. You can't even do what you want to do. That's not the Lord."

"I don't know, but it feels good." My friend was literally trying to get me off the bed.

Holy Spirit I Love You

Despite my friend's views about my experience, I knew it was from God. I'd come home from work cleaning gutters and washing vinyl siding. I was so excited about being in His presence I would run to my bedroom and throw open the door. It was like an electrical force field lived in my bedroom. He was waiting for me. He was just as excited about being with me as I was about being with him. When we were together, it was that same kind of emotional high that two six-year-old kids together on Christmas morning would have.

I would close the door and tears would stream down my face. I would stand for 3 hours and tell Him how much I loved him and I would feel tangible love back. This incredible intimacy lasted from four to twelve hours every day for about three months. The Spirit of God breathed on the pages of the bible. This wasn't the baptism of the Holy Ghost; this wasn't speaking in tongues. This was a Person in my home who, today, is as real to me as the Father and the Son.

Within three months of getting saved, I had discovered that the Holy Spirit isn't limited to convicting people, slaying them in power or manifesting gifts and miracles. The Holy Spirit is a Person I can converse with. I can say, "Holy Spirit I love you and I'm glad that we are partners; together we can bring Jesus to the world. You inspired people to write this bible, help me understand it. Put the scripture in my heart so it's not just words. I can't even say, 'Jesus is Lord' without you." I'd open the bible and I'd feel Him hovering over me. When I talked to the Holy Spirit about Jesus, time would fly by. He's sovereign and He'll do what ever He wants but I volunteered to let Him work through me.

I said to Him, "I want you to open this bible to me and I'm going to take this message all over the world. I ask you for wisdom and revelation. I'm going to talk to you from this day forward. I want you to be my best friend. I want to know your presence and your person in this place. I ask you to come." I loved, welcomed and yielded to the Holy Spirit daily. God was revealing Himself to me as I hungered for Him. It was almost like dating—the freshness of a new love. To this day the Holy Spirit is as real to me as any person. He constantly speaks to me through the inner audible voice of God.

I've been in such communion with the Holy Spirit, where His presence was so real, that when I stepped out of my room, I would feel him moving with me to the elevator. When I got in my car, I would feel a person get in the seat next to me. People would come into my apartment while I was worshiping the Holy Spirit; they would step from the kitchen into the living room, hit an invisible, electrical, force field and bounce back. I'd look at them and ask,

"What happened?"

"Something just zapped me."

At times people couldn't get close to me without falling down. Years later, Shonnah, my wife, was washing dishes while her friend was in the apartment. When I stepped into the kitchen Shonnah went down under the power and her friend screamed, "Your face is glowing." Once when I got in a friend's car, I felt the Holy Spirit moving like a cloud with me. The driver began weeping when I got inside.

I went to a Christian school once and shared about the Holy Spirit and started loving and honoring him and most of the kids fell out in holy laughter. I was like "What's going on?" I didn't know how to move in the flow. People would say, "There's fire coming off you," and I wouldn't feel anything. I remembered reading about some of these manifestations in Benny's book and I'd get so excited. "It's happening to me too."

In those days of growing intimacy with the Holy Spirit, I had nothing to do but pursue the Lord. Mom was deaf and none of my friends understood what was going on in my life.

A Geographical Change

Within this three-month period, I heard God's audible voice clearly for the first time. "I want you to move to Abbotsford, British Columbia," He said. "God, there's no Abbotsford, BC. I've never heard of it," I replied. (Boy did I have a lot to learn). "Besides, my church is sponsoring me to go to bible school— I've been accepted. They are even going to pay for it. I'm going to get a suit and tie, cut my hair, look like the rest of the preachers and meet my wife. Even if there's an Abbotsford, I can't just tell my friends at church I'm leaving." Yet God's audible command to me continued to ring and resonate through my being—it was as if my whole head filled with the idea of Abbotsford. I had heard God so clearly, I remember thinking to myself, "This must be how God speaks audibly." Today, He still constantly speaks to me and I can still hear him whispering in my ear.

In those days I didn't know a lot about Christianity but I had learned that a prophetic word should be confirmed in the mouth of two witnesses. So I told God He would have to confirm my move to the "mythical" town of Abbotsford.

The Charismatic Catholics

During this time I had been hanging out with the Charismatic Catholics. They seemed to be the most alive church group in town. I went every week to those meetings and people were encouraged to practice prophecy and spiritual gifts. During worship I started hearing a few simple words or a scripture. I'd get really excited even though it might just have been, "He loves you." I was so excited about hearing God that I generally waited until I was trembling and shaking before I spoke. Once the Lord told me, "I am here." I could feel His presence and the strength of the word kept building and building until I finally stood up and yelled out, "Thus saith the Lord, 'I am here.'" Then I sat down. They thought I was a great little fireball.

One night at the Catholic meeting the Lord spoke to me Hebrews 12:22, "You have come to Mount Zion and to the city of the living God..." I didn't know what to do with it. I went to the microphone, read the verse, sat down and everyone cheered. I didn't realize that the scripture was for me. (I found out later that when we get revelation we don't always know what to do with it. Sometimes revelation can be progressive and it can be months or years before we get the understanding.)

Misled

Because I was hungry for the gifts of the Spirit I hooked up with a man in the community named Frenchie. He had a reputation of being one that had visitations and moved in extraordinary demonstrations of the Spirit. He lived on

46

a boat at the marina and people brought the sick and they would get healed. He would cast demons out of people and lead them to Jesus. It was rumored that he could tell people in detail what they had done that morning. The church called him an independent, lone wolf and, in many ways, he was. He was anointed, but he was rebellious and had issues with authority and leadership.

I was very interested in learning from him because he was moving in the Spirit in a stronger way than what I saw happening at the church. Frenchie usually didn't go to the church because he saw them as "too religious." Now when I look back, I understand that although He had a God-given gift, and a lot of charisma, he wasn't solid in issues of character. But I didn't understand those things—I was just hungry for the supernatural. I talked to my dad on the phone one day and when I went to see Frenchie on his little boat he told me about the conversation in such detail that I knew he had a true gift from God.

Later his character was revealed to me. Before I met him he had married and divorced two or three women and had multiple affairs. He'd get angry and violent with the wharf manager and curse at him. He got his food from the dumpsters at the Safeway grocery store at night when the leftovers and outdated breads, meat and food were thrown out. It took me a few months to see his flaws. Frenchie did help me to move into the things of the Sprit. God used that experience to teach me. "Todd, I want to anoint you and use you," He said, "but I want you to be one who loves Me, knows Me and wants to be like Me more than one who wants My gifts and My power. If you will always remember to dwell, rest and soak in My presence, I will use you to shake the nations. But, remember, I am more concerned about what I can do in you than through you."

The Lord showed me through Frenchie's charisma, gifting and lack of character that it's possible to have His power but not be in right relationship with Him. I don't want to be like the foolish virgins or the ones who prophesied and cast out demons in His name. What did He say about them? "Depart from me I never knew you," or literally, "Depart from me for I once knew you but you have since not allowed yourself to be known" (Matthew 7:23). Although I was beginning to move in the gifts quickly, I pressed in even harder to the Lord.

Geographical Guidance

A few weeks later I was out in the woods, in the middle of nowhere, with my boss, Barry. Remember, to get to the Sunshine coast you have to take a 40-minute ferry ride. We were miles from anywhere in the bush, sitting on a picnic table when God sent me a messenger. Some guy had decided God told him to bike across Canada and, for some reason I have never learned, he decided to take a 45-minute ferry ride to the island and pedal for more than 40 miles to where we were in the woods. He didn't know we were there and I had never met him before. He pedaled up to us on his mountain bike and recognized my boss.

"Barry, I can't believe it's you. When did you move here?" Then he said, "You're not going to believe what's happening. There's an outpouring of God in Abbotsford, BC. You've got to come to Abbotsford." It was the voice of God. This man had no idea the Lord was using him. Barry turned and said, "Todd, do you want to go to Abbotsford? We can get an apartment together." I said, "Praise God. I got a prophetic word about Abbotsford."

That's how God moved me supernaturally from one community to the next. I ended up sharing a basement apartment with Barry in Abbotsford. Next I needed a church and there were over 100 different ones to choose from. Abbotsford is the bible belt of Canada. Barry recommended the church he used to attend, a little church with about 50 members. I walked in the door, a little late, and stood in the back. "Friend," said the pastor as he opened his sermon, "You have come to Mount Zion and to the city of the living God." I fell out under the power in the back of the church. He wasn't even speaking directly to me and certainly didn't know about the scripture the Lord had recently given to me.

"Now I'm saved and I know the Holy Ghost," I said, "I'm in my city and I'm in my church. We're talking destiny here. Someone's got a hold of my life and He's a lot bigger than I am. And it looks like He knows what I'm doing before I do it."

Chapter 6

HERE COMES THE BRIDE—RELUCTANTLY

"Barry what's to do in this Abbotsford town?" He mentioned that there was a citywide youth revival called God Rock in an old shopping mall on Friday nights where they worshiped God with heavy rock-style music. This youth revival was birthed out of the Toronto outpouring. God was moving in power on Generation X. Hundreds of young people in their teens and early twenties gathered. They came from every imaginable background and subculture—punks, metal heads, preps, Goths and Kool-aid kids with green or pink hair.

Since I didn't have a license or a car, I asked Barry to find a ride for me. He made a few phone calls and eventually contacted Shonnah, a girl from my new church. She agreed to drive me to God Rock. Later I found out that she had second thoughts and complained to her parents that she didn't want to pick me up. "I don't know this guy," she said, "Who is he and why can't Barry take him?" She toyed with calling to cancel. She tried to convince her best friend, Roswetta, to ride with her. Roswetta (pronounced Rosevita) was a little conservative

This is how I looked when Shonnah and I met.

at the time and thought Shonnah was in a cult, as did Shonnah's parents, and even the pastor of our small church. When Roswetta wouldn't come along, Shonnah finally resigned herself to her fate, came to my basement apartment and knocked on my door.

Shonnah had grown up Catholic. She got saved at 16 when the Lord healed her of bone cancer and a spot on her lungs. Several Christians, including some ministers, prayed for her over a period of several weeks and God blessed her with a miracle. The nurturing of the church impacted her immediate family and they all got saved too, including her dad who had been an alcoholic over 20 years.

Shonnah is seven years older than I and had been waiting and praying for a husband for ten years. She and I were complete opposites. I was loud and outgoing and she was quiet and conservative, especially in speaking to guys. She had a job and a driver's license; she'd never touched drugs, never dated steady or even kissed a guy. Yes, Miss Goody Two Shoes, the reserved Catholic girl, was knocking on my door.

On the other side of the door, sporting a big goatee, long hair, earrings, bandanna and ripped jeans was me. I looked like a Hell's Angels biker. I hadn't bothered to change my look since Dad and I partied with them a while back. In the natural, I was the last person that you'd want your daughter to marry. We couldn't have been more different. (God has such a sense of humor).

I opened the door and sucked in a deep breath when I saw her. She was beautiful. I tried to regain my suave and debonair persona by blurting out, "Just a minute," and slamming the door in her face. I ran to Barry ranting about her beauty and how I'd have no chance with a woman like that. She was a preppy and I was a hood. Well, I finally opened the door. During the ten-minute ride to God Rock, she was silently praying, "Oh God, help me. Help me." She was so scared. I think she thought I was going to mug her.

We walked into the meeting, which was already in progress—loud music and dimmed lights like a club. I asked where she wanted to sit. "I don't know, just pick somewhere," she said. I pointed to some chairs and, as I discovered later, we ended up sitting directly in front of Chris, a guy she had a crush on. In fact, she felt that the Lord had told her that they were going to marry. She was thinking, "Oh great. He's going to think Todd and I are together." To make matters worse, when the pastor had us turn around and greet the person behind us, I immediately whipped around and shook this guy's hand. It must have appeared like, "In your face buddy. She is mine now!" But, I had no idea they were even friends.

A few minutes later Roswetta showed up at the meeting; she had decided to join us and help her friend. Roswetta, being a conservative Mennonite girl, wasn't sure about these spiritual manifestations in the meeting: drunkenness in the Spirit, falling on the floor, shaking, groaning, laughing, and crying. Remember, this was in 1994 when the spiritual renewal movement, or the "Toronto blessing," was going all over the world. This meeting was the first time that I had even seen the manifestations of the Spirit outside of my apartment. During the worship there was a call for prayer and Shonnah went forward. I remember her bending backwards and forwards like a tree swaying in the wind. I thought to myself, "Why is she shaking and doing the Gumby?"

Suddenly, I felt an anger churning deep inside me. I tried to squelch it but it rose from inside with violent thoughts. I was overcome by a demon and I ended up throwing myself at the chairs and knocking them flying. I was screaming and cursing, writhing on the floor like a snake. I began rolling and screaming, trying to avoid the four or five guys trying to restrain and deliver me. Fortunately, Shonnah was oblivious to what was happening with me. However, Roswetta had a front row seat for my performance—it certainly did little to quell her fears that this meeting was some "cult movement" and didn't leave her with the best first impression of me. (The good thing about this incident—I received a powerful deliverance from some lingering demonic bondages.)

The Pursuit

I was totally infatuated with Shonnah after this meeting, so I devised a plan. I started observing whom she hung out with and found we had some mutual friends. Coincidentally, the next few weeks we ended up in the same group of friends and in the same restaurants after revival meetings.

A friend of mine, Gerard, was a friend of Earl and Val, Shonnah's parents. After a few weeks I told Gerard how I felt about Shonnah. We hung out together at his apartment and we'd end up doing "carpet time" together, enjoying the presence of the Holy Spirit. I worked with him part-time doing renovations. When I was with him it was "Shonnah this and Shonnah that and Shonnah, Shonnah, Shonnah." It used to be, "Jesus, Jesus, and Jesus." Gerard finally got fed up and said, "If you don't ask her out I'll do it for you." So the next time he saw Shonnah he said, "The new guy, Todd, likes you and wants to go out with you." Shonnah replied, "No thanks. He's too wild. Will you please let him know I'm not interested… but please be nice about it."

I was perplexed but not in despair, struck down but not destroyed. I kept arranging meetings just to be near her but acted like I just wanted to be friends. She thought I'd lost interest, which was absolutely fine with her. She picked me up a few more times for God Rock and we even did prayer ministry together. She loved to hang with me because she liked my fiery preaching, evangelism and anointing. I was everything she wanted in a Christian, but nothing she wanted in a boyfriend. There were times that we got together at 10:00 am and hung out until 3:00 am praying and ministering with others.

On a previous occasion, the Lord had actually shown me an open vision of Shonnah. It was my first open-eyed vision. I was in my living room and my fireplace mantel opened up, kind of like a TV screen, and I saw us embracing in a wheat field that was ready for harvest. We were both weeping and I was wearing a tux and she was in a wedding dress. At the time I had the vision, her friend Roswetta (who was now my friend) was talking with me in the living room about Shonnah. I described the open vision to her as it unfolded. The presence of the Lord fell and we both wept. Roswetta said, "I can't see it but I can feel goose bumps." During this vision I also received an anointing of creativity, poetry and writing. In fact, I even received a three page prophetic poem that I read at our wedding. I still write prophetic poems for my wife to this day.

A woman in our church named Helen had a niece who was vexed with an evil spirit and was slowly dying. She asked me to come pray for her and I asked Shonnah to come along. Returning from prayer time, Helen was driving us home and I asked, "Helen, how do you know when you've found the right one?" All three of us engaged in an enthusiastic conversation about marriage. Shonnah was really getting into it because she still felt like the Lord had told her she was going to marry Chris. She wondered why I was asking all these questions. Then she remembered a conversation we'd had a few weeks earlier at a restaurant. Shonnah overheard me tell my friend Steve that the Lord had showed me who I'd marry. They badgered me at the table until I gave a description of the one the Lord showed me. Apparently, Shonnah was sitting there thinking, "I sure hope it's not me."

I interpreted Shonnah's enthusiasm for the marriage conversation as a hint to me that she had re-thought her decision and was now interested in me. I thought maybe the Lord had shown her our future marriage the same way He had shown me. On her part, Shonnah brushed off her fears that I was still interested in her because I had "backed off" in recent weeks. Helen dropped us off at my apartment where Shonnah's car was parked. We got in the car to go somewhere and, because I was so encouraged by what I *misperceived* as her "hints" to me, I blurted out, "The Lord has shown me that you are going to be my wife."

It didn't go off quite like I'd played it over and over in my mind. Instead of the tearful embrace, enthusiastic laughter and excitement I was hoping for, she said, "No way. God has not spoken to me at all. I don't see it." Ouch!

In the natural I wasn't that great a catch. I didn't have a job or work skills and I wasn't interested in one because I was doing the "work of the ministry." I saw it as living by faith while I was cashing my welfare checks and living off everyone else, including my roommate. My pastor, Henry, who was discipling me, tried to encourage me toward employment... but the message wasn't getting through. He and others recognized the evangelistic call on my life but they knew it was in the future. I thought it was for now. Besides my unemployed status, other black marks against me included my wild background, my very recent conversion and a less-than-distinguished grade-eight education. Also, I didn't have a driver's license and lived out of a backpack. Another very legitimate concern was whether my zeal would burn out, causing me to backslide and return to my previous lifestyle. At the time, I had been walking with the Lord for less than a year.

Letting Go Of Expectations

Shonnah had a list she'd made of the characteristics she wanted in a husband. She'd been praying over it for ten years and also had ladies in the church praying for her future spouse. I exceeded all the spiritual requirements but she'd also been praying for a good-looking virgin and she didn't think I fit either of those criteria. I wasn't a virgin, for sure, but I was hoping I'd squeak by on the other qualification. (This is known as denial and wishful thinking.)

Shonnah's parents and my pastor knew that she was the one for me. One of the elders had a dream confirming it. Shonnah's brother knew it. I wondered why God wasn't telling the one person whose opinion *really* mattered. It did seem to be a bit of an obstacle.

Shonnah worked the graveyard shift at a bakery. With the help of her friends there, she came to realize that she talked about me all the time and that she missed me when we were apart. One of her friends at work said, "I don't believe you aren't interested. You like him; you're just not admitting it."

"No I don't." (This is known as denial and wishful thinking.)

She kept getting hung up on her list of requirements. Then she read a book called *Passion and Purity* in which someone asked how important it was that her potential spouse is good looking. The reply was, "What if you are the tool God wants to use to bless someone else with what they want? Get your eyes off yourself." The Lord led Shonnah to ask, "What if God wants to bless Todd with me?" She had been living in a fairy-tale world and her friends had to help her see her true feelings because she had an expectation of what "it" would look like.

The most important characteristics are love, devotion and passion for God. Yes, beauty is in the eye of the beholder. Yet God can help us see the beauty in others. I believe it's important to have expectations regarding a mate but not to hold God to our unrealistic expectations if they aren't His requirements. I encourage single Christians to ask the Lord what their ideal husband or wife looks like for them. There are a lot of single people who won't accept the spouse of God's choosing because of a physical flaw. Deciding on a life's partner needs to be by the Spirit, not by the flesh, natural attraction or lust. The Lord isn't against dating, but God has a choice for each one.

Dear reader, if you're single, I want to encourage you to keep your eyes on Jesus and ask Him to help you make your list. If you're married and your original motives for saying "I do" were not right or from the Lord, don't think my previous comments are an endorsement for divorce. Invite Jesus and His principles into your life and He will bless and honor your covenant as you do the same. The issue of divorce and remarriage is a whole topic in itself and I won't get into it right now. (Now, back to my story—sometimes I just can't help lapsing into a sermonette.)

Finally!

Shonnah finally believed that I was God's answer to her ten years of prayer. Since everyone else believed this too, we decided not to have a long engagement. I whole-heartedly embraced Paul's philosophy, "better to marry than to burn". Long engagements are fine but if both parties, pastoral leadership and those you are in relationship with feel you're making a good decision, then why give room for the devil to attack? We decided to get married in five weeks, on May 22, 1995.

We were so on fire in those days that even at my "bachelor party," we did evangelism. At the restaurant, they dressed me in a white shirt that said prisoner of love, put a ball and chain on my ankle and put a toilet seat around my head. Then they said, "You have to go to the Save On and buy toilet paper and Hershey's chocolate sauce for your seat." We were so passionate about reaching the lost that

54

the pastor, a few of the friends and I just stood out in front of the store for a while and shared with people about Jesus. "What are you doing?" they'd ask. "It's my bachelor's party and I want to tell you about Jesus," I'd say. (Even years later in my ministry as I travel doing big crusades, we still take people into the market to do prophetic evangelism.)

The night before my wedding, I barely slept. I had butterflies in my stomach. My friends stayed the night. In the morning my mother came over and, sure enough, we got into one of the biggest fights we'd had in years—and believe me, we'd had some doozies. (There had been times that I violently abused her and she had gotten so upset that she'd pull out a knife to try and stab me.) In the midst of our fight that day I said, "Mom you're wrecking my wedding day. How can you make me feel like this? How can you be so selfish?" But by the time I was ready to leave for the church I had gotten down on my knees and apologized for all the ways I'd hurt her then and in the past. We wept and prayed together. God wanted to expose some things in my life and be sure I was ready to "leave and cleave".

From that day forward I had an open door to minister to her. She read my newsletters and began watching Billy Graham on TV. She read all the Christian material I brought to her. She would even let Shonnah and I pray for her.

The Most Beautiful Bride in the World

I arrived at the wedding hall, nervous and excited. I wondered what would happen when I saw her for the first time in her wedding gown. I remember the moment the music began to play and the door opened. My most vivid memory is of the moment she stepped out into the aisle with her dad. She was beautiful. My breath was literally taken away. I just about passed out. That moment was as dramatic as it could be. My best men looked at me and asked, "Are you all right?"

We had a beautiful reception. The church was like a family for us; they prepared the hall, put together all the details of a perfect wedding and pulled together a potluck reception. They even blessed us on our way by stuffing my Dayton boots with money (a collection from family and friends). That day we left for a short honeymoon to Qualicum Beach and yet, today, the honeymoon continues. (It's worth the wait my single friend; God has a mate for you.)

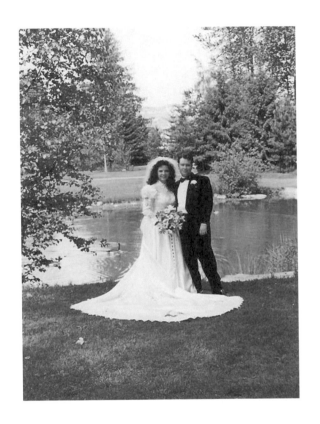

Chapter 7

THE CLEANSING PROCESS

As in every believer's walk with Jesus, my conversion was only the beginning of the transformation. Then came the working out of my salvation with fear and trembling. One of the first things to go in my ongoing cleansing process was a poverty mindset, the idea that God probably didn't want me to have anything at all. My attitude was, "I won't presume on God, whatever He gives me is OK." I had a "crumbs-from-Your-table-are-good-enough" mentality. I was just thankful that I was saved and not going to hell but I really didn't expect much from God. I felt so unworthy of anything good and pure because I knew how many lives I had destroyed. I struggled daily with rejection.

God used my relationship with my wife to teach me about His unconditional love for me. Shonnah was 16 when she got healed of cancer and born again. At that time I was ten and dabbling in the occult. I was a child and my wife and the intercessors were already praying for me. I was overwhelmed that God would keep a woman pure 26 years for me. She never did drugs, drank or smoked; she kept herself from men and was on fire for God. She was everything that I ever could have wanted in a woman and I felt totally unworthy. I really struggled with thoughts like, "How could I have someone so pure? I'm going to corrupt her."

Once, when I was newly married, a woman in church said, "Todd Bentley, you are not for Shonnah but Shonnah is for you. God kept Shonnah all these years as a gift to give to you." She was a tangible evidence of His love for me. God used Shonnah's love, time and time again, as I struggled with guilt, condemnation, unworthiness and rejection. I'd mess up, come short of my expectations, hurt her and feel terrible. It was like Paul's struggle—what I wanted to do I didn't and what I didn't want to do I did. At times I'd be insensitive and she'd be right there to say, "I forgive you." Then I'd fall, sin against God and feel such condemnation. She would say, "If I can forgive you every day, then why can't God?" Then I would think: "My wife loves me so much—surely His love is even greater!"

Employment

I'd always struggled to hold a job and be financially responsible. Most of my life I didn't even care about working. In the past I worked and collected welfare at the same time. I saw the government as my enemy and I was going to keep every dollar I could. I thought that God would call me into the ministry any second but others convinced me that I needed to work and support my family. It was a struggle—I'd get a job and get laid off, then I'd get another job and the place would go bankrupt. I'd start my own business and it would go well—for a while—then the bottom would drop out. It really wasn't until I got into the ministry that I began to believe that God even wanted me to be blessed and to enjoy His goodness in my own life.

Deliverance

In the first couple of years after I was born again, God dealt with me over and over again, bringing deliverance, imparting a greater revelation of my acceptance and pouring out His cleansing grace. Before I move to Abbotsford, I was at the home of some Catholic friends, in the middle of bible study, when the Lord told me I had a demon of fear. "Oh God, what am I going to do?" I asked. He told me to talk to Frenchie who was there. I walked up to him and said, "Frenchie, I have a demon of ..." When I said "fear", I started contorting, flailing, screaming and writhing like a snake. People jumped on me but I threw them across the room and started ripping furniture. Five people finally sat on me and took me through deliverance for more than two hours. This was the first deliverance session the Lord divinely arranged for me (as referred to earlier in the book).

Another time, God touched my life during a Vineyard revival meeting. I was at the altar to get prayer ministry when churning emotions rose up inside me. Destructive thoughts overwhelmed me: "I just want to kill myself." Anger, murder, death, suicide and violence raged inside me. I ended up on the floor writhing and screaming. It was a spirit of death and it was connected to my fascination with Jim Morrison and my drug overdoses. I went through deliverance until one in the morning.

Once more, I was at my local church during a city prayer gathering. During the worship service I started screaming at the top of my lungs for my father. Picture that, right in the middle of the service and I'm yelling, "Dad, daddy." Here I was, Mr. Cool, still looking like a biker and believing that "big boys don't cry". This time it wasn't a demon; it was just the pain, the ache, the loneliness of not knowing the love and acceptance of my father. The whole place, about 30 people, started interceding for me. I ended up like a lump of weeping mush on the floor. I was crying like a baby but I was dressed like a biker. After bawling for hours I was overcome with the revelation of the Father's love for me. My friends had to carry me to a vehicle, drive me home and carry me into my house I was so intoxicated with the Lord's love.

Outside of my own prayer life, I had many other tremendous encounters in which God set me free from bondages, brought me a revelation of His love and dealt with my past experiences. I believe the Holy Spirit was saying, "This is My fish. I want to get him clean and get him on the market as soon as possible." So God did a very quick work in my life.

Children

Like my wedding and cleansing process, most events in my life seemed to happen fast. So Shonnah and I asked, "Why not have kids right away too?" As a result of Shonnah's past fight with cancer, the doctor said she'd have a one percent chance of conceiving. After trying for 14 months we were convinced the doctor was right.

Shonnah got prayer from a prophet who had a word of knowledge for barrenness. The power of God went through her and seven days later she conceived. I was so excited when we discovered that Shonnah was pregnant—from then on, every day for me was like waiting for Christmas. One day I was in the bathroom; the due date was still a few months away. "I just can't wait any longer for this child," I said to God. "Can You bring the labor on early?" Everything else God had given me had come fast, so I was in my bathroom begging. "Give me the baby; You can give it to me in half the time and it can come out done."

Then I heard an audible voice that said, "I'm even more excited and more passionate about your child than you are." I broke down and wept.

God taught me so much
when I became a dad.
Lauralee at one and a half
months old.

"Look at you; look at how excited you are about having a baby," the Father said. "You can't wait. That's what I'm like. Every morning I'm just as excited about fellowshipping with you. Would you come and be with Me?" Those words wrecked my life.

The Lord also used Lauralee's birth to show me the love of the Father. When she was born, I would hold her while I walked up and down the halls singing spontaneous love songs to her. The Lord said, "The way you see this child is how I see you. Is there anything she could ever do that would make you stop loving her? He used the emotions of how I felt toward my daughter and related it to His feelings for me. "That's how I sing over you, that's how I delight in you and rejoice over you with singing." This powerful message freed me from the feeling that God was angry with me.

Today, as I write this book, Lauralee is six. Later we had Esther and Elijah ten months apart. They are four and three now. Then my prayer became: "God can we turn it off now?"

Visualizing the Future

My pastor, Henry Schmidt, continued to disciple me while I headed to the skateboard park or the street to evangelize. I was still wearing my hair long with a beard, leather jacket and ripped pants for extra effect. I had this voracious appetite for God and as great a desire to share with others the treasures I had found in relationship with Jesus and the Holy Spirit.

I began to have lots of opportunity to share Christ as well as my testimony: youth groups, Christian schools, a coffee house, and the skateboard park. I set up a tract booth outside of the mall. I'd give a tract or magazine to everyone who was "foolish enough" to walk close by. Many days I was in the street for up to four hours. I made opportunities. I took teams into the street and had open air crusades Saturday evening in the park whether people wanted to listen to me or not. I was on fire. The world was my parish. I didn't wait to share until someone offered me a stadium. I soon came to understand that what you do in secret, the Lord rewards openly.

A desire for God to use me in the nations began to grow; I used to lie on my bed and have, what I call, Holy Ghost fantasies till 12:00 or 1:00 a.m., or sometimes until 3 a.m. Sometimes the sun would be coming up and I would still be dreaming about what I would do that day and imagining it in my spirit. Although awake, I would imagine myself preaching in Africa and would picture stadiums filled with multitudes or see people healed and raised from the dead. It was like a sanctified daydream. Even King David, in Psalm 63:6-7, speaks of lying on his bed and meditating on the Lord in the night watch (which was 3 a.m. to 6 a.m.). I also believe that, during these night watches, David was reliving in his imagination all that God had done in the past—how God delivered him, guided his life and provided for him. Here is David, in the early-morning hours, meditating on his destiny, dreaming about what it would be like to fulfill what God had said would happen in and through his life. I see David even recreating the scenario, in his mind, of what it would look like when God defeated his enemy.

When I was a newly-saved Christian of only two months, I knew what the prophetic word over my life was and the promise of the Bible about my destiny. So I would lie on my bed and daydream that tens of thousands were streaming to the altars, asking Jesus to be their Savior. In my imagination I'd picture myself praying for the deaf and I'd hear the crowds screaming. I would see the mother whose son was just healed of deafness say, "my son can hear" as tears rolled down her face. Day after day I'd have these big dreams from a big God about big stuff. I see now that I had a big, God-inspired imagination. Yet, back then I would say, "Lord forgive me for my pride. It is wrong for me to think of something this great." Then I'd think to myself, "Who am I that God would use me?" With these condemning thoughts came a sense of guilt about wanting God to fulfill my dreams and do great things in and through my life. (I realized later that God was initiating my dreams and desires and that the devil was trying to discourage me from them.) But the God-dreams became stronger— the next day, there I was again in Africa and India holding crusades like Reinhard

Bonnke and Benny Hinn.

Eventually, as a result of surrendering my sanctified imagination to God, I learned to release destiny by seeing myself preaching in stadiums or healing the sick. I believed in a big God and I had big dreams. I was actually, according to scripture, calling forth the things that weren't as though they were (Rom. 4:17). I was cultivating the promise of God that He had birthed in my heart; I knew I was called as an evangelist. This principle of, "calling things forth" (which is a kind of prophecy) became a major key in birthing my ministry.

I'll share two biblical examples of this visualization process: Even though Abraham and his wife were past child-bearing years, God had a destiny for them. God told Abraham to look at the stars to illustrate how numerous his descendants would be (Gen. 15:5). He had to visualize it to help get it in his spirit. We see the same principle demonstrated in Genesis 30:31-43. Jacob increases the flock of spotted goats by putting striped or speckled branches in the watering troughs so that the goats would see them when they came to drink and when they mated.

In the New Testament, the Apostle Paul echoes this truth: "But we all, with unveiled face, beholding as in a mirror the glory of the Lord, are being transformed into the same image from glory to glory, just as by the Spirit of the Lord" (II Cor. 3:18). As I like to say, "What you see, you be."

In the beginning I didn't understand this principle and I'd repent after I started seeing myself preaching in stadiums. "Lord, forgive my pride," I'd say, "I'm hungry for You, but I also want to be faithful to what You've called me to now." I'd walk down the street in Abbotsford preaching to the trees along the road, pretending they were people. Really, it wasn't my pride; it was the Holy Spirit putting destiny in me.

Foretaste of Things to Come

On one occasion, I was invited to speak at a local Mennonite youth group. I gave my testimony and taught about the Holy Spirit and intimacy with Him. During the altar call, young people fell under the power of the Spirit—some shook, while others were touched in many other ways (all spiritual manifestations were quite foreign to this group of youth). Thus began a revival in that youth group; it grew from about 25 to 100 in less than a year.

Some time later, I was introduced to Kevin Paterson and a group of local youth pastors who had been meeting for over a year for weekly prayer. They felt led to start an inter-church revival meeting called Fresh Fire. In 1997, they began to meet in a storefront church with a small group of spiritually hungry young people. Their vision was to pray, worship, prophesy, hear God and ignite a revival fire through youth of the city.

I shared once at Fresh Fire and they invited me to come with them and a team of youth to minister at "The Street Church" in Vancouver. I spent about two eight-hour days in prayer, preparing for my evening message. Since I had no religious training I didn't realize that, to many Christians, this would be considered excessive. That evening the youth ministered with drama, music and testimonies. I got up to preach and the Holy Spirit fell. Halfway through my sermon, people started coming to the front, falling on their knees and calling out for the Lord. Many street people were saved and healed that night. After that experience, I began to preach more regularly at Fresh Fire meetings.

These two experiences, one with the Mennonite youth group the other at the street church, were some of the initial evidences of God's hand on my life for ministering in the supernatural. I believe God was giving me a foretaste of things to come.

Chapter 8

MARINATING AND PICKLING IN THE HOLY SPIRIT

I'd been saved almost four years. I was still preaching in the streets. I had a daily prayer life and was regularly spending extended days, hours and months waiting in His presence, fasting, and studying the bible. I was still hungry for more of God. I wanted Him to use me. I knew that one day He would. Two months after I got saved someone told me that I had the mantle of an evangelist and I was called to reach people. I never doubted that.

However, I always struggled as to whether I needed to work a secular job because I knew that I was called to the ministry. I believed the call was now and that I should live by faith. I remember having to come to the place where I died to my vision of full-time ministry. I said, "God I want to thank You for my wife and children and I'm going to do what I have to do to be a mature Christian man, husband and father.

I worked in a sawmill stacking lumber; they called it the "green chain". The lumber came out of the saw cut to different sizes then down a conveyer belt where I grabbed the lumber, pulled it off the green chain and stacked it according to length. It was a good job with good pay. The best I'd ever had.

I learned that it wasn't so much about who I was in the pulpit as much as it was about who I was in the home and in the marketplace. I wanted to be a witness. I wanted to know Him and seek His face and not His hand. I had to let Him work character in me. Yet, I still couldn't shake the passion inside for doing Christian ministry. I was consumed with God and His call.

Every day I would go to the mill, but there was still a vision, a passion, a knowing that God was going to use me in the nations. I wanted to see thousands saved and be used by God in miracles and healings. The great evangelists throughout history inspired me. However, I had to die to these dreams regularly and say, "I'll love You and I'll serve You Lord whether or not You use me in 'full-time ministry.'"

Within months of giving my passion for ministry to Him, He resurrected it and gave it back. I felt like Abraham laying Isaac down on the altar. The test was, "Will you love me more than you love the vision?"

My Second Season of Visitation

Soon after, I was introduced to the youth pastors of Fresh Fire. After the powerful experience at the Street Church, I was so excited about what God did that I resolved to spend more time in prayer and in the presence of the Holy Spirit. I was being asked to preach more at the Fresh Fire youth meetings, which soon moved to the basement of the Anglican Church at the invitation of the youth pastor, Jean-Marc Russi. I desperately wanted God more and desired to see Him pour out His Spirit through me at these youth meetings.

Around that time I got tendonitis at work and went on compensation for what ended up being three months. I began to cry out to the Lord: "Oh God, please visit me in power again like You did in that first extended season of visitation when I was introduced to the Holy Spirit." I purposed in my heart that I would pursue an encounter with God. I committed that the time I would normally spend working, I would spend with the Lord. I pressed in each day in desperation to sense His presence. I wanted to hear His voice. I was crying out for a life-changing encounter with His Glory.

"If I draw near to You, You said You would draw near to me," I would say to God. Every day I would cry out for Him to fulfill His promises. You said, "If I search for You with all my heart then I would find You." I sensed moments of His presence but inside I was never satisfied—I wanted more. For about two weeks I did everything I'd learned—praise, worship, speaking in tongues, interceding and everything that I knew about prayer. There was something of a routine to my prayer life. It consisted of a half hour of speaking in tongues, a half hour of praise and fifteen minutes of spontaneous prayer. "God I want to feel Your presence," was my cry—I knew there was more.

Then one day it happened. At home, in my living room, I was desperately crying out for His presence, "Visit me Lord. Come a little bit closer." In the midst of my desperate pursuit of a breakthrough, suddenly, without warning, a wind filled my lungs. I became supernaturally mute, just like Zechariah in the temple. The atmosphere of my room changed. I became aware of a strong presence of the Lord. I saw the smoke of His glory moving toward me—like liquid honey, like a warm blanket it enveloped me. I felt electricity begin to move through my body and I was overwhelmed by the intense, weighty presence of God pressing on my body. The apostle Paul talked about that "weight of glory" in II Corinthians 4:17. The glory settled on my body and weighed me down. It was almost like I was entering into sleep. This heavy glory caused me to fall off my chair onto the carpet.

I was powerless to regain my strength. I was reminded of when the glory fell in Solomon's temple and the priests couldn't stand to minister because of the cloud. I felt wave after wave of the Lord's presence and electricity moving through my body. Hours later I got up and my voice returned. "Something's happened to me," I said.

"More Lord"

There was a new excitement in my spirit in prayer, a fiery passion in me to repeat yesterday's experience. I was wrecked. I didn't want to do anything except spend time with the Lord. For four to twelve hours each day I would seek the Lord in my apartment. Most of my time with Him consisted of laying in His presence, soaking and marinating in the glory, allowing the Holy Spirit to saturate me. I grew more intimately acquainted with the heart and voice of the Spirit as He visited me in sweet, loving ways and in dramatic encounters. Each day when I finished praying and soaking, I would eagerly anticipate what would happen the next time I prayed.

I distinctly remember day two of this visitation. "Shonnah," I said, "I'm going to take some time to enter the Lord's presence." I opened the door to my prayer room, stepped inside and closed the door; when I turned around I became aware of not just the presence of Jesus, but the presence of the *person* of Jesus. He was standing in the center of the room. I mumbled, "Thank You Jesus" a few times as I began to shake and weep. This time it took no effort to enter into the glory; the glory was waiting for me.

The third day I was getting ready to pray. "What's going to happen today?" I wondered. Before I prayed, I went to get a glass of juice, opened the refrigerator and began pouring when I became aware, again, of the presence of a person walking up behind me. "I know it's You Jesus," I cried out. Though I could not see Him with my physical eyes, I fell to my knees, juice, jug, and all. The fridge door was standing wide open. I wept… and I knew I was weeping on His feet.

Vision of Gethsemane

In a vision, He took me to the garden of Gethsemane. I watched the crucifixion, the suffering and the intensity of Jesus' emotions. During this encounter I was aware of all of my natural senses. I wept and felt the deep despair of the moment.

It was through that experience that I understood the intensity of the Father's love and desire for me. As I watched, Jesus asked if the cup could pass from Him then said, "nevertheless, not My will but Your will be done." With great intensity, the Father sternly said, "It is My will, drink the cup." It wasn't stern as in "angry", but stern as in "urgent", birthed out of passion. "Yes, take the cup," the Father seemed to be saying, "because I can't wait to get the world redeemed; I long to be with them, to have them back in intimacy with Me." He was feeling the agony of His one Son but wanted the others as His children too.

Jesus was sweating great drops of blood, wrestling back and forth, and anticipating the awful agony of taking the cup. It was so intense. The revelation began to sink into me: Jesus abandoned His life because of the Father's great desire to delight in me. As the Father loved the Son, I realized, He loves me with this same fiery passion I was seeing.

"May they be brought to complete unity to let the world know that You sent Me and have loved them even as You have loved Me" (John 17:23). This scripture reinforced that love I was seeing in my visionary experience. John says that the Father loved me as He loves Jesus—Wow! Then I started applying this incredible divine truth. If God hears the prayers of Jesus, then He must hear mine. The revelation came in great waves—even though I was desperately seeking intimacy with Him, His intense passion to be with me was even greater. This heart-level truth dealt a major blow to the enemy's hold on me concerning my past.

The experience left me numbed and with a deep conviction that I needed to completely abandon my life to Him. I felt an intimacy and a new oneness with the Lord, realizing that He would bleed and endure such agony and suffering for me. Day after day I sat at His feet and enjoyed His presence—in this place, numerous encounters followed, each one as powerful as these initial three visitations. There were times the encounters happened daily. God would visit with visions, trances, dreams, revelation, angelic visitations, and even His audible voice—things I'd read about in the bible but was now experiencing. Yes, the "God, who at various times and in various ways spoke…" (Heb. 1:1) was now speaking to me in various ways too.

A supernatural God, I believe, wants the supernatural to be natural and common. Realize that when I speak of visions, trances, visitations, miracles and visits to the third heavens… really, I haven't known anything else since I was saved. All that I've known is the gospel. It was only when I got involved with Christians that I found out how out of the ordinary it was for North American believers to experience God in that way. When you read the bible you find out that all these experiences should be ordinary.

This intense season of soaking in His presence and receiving revelation lasted three months.

Chapter 9

COUNTDOWN TO SPIRITUAL BLAST-OFF

During those three months the Lord dealt with me on five issues: Intimacy, the Prophetic, Healing, Evangelism and Repentance. Since intimacy is such a huge part of my life and I want to share some teaching, I'm dedicating this whole chapter to it and will pick up the other four subjects in chapter 10.

Intimacy

For three months I did carpet time. I purposed that I wouldn't ask the Lord for anything. I practiced just being and beholding the glory and worshipping. I waited and listened more than anything. The Lord taught me how to empty my mind, to sit at His feet like Mary, to gaze upon His beauty and to soak and be still. He showed me Isaiah 30:15— "...In returning and rest you shall be saved; in quietness and confidence shall be your strength...."

The Holy Spirit taught me that I didn't need to do all the talking, praying and the "charismania" acts to make Him come down—the praying in tongues, devotions and intense prayer. He wanted to be with me more than I wanted to be with Him. All these disciplines are important but during this season of soaking God wanted me to come and just be in His presence without a list of needs or the sense of duty expected to accompany prayer.

I remember thinking, "But if I stop talking, God's going to forget that I'm here wanting to be in His presence. Because the only time I'm with God is when I'm praying." I thought that the minute I stopped speaking in tongues, praising, worshipping, or reading the Word, the presence of the Lord was going to wane.

But the Holy Spirit wanted to teach me the place of resting. Later I would understand that the Spirit was preparing me to be part of the great contemplative prayer movement that He was raising up. The Lord began to teach me about resting through scripture. He showed me that He "acts for the one who waits for Him." (Isaiah 64:4) and that "...they that wait upon the Lord shall renew their strength; they shall mount up with wings as eagles; they shall run, and not be weary; and they shall walk, and not faint" (Isaiah 40:31). He also whispered to me: "Be still and know that I am God"(Psalm 46:10).

I was excited about growing in rest and intimacy with the Holy Spirit—I knew from experience that in that place, even without praying sometimes, God begins to give us the desires of our hearts. I walked in such intimacy with Jesus when I first got saved. I remember one time I was walking from my kitchen to my bedroom, and I thought, "Oh, I've got to have a peanut butter sandwich." I went to the cupboard and there was no peanut butter. So, I thought to myself, "Oh, man, I really want peanut butter", and I went to bed. Shonnah got up the next morning, opened the garage door, and there was one jar of peanut butter sitting on the steps.

Positioned in Quietness

During this season, I learned that soaking in His presence releases prophetic revelation into our lives. Just like Mary, who sat at Jesus' feet and listened to His teachings (Luke 10:39), I was positioning myself in quietness and stillness before Him so I could hear His voice. Many believers don't hear God's voice because they don't practice quietness, stillness or soaking in the Lord's glory.

First Samuel 3 indicates that the key to Samuel's hearing was positioning himself, lying down where the ark of God was: "…in the tabernacle of the LORD where the ark of God was, and while Samuel was lying down… the LORD called Samuel" (I Sam. 3:3-4). In those days, the bible tells us, the word of the Lord was rare and there was no widespread revelation. Yet the word of the Lord and the revelation of Jesus came to Samuel while he was lying where the ark of God was. That's where God wants to bring us—to the place of His presence. Once, while I was lying on the floor I said,

"God, how I want You. You don't know how much I want You and Your presence."

"I want yours more," He clearly replied.

"Lord, You want me more than I want You?" I questioned. "Oh God, how many times have I withheld myself from You?"

The Genesis account of God's first relationship with man confirms this divine passion for relationship with His children. Oh how the Father loved to come down and walk in the cool of the day with Adam and Eve. The Father even went searching for them when that sweet relationship was broken. "Where are you, Adam? Where's our intimacy?" I can imagine God asking. "What happened to our times of just being together in the garden and talking? I miss it. I want your presence more than you want Mine."

Desperate for More

There was a time when the Holy Spirit fell on me with a spirit of holiness and desperation. I felt like I didn't know God; I felt like God was a million miles away, even though I knew I had a relationship with the Holy Spirit. People around me said, "Todd, if I could only have half of what you've got, I'd be satisfied. Who are you to hunger for more?" In response I would say, "Compared to how deep I know I can go, I'm not really deep at all." A passion and holy desperation fell on me as I came into this valley of death, this wilderness. At the same time, I was still experiencing God's manifest glory on me. Yet, I knew I had only begun my journey of intimacy. "No, Lord, I know there's more."

For a few days I was in prayer from the moment I woke up to the moment I went to bed, seeking, drawing near, saying, "Lord, more. Oh, deeper." I locked myself in the bedroom, prayed in tongues, read the Word and worshiped for hours with a worship tape. I was on a quest. I wasn't satisfied with where I was or where I had been. I was looking for the next realm in Him, that place of glory to glory. Whatever got in my way was going to get out of the way because I didn't have a shovel in my hand—the hunger inside me had the force of a bulldozer. "Either You touch me God, or I'm going to Heaven. That's it!" I was so hungry I literally felt like I was about to die if God didn't visit me. It was an unquenchable thirst.

I was on the floor day after day, resting in His presence, drinking in the wine of His Spirit. I also attended every revival meeting or conference that I could get to, yet I still hungered for more. "I've got to go deeper. There's a well I haven't touched," was my heart's cry. I stirred myself up to take hold of God.

"God, I'm seeking You, I'm searching for You with all of my heart. You said I'd find You. You said if I'd draw near to You, You'd draw near to me. Fall on me!"

This season of intimacy was so wonderful that, at times when I woke in the morning, I would still feel the lingering presence of the previous day's meeting with God. It was like dew resting on me.

Stay Holy Spirit

During these times of visitation, I was afraid that the Lord's fellowship would leave. I said, "Oh no, the Lord's leaving, fellowship is over." But one particular time I was so hungry I yelled, "No!" I jumped up off the floor and said, "God, I'm going to take hold of You." I chased after God and stirred myself up. "Draw near to me. Fall on me again. Who are You to make me hungry and not feed me? Who are You to make me thirsty and not give me to drink? You fall on me with this Glory, and then You just take Yourself away? Forget it, God. I'm going to seek You until You fall on me again."

Then, I'd pray in tongues and seek the Lord for another hour. Wham! I would be sandwiched to the floor again for another four hours. Then the presence of the Lord would lift again. I felt like a wild animal going after my prey as I jumped up and said, "Lord, No!" I'd chase God down again and then wham, I was on the floor once more. I had times with God like that which lasted up to 12 hours.

The Holy Spirit was re-emphasizing, "Todd, I'm trying to teach you how to receive. You don't have to strive. I know you're hungry but I want to reveal Myself to you more than you want Me to reveal Myself. You've got to quiet yourself. You've got to become still. That's why I took the words out of your mouth. It's to get you positioned in quietness at My feet and in the place of stillness so I can speak to you." I finally caught the picture. It's like this, if you and I were having a conversation and we were both talking at the same time, we wouldn't hear each other. There are times for talking, times for listening and times of just enjoying sweet fellowship.

Then I went back into prayer that evening and prayed, "Come Lord. I just want to lie in Your Glory, to lie in Your river." Wham! God's glory for four hours!

Even to this day when I soak I say, "Alright, Lord. You know I'm here. I don't have to tell You. You're not dumb. I'm just going to get on the floor." The Lord shows up with His glory presence.

Soaking Party

We started having "soaking parties." People asked if they could come over and lay on my carpet so we could soak together. Many times Shonnah and I would soak with our friends. One time I had eight people in my house including one of my pastors. After a time of worship, the presence of the Lord was resting heavily. It's hard to describe but I'll say it was like an electric, honey blanket came upon the room. I knew in that moment I was about to be taken into a trance. "Let's just be still in His presence," I said. Then suddenly, the walls of my apartment seemed to disappear.

I was overwhelmed with the presence of the Lord. All of a sudden I shouted out, "The grass! Can you see the grass?" I could feel it coming up through my toes. When I looked at the grass it moved and it had life—the glory came off it. It was greener grass than you've ever seen before. As I stepped on it, I could feel it under my feet. I could feel the Presence tingling through my body. It was as if the grass itself was alive and had personality. I'd look at it and it would say things to me even though there was no actual conversation. There was life in that grass; it was as if God Himself was in it. At first, everyone in my home thought I was crazy! Then they also began to experience aspects of the vision.

When I looked out, I saw a forest and trees that went further than my eyes could see. My carpet had become grass and there were river banks on both sides. I was fully conscious and I saw nothing but the paradise of God. Every time I looked at it I was overwhelmed with another wave of glory. I became intoxicated with God's presence. "He gave showers of blessing and grass in the field for everyone," I thought.

People started getting scriptures—the moment I'd share something, the Lord would bring a verse to them associated with the vision. It became so real and vivid that, with my eyes wide open I saw water an inch deep come pouring in out of the kitchen and across my carpet. The carpet actually looked wet—I thought my wife had left the bathtub or the dishwasher on. "The river just came into my living room!" I screamed. Nobody else knew what to do. Then the pastor jumped off the couch and threw himself onto the floor into this revelatory river. I saw it rise a couple of feet and start flowing across his back. The river was flowing, vibrant, rushing across him. And there was grass and trees—a full-on interactive prophetic experience. The more I shared the vision and the more the others allowed themselves to be taken into what I saw, the more it grew. By now there was a guy lying on his back, under the power, and the others were having experiences too. They weren't seeing the vision like I was; they were experiencing it in realm of emotions. I saw it and experienced it with all of my senses.

The next thing I saw was a huge tree in the center of my apartment. The body of the tree was like a mass of stalks intertwined together to form one massive trunk. The stalks represented elements of the glory of God. Some were gold, silver, bronze or amber. They shimmered with the golden light of His presence. The huge branches of this tree were weighed down, heavy with fruit, about three feet off the ground. The tree was covered with massive, ripe fruit like the fruit that Joshua and Caleb brought out of the promised land. I realized I was seeing the tree of life. Some of us began to eat from that prophetic tree and experience its fruit. As I described the fruit, the pastor on the floor swimming in the river responded with delight at the taste of the fruit. Although he had not seen the tree, he was acting as if he was eating fruit. I could hear his lips smacking, "Umm umm, yumm." As others ate the fruit there was an explosion of joy and laughter. I heard the joyous outbursts and groans as others were overwhelmed by tastes of His glory.

Then I said, "shhhhh" and there was nothing but silence. In the midst of the silence, from a different realm, I could hear a sound, like a bass note going off on the inside of my spirit-man. So I asked, "Can you hear it?" However, they couldn't hear the sound. The same thing happened on the road to Damascus. Paul's companions saw the light, but they couldn't hear the voice. But this experience was so real to me that I thought for sure the others could hear it too. In that moment I heard the sound of the Lord God walking in the garden. Eventually, I realized I was in the Garden of Eden, in Paradise. Then the experience changed, it was like we were playing hide and seek with God and He was searching for us. "Adam, where are you?" I knew this was an invitation to walk with God in the cool of the day. The Lord was inviting us to intimacy and to taste and see that He is good.

Another time, several of us, including several prophetic people, were basking in His presence at Patricia King's house. We were just waiting to see if the Lord would speak to us. After worshipping for a while, everyone in the room, with their eyes open, saw flashes of light followed by a lighting bolt in the living room. Patricia screamed, "Did you see that? What was it? I think it was lightning." Someone suggested that the florescent lights had flickered. So we dimmed all the lights and continued waiting on the Lord with only candles. Yet, the lightning continued to flash for some time. Following the lightning experience, a corporate wave of intercession fell and we spoke in Chinese tongues. Several actually saw themselves preaching in China.

Angels, Angels, Angels

Do you know what started happening to me during my private soaking times? Angels started coming into the bedroom as pillars of shimmering light moving to and fro in the room. Shonnah saw them too. We both trembled and wept together holding hands in bed.

On another occasion, a huge angel showed up in my living room. He stood about 20 feet tall, towering through the ceiling of the apartment above me. His chest was level with my ceiling. It wouldn't be until several years later that I understood the significance of the visitation of this angel, which came just weeks before I was commissioned into the ministry.

Resting in His Presence

During this time, the Holy Spirit emphasized again and again the importance of resting in His presence. I learned that God never leaves. We only leave Him when our mind wanders or strays into worry and concern. But, did you know it is possible to live in God's glory? In his book, *Practicing the Presence of God*, Brother Lawrence describes how he learned to live in the Presence. (I encourage you to read this book—it has blessed me greatly.)

Another reason people can't get into God's presence, even when their mind is on God, is because they're too busy trying to find God when He's actually right there. Mike Bickle says, "It's like trying to get into a room you're already in." Once I prayed, "God, I'm running after You, I'm looking for You." He responded, "I'm right here. I live inside of you. All My glory, the same Spirit that raised Jesus from the dead, is inside of you." Quiet yourself and think about entering into that glory that's in you. Each of us is a New Testament ark of the covenant; God's presence lives in us. The key is to be still, to be quiet.

Listening prayer became my greatest weapon. I wanted (and still want) Jesus more than anything. I spent more time in His presence than anywhere else. I exercised my spiritual senses by listening to the Spirit. I was dwelling in the secret place of the most high, focusing on Jesus. Today, I have a grace now to call others into a "God hunger." This soaking season was really a special time of personal revival.

The Secret Place

Resting in His presence equipped me for the work of the ministry. God used that three- month period to impart the anointings I carry in ministry now: power, healings and prophetic blessings. The thrust of our whole ministry is built on the foundation of this season of soaking.

As I cried out for more intimacy with the Holy Spirit I entered into a place where I grew dramatically in receiving spiritual gifts. I call this the Secret Place—it was living here that I received revelation. The Lord gave me prophetic insights into the kingdom in that place.

I still remember one of the most revelatory messages I preached early on—it's still one of the most sought-after tape series, *The Secret Place*. During this time, in a matter of two minutes, I received a prophetic revelation, which I call *The Father's House*. It's about nine rooms in a house that correspond to nine levels of intimacy with the Father. Oddly enough, when God gave me this revelation, I was in the bathroom brushing my teeth and I went out in the Spirit. I was taken into the Father's House and permitted to go into those nine rooms.

Contagious Fire

Those first nine months of my personal revival I preached on intimacy, God chasing, holy hunger, soaking and Holy Ghost visitation. During this season, I continued ministering each Friday night at the interdenominational Fresh Fire youth meetings in the basement of the Anglican Church. These meetings were attended by youth from Baptist, Mennonite, Pentecostal, Anglican, independent charismatic, and various other evangelical churches. I preached a few times at these meetings while I was still working at the mill and then continued through my soaking season. During this three-month encounter, the youth and youth pastors watched my life change almost overnight. Every Friday night I shared what was happening in my apartment. I had new favor on my ministry and the presence of the Lord would break into the meetings in powerful manifestations.

In the Friday meetings, I simply shared the testimony of visitation with these youth. When they saw the hunger and desperation I had for God, it became like a contagious fire. I taught them how they could come into the same place of intimacy. As I ministered, God would use me to usher His presence into these Fresh Fire meetings and to draw others into the same place of intimacy. In His presence, the Holy Spirit would powerfully touch youth and various manifestations would begin to break out, including "falling under the power of the Spirit", drunkenness in the Spirit, shaking, and laughing. These phenomena happened sovereignly as the Holy Spirit visited us, without any hype or prompting by the leadership. What was even more amazing—the majority of these young people were from very conservative backgrounds, had never heard of these types of manifestations and were just beginning to learn about the Holy Spirit.

Once, there was such a profound outpouring of the Holy Spirit that about 30 Mennonite youth ended up on the floor in travailing intercession, in fits of holy laughter, or just screaming as God touched them. The meeting had gone late and parents were starting to come down the stairs to find their kids. I remember Kevin running around saying, "Pray for me guys. I'm going to go talk to the parents and try to explain what God's doing in their kids. Their parent's don't believe in this. They're conservative and don't express themselves like that. Try and get the kids sober." Some of the youth had to be helped up the stairs to their parents. I remember thinking, "We'll get phone calls on this," but they never came. Although some kids didn't return, many more came, hungry to experience what they heard God was doing among their peers.

Chapter 10

SPIRITUAL BLAST-OFF
(Growing in the Prophetic, Healing, Evangelism and Repentance)

Prophecy

The season of intimacy eventually grew into another level of God's preparation in my life. During my hours in the Holy Spirit's presence each day, I continued to cry out for more prophetic insights. Once I had tasted the anointing for ministry, each day I would pray, "Lord I want to prophesy over someone today." I wanted to give it away.

I started prophesying to all the youth on Friday nights. At times the Lord would give me specific words before I prophesied and other times I would just step out in faith, begin to prophesy and hope the Lord would join me. "If (you have the gift of) prophecy, let us prophesy in proportion to our faith" (Romans 12:5).

I had become so full of God's presence, I had to give it away. I remember sitting with two other youth pastors in the church office and the Spirit of Prophecy fell on me. Literally, a mantle fell—Whap! "I'm going to prophesy," I said. I'd given little words here and there but this was like a torrent. I felt the prophetic bubble up in my spirit. I prophesied over them and I got so intense, I opened up the door and ran down the hallway into the church and said, "Is there anyone out here I can prophesy over? It's flowing. Where's the secretary?" I was looking for more targets... I mean, people. So I prophesied over everybody there in the church. It just kept flowing—people were going out under the power and they were weeping. It was like Saul (I Samuel 10:10) when the Spirit of Prophecy fell on him and he prophesied non-stop from morning to night.

At times I would prophesy over the majority of the youth at Fresh Fire. Meetings would go late into the evening and I would often minister, pray and prophesy for hours. Lives of young people would be dramatically changed as God began to prophetically speak life and destiny into their lives. In this prophetic season, I was invited to speak to a group of youth holding a Saturday night prayer meeting at a Mennonite high school in town. During the worship time I began to receive visions from the Lord for the group as well as specific prophetic words for individuals. Most of these youth had never heard a prophetic word. When I began ministering prophetically, both the leaders and youth were deeply affected at the powerful and accurate words from God. Some youth were touched by the Holy Spirit and fell under the power; others began shaking or weeping—right in a Mennonite high school! One of the youth pastors and I prayed prophetically over most every young person in the place and then invited them to our Fresh Fire meetings. Over the next few months the youth revival continued to grow. Many of the Mennonite youth from the high school began attending the Fresh Fire meetings and were transformed by the Spirit's power.

Healing

The second clear season I entered into during my preparation for full-time ministry was a period of growth in faith for healing and miracles. Even before my soaking season started, I had a foretaste of the healing anointing the night we took the young people of Fresh Fire to the Street Church in downtown Vancouver. As I spoke of this church in an earlier chapter, it was a ministry to the homeless, criminals, street kids and prostitutes. It is significant that my ministry to these broken people was the springboard that launched me into my season of intimacy and the powerful things to follow. (Scripture tells us that God has compassion on the broken and poor in spirit.)

This meeting was my first real, "crusade-type meeting." I still remember the smell of alcohol on people in the little storefront church. It was in March. It was cold. People were lined up on the street. I said "God, the food tonight is hot dogs. I love hotdogs!" I was excited. I thought, "I'm going to share my testimony and ask God for the same kind of power we've seen on Friday to be here tonight." During my testimony, before I gave the altar call, four guys and one woman were moved by the way the Lord touched my life and came and stood at the altar. I gave my youth team a look that asked, "What's going on? Find out what they want." I thought that they were coming to interrupt the meeting because they were drunk.

I was still preaching and one of the team members yelled out, "They want to get saved now." The woman said, "I'm a prostitute. I'm a drug addict and I have AIDS. I feel dirty and I want to be clean." I led her to the Lord. I remember how she screamed, wept and shook as a demon came out. She fell to the floor and vibrated under the power of the Holy Spirit. I can still remember the change of her countenance.

Then I opened the altar for everyone and others came and got saved. I left that meeting and as I walked to the bus I said, "I want to do this for the rest of my life. I'm hungry for God's power." I got a testimony a few weeks later that that woman was completely healed and delivered from her addictions.

Later, during my soaking season, God began to stir up an even greater desire to be used in healing and miracles. I began to read about healing. The Lord also began to give me more revelation regarding healing as I studied His word. Soon, just reading about healing, hearing wonderful testimonies and meditating on the powerful scriptures was not enough. I was compelled to begin stretching my faith and begin praying for the sick. I would pray for the sick at every opportunity, as I met sick people throughout the day or at the youth meetings. I would even visit the sick in hospitals sometimes so I could begin activating the scriptural truths I was learning.

A Grandfather is Healed!

On Friday nights, the fire of God would fall and ignite the lives of youth from many denominations. I remember preaching on radical faith for the impossible one night. "Todd you've got to pray for that girl over there," said the Holy Spirit. That same 14-year-old-girl, Julie, came to me after the service. She asked if I would pray with her. Her grandfather in the U.S. had experienced a stroke that had left him mute and his left side paralyzed. "He doesn't know Jesus. Pray that he would be healed and know Jesus was the one who did the miracle."

We agreed and I prayed, "Jesus I ask You to heal Julie's grandfather." Just then Jesus interrupted my prayer.

"What are you doing Todd?" I heard Him ask.

"I'm praying."

"You just preached on radical faith for the impossible—what are you going to do about this?"

80

I knew in my heart I was only praying a courtesy prayer. But my faith changed as I prayed and suddenly I was translated in the Spirit to this man's hospital room. I saw him lying before me on the bed asleep. He was hooked up to IV's and a heart monitor. I laid my hands on him and rebuked the effects of the stroke. Immediately, I saw that man rise up out of his bed and run down the hallway with the IV still in his arm.

Within hours the telephone rang back in Canada. Julie answered it, and heard these words, "Praise Jesus, praise Jesus, I've been healed." Her grandfather shared how the power of God came into his body and how he was supernaturally healed of every trace of that stroke.

When she told me, I couldn't actually believe it. She shared it with me three times. I really thought I had just visualized the scene in my mind since I knew he was hospitalized. When I finally believed it I thought, "Wow this is cool, but why me?" Countless times I've asked that same question, "Why me?"

Then on Friday, healings and miracles started through the word of knowledge and the prayer of faith. Before I would go to the meetings, I would wait on the Lord. I began to have pictures and scenes in my mind of people's faces or of healings that would happen. I would see people bending over and touching their toes or taking a brace off their leg. Then I would simply go to the meeting and tell people what I'd seen. Occasionally I would feel someone's infirmity in my body.

I specifically remember one 16-year-old girl with such a severe case of scoliosis that she couldn't stand up straight. As the Lord touched her, there was a cracking sound. Her spine straightened, she began to cry, her leg became normal, her bones adjusted and she stood straight. Others were healed of various pains as well as shoulder, neck and back conditions.

Week after week the youth would press in with hunger for more of the Spirit. The Holy Spirit would fall and it would be as if He was supernaturally conducting the meeting. At times, some youth would be praying and crying out for souls, while in other parts of the room others would be worshipping passionately, some would be dancing to the Lord and others would be gathered in groups prophesying over each other. It seemed that even this prophetic anointing was being caught. The Spirit of prophecy would come on the place and youth would begin to prophesy spontaneously under my mantle, similar to the story in

I Samuel 10:10 of Saul prophesying when he came into contact with the prophets. As the youth continued to earnestly desire spiritual gifts, according to I Corinthians 14:1, they began to grow in the prophetic anointing too.

We were all amazed at God's powerful workings as He orchestrated our small meetings; young people were being saved almost every week. He imparted a new passion for Jesus and changed their lives as prophetic destiny was spoken over them.

Stretching My Faith

It was T.L. Osborne's book *Healing the Sick* that would further ignite and activate my passion to walk in God's power. I began to read through this book one chapter at a time. I would preach the book and pray the healing scriptures out loud, proclaiming them by faith.

There was no specific call by a prophet, vision from the Lord or visitation of an angel that said, "Todd I've called you to healing ministry." All I had in those days was hunger. The bible said to earnestly desire spiritual gifts and I did. Fueled by stories of others whom God had used in the past, I said, "Healing is for me." After all, Jesus clearly told us: "I say to you, he who believes in Me, the works that I do he will do also; and greater works than these he will do, because I go to My Father" (John 14:12). He also promised us that signs would follow those who believe:

> ...in My name they will cast out demons; they will speak with new tongues; they will take up serpents; and if they drink anything deadly, it will by no means hurt them; they will lay hands on the sick, and they will recover (Mark 16:17,18).

In James 5:15, I also saw that "the prayer of faith will save the sick, and the Lord will raise him up..." I wondered why I couldn't pray the prayer of faith if healing was so clearly a powerful truth in scripture. "Why can't I preach healing like those other guys and pray in faith for the sick; why wouldn't God do for me what He did for them?"

In my journey into the ministry of healing I continued to discover new truths. "God," I said, "there has to be a release of Your power that comes through fasting." I remember going on three-day fasts. I didn't pray a lot; rather,

I read over and over every account of the healing ministry of Jesus recorded in the gospels. I would only read those accounts. I didn't stop; I just read every story about Jesus the healer again and again. I prayed that His stories would become real in my life. I did this day after day, over and over. "What did the healing look like? What were His motives?" I would wonder. Then I would examine His language.

Because I had learned this whole new dimension of expressing myself in prayer called soaking, I had become very receptive to the Holy Spirit. Often a day or two before the next youth meeting I would wait in His presence and say, "Lord, show me the things You want to do in the meeting tonight." During these moments of seeking direction in quietness, I had mental pictures (which we call visions) of people's faces or of illnesses. I would see the service and the altar call.

As I continued to step out in faith using the T. L. Osborne model of teaching and the Oral Robert's healing line model of laying on of hands, more and more people began to be healed and the healing anointing increased. I began discovering that the key to the healing ministry was persisting in prayer whether I saw results instantly or not. My motto was, "It's our job to do the praying, it's God's job to do the healing."

As God began to release more and more healings, I experienced something I hadn't seen yet in my meetings. A woman was healed in her seat without the laying on of hands. She was healed of chronic wrist pain just sitting in the meeting under the anointing. She yelled out, "My wrist pain is healed!"

As the healing and prophetic anointing increased in our meetings, I began to feel a desire to take God's power outside the church walls.

Evangelism

As God stirred up a greater passion for evangelism in me once again, I especially longed to take this increased prophetic anointing to the streets. "If it works in the church why can't it work in the market place?" the Holy Spirit asked one day. He began to illuminate a passage of scripture to me:

> "But if all prophesy, and an unbeliever or an uninformed person comes in, he is convinced by all, he is convicted by all. And thus the secrets of his heart are revealed; and so, falling down on his

face, he will worship God and report that God is truly among you" (I Cor. 14:24, 25).

One Friday after the Fresh Fire service I asked, "Who wants to go out into the market to do prophetic evangelism?" Then some of the youth and several of my friends went out believing for a prophetic anointing to impact the lost. Some of us ordered sandwiches at a Subway sandwich shop while some of the youth went to Tim Horton's, two doors down.

In Subway, we were talking loudly about the healings and prophetic words at the meetings when two of the employees, overheard us. They asked a question about psychics and I said, "Forget about psychics." I asked if they knew that God spoke today. After I described some prophetic experiences, I asked whether they wanted to hear from the Lord. "God created you and He has a plan and a purpose for your life. I'm going to ask Him for just one thought that He has about you."

In that moment about four others kids came in to get sandwiches and asked, "What's going on in here?" I answered, "You know how psychics can sometime tell you details of your life? I've got a gift like that from Jesus and it's called prophecy. I'm going to tell these two people about their destiny. If you want to hear yours get in line."

The first employee volunteered quickly but the young woman was hesitant. The other four were watching to see what would happen. I told the employee about how hurtful it had been when his father left recently and his parents divorced. I also told him about what was going on in his life with drugs and that he might go to prison. Tears welled up in this young man's eyes and he had to go compose himself.

The Lord also really touched the second Subway employee, a young woman. As I laid hands on her I was able to describe the inside of her bedroom right down to the last detail, including her stuffed animals. She was so afraid; she got freaked out and ran back behind the counter. I wondered why the Lord gave me the most intimate room in her house. I was concerned she might think I was a peeping Tom or had been stalking her. The Lord told me that He wanted to bring her into the most intimate place.

The other young people were amazed and lined up. Next, the toughest of the kids challenged me. "Do me!" The Lord revealed that he was an avid athlete and football player and that he had broken up with a girlfriend many months before but still deeply missed her. This young guy turned to look with wide-eyed amazement at his friends, "Did you hear that?" They all laughed because they knew it was true. Then came the softening word. I began to tell him how that he was tough on the outside but soft on the inside and that no one knew that he would sometimes cry on his bed at night. This young jock and his friends were all deeply touched that night over their prophetic words.

The youth that were with me ran over to Tim Horton's and we all met in the parking lot. The four unsaved kids actually went to find their friends to see if it would work for them. "Do this guy, do this guy." The first Subway worker got saved and another one of the youth got saved and fell out under the power. I invited them all to church. This was our first encounter with prophetic evangelism during my soaking season.

The interesting thing about this encounter was that weeks later, on Halloween night, one of the young men I prophesied over at Subway came to church with two friends and asked me to prophecy over them. One of them came to the Lord, most of them heard the gospel, and all of them had an experience of the reality of God which they would never forget.

A Word for the Waitress

Many other times, in those days before I was released into full-time ministry, I had watched God touch the lost through prophetic words. Another occasion Shonnah, my friend Steve and I were in a restaurant and I asked myself, "Why can't I, in faith, ask the Holy Spirit for a word for the waitress?" I said to everyone at the table, "Let's ask God to give each of us a piece of information for the waitress." When I prayed, I felt an impression that she had grown up in a religious environment and that at about 11 or 12- years-old she was a victim of abuse—she was now angry with God, blaming Him for betraying her. I told her, "The Lord tells me things about people sometimes," and shared what I felt. She was taken aback and said, "Yes." She didn't know what to say, so she walked away.

When she came back with our drinks, I asked Steve, "Do you have a word for her?" Steve said, "No, I've only got a picture in my mind. I saw a birdcage out on a balcony, with a bird in it." The rest of us were rolling our eyes. But she said, "That's my apartment." God was using that picture to show her that He knew every detail of her life.

Immediately I shared another word of knowledge: "The reason you don't want to give your life to the Lord is because the boyfriend you live with doesn't want anything to do with Christianity and you're afraid you'd lose him." Although she didn't give her life to Jesus that day, we prayed together that the boyfriend would give his life to God. By the time we left, she knew that the Lord was speaking to her and that she had a call on her life.

The Convenience Store

In those early days, even before my season of soaking, I had such a heart for evangelism. One time I went into a convenience store late in the evening to pick up some junk food. I got into a ten minute, one-on-one conversation, with the clerk who had asked me "What are you doing tonight?"

"I just came from this radical youth service called God Rock"

"I don't believe in that God stuff; I'm an atheist."

I shared my testimony and it seemed to go OK. I ended my story with, "When you're alone sometime, ask Jesus to reveal Himself to you." I figured I'd sewed the seed and I left. Weeks later, after another one of these God Rock services, Steve, Shonnah, Roswetta and I, (the same group from the restaurant story), decided to go with me back to the convenience store to get some food and see how my seed had been growing. We pulled up and Steve and I went in. Steve went to the sandwich bar at the back. I just said "hi" and walked by on the way to the Slurpee machine. "Oh look, it's the God fanatics!" yelled the clerk sarcastically—it was a challenge.

Two of the clerk's friends were also in the store. They were wearing the 80's rocker look—ripped jeans, jean jackets, long hair, AC/DC t-shirts and trucker-type hats. They reeked of alcohol and marijuana. The three of them were mocking and scoffing. The clerk was saying, "Come over and tell them what you were telling me." Steve and I were both on the way to the counter to pay for our food. I felt something in my belly like a deep groan or a cramp. I felt like something was going to come up or erupt. I'd heard in meetings about people roaring like lions, and I'd always thought it was ridiculous. I was thinking, "Don't do it. Don't do it". All of a sudden, it was like a river came out of my mouth and I fell to my knees roaring.

The moment I fell under the power, Steve was also hit and his arm went up in the air. As he held his sandwich over his head, his hand was shaking and lettuce was flying out. Steve is naturally, quiet, reserved and introverted. He's a humble, soft-spoken, nice guy who doesn't usually command attention. But all of a sudden, it was as if he was an old time, turn-or-burn revivalist. Even his voice changed. "If YOU DON'T CHANGE YOUR WAYS, YOU WILL GO TO HELLLL!" he yelled out. The Spirit of fear hit the place. The clerk and his friends dove behind the counter. Finally the clerk stood to his feet, pointed over the counter with one finger, shaking and asked, "Is that your God?"

No one was mocking now. Steve and I calmly put our food on the counter. Right then the door opened and an old, dirty bum walked in with a couple of pop bottles to get his refund. He put the bottles on the table, got his money and said, "You better listen to what these two guys are telling you because it's true." Then he turned and walked out. Shonnah and Roswetta were waiting in the car and we asked them if they saw the bum. They said that no one had gone in or out.

Thrown Out of the Donut Shop

We did radical evangelism in these days. Once when my friends Steve, Brian and I went to Tim Horton's donut shop, wanting to witness, we went from table to table with no results. In the shop there was one little side room where you could smoke and it was packed. They encouraged me to preach in there, "You could stand on the table and preach." It was midnight. I went into the room and stood on a chair, "Do you believe in Jesus? I was a drug addict but now I'm a new creation. You can become a new creation too." People were like, "Shut up!" We were kicked out but we congratulated ourselves on our obedience to the Lord. Steve had so turned into an evangelistic fireball that it actually got to the place where no one wanted to go with him to the movie or the store if they were on any kind of a time schedule. He would show up two hours late and he would say, "I picked up a hitchhiker and led him to Christ." If you went to a restaurant with Steve, just wanting to eat, he would share with everyone as he made his way to the table or he would hand out tracts.

Repentance

During the three-month visitation season God continued to pour out His Spirit of intimacy, stir up the prophetic, increase the healing anointing and impart evangelistic zeal. Many of the Fresh Fire youth caught the fervor and would go out with me to witness and prophesy to the lost.

Besides the four impartations already mentioned, God took me into a fifth area—I think of this part of my visitation season as the Holy Spirit boot camp of deep repentance. The intimate times of soaking continued as the Lord gave me specific scriptures which applied to the youth ministry and to my calling. Once I was in prayer and I had an open vision of one single red rose. In the vision, I was looking at the rose, wondering if I could touch it, when it exploded into a ball of fire. I thought, "What does that mean?" The Holy Spirit spoke this phrase, "The desert shall blossom as a rose." Then He brought to my remembrance Isaiah 35. I realized that would be my ministry mandate. The three major themes of this scripture passage are 1) The revival mandate to bring glory, refreshing and wine in the wilderness so the deserts "shall rejoice and blossom." Everything was about the presence of the Lord. 2) Then the miracles happened—"the eyes of the blind shall be opened… and the tongue of the dumb sing." 3) The next theme of this passage was the "highway of holiness." Week after week I preached the conviction of sin, repentance, holiness and the consecrated life. I realized that the highway of miracles and glory was the highway of holiness.

In the early days of my Christian life the Holy Spirit sternly dealt with me about ungodly music, sexual purity, and a set-apart lifestyle. Now I began to see the lukewarmness in the Christian youth of the city—compromise, toleration of sin, unclean movies and ungodly music. This time of refining was crucial for my future ministry. I began preaching fiery messages on repentance and on dying to self. Many youth repented and began embracing set-apart lifestyles. Some even destroyed ungodly music, fetishes, and charms. There was a real passion in many youth to become extreme radical disciples and to ask themselves, "What would

Jesus do?" They wanted to obey the Lord no matter the cost.

Each week backsliders were turning to the Lord. The Spirit was warming cold hearts. Young people were lying on their face weeping at the altars. I remember praying, "Oh God don't let me be a fiery, long-bony-fingered, John-the-Baptist-style, prophetic, repentance preacher for the rest of my life. Let me preach love and soaking." However, there was a desperate need for this message at the time. Today, we still need to see this kind of preaching in the church.

Preparation for the Nations

My ministry involvement with the Fresh Fire youth group lasted about five months in total, until I began traveling regularly and taking the fire of God on the road. Together, we had all grown and learned through those five main lessons the Holy Spirit was teaching me: intimacy, prophecy, healing, evangelism and repentance. A revival began in that interchurch youth group; it grew from about 25 to 50 and over 100 at times. Over those months, hundreds of hungry youth came to that Anglican church for a touch of God's fire. Sometimes the Spirit would come in such intensity that it was complete Holy Ghost chaos (in an orderly way of course). Some enjoyed the joy of the Lord; others fell out under the power. There was shaking, travailing for souls, worshipping, dancing and prophesying. The power of the Lord changed lives and imparted a hunger for Jesus.

The revival ministry with the youth group and my prophetic vision of the Isaiah 35 fiery rose confirmed that there would be three measures of my future ministry—first revival (through intimacy and God's prophetic voice), then healing and finally a strong preacher's anointing for holiness, repentance and the abandoned life. I realized, from that vision, that one day the ministry we had in the church basement would become Fresh Fire Ministries International; but I didn't know when.

Chapter 11

LAUNCHING INTO MINISTRY

Patricia King, a prophetess from British Columbia, heard about the experiences in my prayer closet and how it was spilling out in the youth meetings. She was excited. Though I had been to many of her conferences over the years and had been to her house once with a group, we didn't have a personal relationship. Patricia just thought, "Great, the Gen-X revival generation. We've got another young guy. He's one of thousands that God will raise up and he's right here in my area." In May 1998, she decided to ask me to share for 10 minutes at a women's conference to encourage mothers whose sons might be backslidden or living a lifestyle similar to mine before I met Christ.

I woke up on Mother's Day 1998 and I was preparing for my ten minutes that evening. This was the end of my three-months of soaking. I was still on compensation and planned to go back to my job at the mill. I was used to praying four to eight hours in preparation for most ministry opportunities. I wanted my ministry to be from the Lord and not me. As I waited on God, I immediately sensed in the Spirit that something was different. There was something in the air, an expectation, like Christmas morning. I felt that I was in for an intense visitation or something. "What's up God? What are You going to do?" I felt like something was going to happen that was beyond what I'd experienced before.

The Holy Spirit said, "I want you to pray in tongues." I felt an incredible burden. Something hit me in my spirit and I felt like I was birthing destiny, loosing something and setting something in order—calling things that are not as though they were. It was like I was pulling something out of the heavens. I felt purpose. I felt that what I was doing now determined what was going to happen later in my life. It was as if I was releasing a city whose builder and maker was God. I knew that I was putting things in place for my destiny. I had a sense that I wasn't just birthing one meeting tonight; I was birthing invitations to do meetings around the world. This was unlike any other time I'd prayed in the Spirit. Something was happening right now!

I'd never had that sensation before and it was very confusing. I prayed mysteries. I was pacing back and forth in the living room. Then my mind kicked in. "Why are you doing this? You're not a minister and you've never been to bible school," my thoughts scolded me. "You're going back to work in the mill. No one knows who you are. You're in a church with 50 people. Why do you think you're building a ministry?"

On one hand, I had a vision from the Lord. However, on the other hand, I thought, "I can't do this; the situation isn't right. This is foolishness; I'm only 22 years old. I'm invited to do one meeting… and only for ten minutes!"

My body began entering into deep groans, almost like contractions. Then I would pray in English, decreeing in the Spirit the thoughts that were breaking in, "God I call forth right now, those You've called to be partners with the ministry. I birth them and I pray they will have the money they need." Then my brain would say, "You don't even have a ministry and you certainly don't have any partners." I'd go back to praying: "God I pray now that Your miracle, healing power would come upon this service and would continue into other meetings."

My brain would kick in again and say, "God I don't have any meetings." The Holy Spirit would respond, "You're building a city whose builder and maker is God. You're doing it on the level of intercession. You're loosing it in the Spirit now so it can come forth in the future, even though it may be 10 years down the road." It was very confusing, like a spiritual battle was taking place in my mind. Just then I heard Shonnah wake up. I went into the bedroom and she said, "I just had a dream and I was walking really fast praying in tongues and someone said, "Why are you doing this?" Then I said, "I don't know, but I know it's the right thing to do." Then she rolled over and went back to sleep. (Although she claims she was entering into the rest of the Lord.)

At the end of that visitation, after about four hours of praying in the Spirit, I felt peace, heat and electricity. I had a sense of someone looking over my shoulder. I realized I was having a visitation of the Lord Himself. He wasn't in physical form but I could feel His wonderful presence behind me. Every time I tried to see Him He was always behind me. But I knew it was Jesus. I heard Him audibly say, "Watch and see."

I sensed something big was up. "Watch and see what? Does it have something to do with the meeting tonight?" Three or four times I asked. All He would say was, "Watch and see." I remembered Genesis 18:17: "And the Lord said, 'Shall I hide from Abraham what I am doing, since Abraham shall surely become a great and mighty nation, and all the nations of the earth shall be blessed in him?'" I pressed in and prayed, "Lord, don't hide from me," when a vision opened in which I saw a woman at Patricia's meeting get healed of cancer. Then I received several other healing words and saw the service—it was like I was there already. I prayed for the sick and then I saw myself laying hands on hundreds of women. They were falling out under the power.

Then I saw Patricia King—she called me out and I saw her prophesy over me and my ministry. The Lord said He would use that night's service to launch me into an international ministry and I wouldn't go back to my secular job. I had no understanding of what was taking place, but I prayed and the Lord reminded me of Acts 13:2: "Separate unto me Barnabas and Saul for the work to which I have called them."

"I'll tell Patricia tonight in the service to take up an offering, ordain you and call you into the ministry by a prophetic word," the Lord said. "You will quit your job. And as a sign to you, I'm going to heal a woman of cancer in that auditorium." I thought, "Oh God, how's it going to happen? I've never been to bible school. I don't have any finances. No one knows who I am. What am I going to tell my wife?" He said, "Watch and see. My power is going to fill that auditorium."

For the first time I had a great job working at a mill run by a Christian. I even had medical and dental benefits, for goodness sake. I was making great money and taking care of my family. I was content to be faithful in the small things and worry about what God had for me later. I had been very zealous for ministry but I laid it down about three years before. I had wanted things to happen quickly but there was too much selfish ambition in me so He had to kill it. Now that the full-time ministry desires had died, He said, "OK, I can give it to you now."

I'd never spoken in a meeting like Patricia's before. I showed up in my typical attire, ripped jeans, bandana, goatee and earrings. She emphasized the time restriction again: "Can you keep it to ten minutes Todd?" I immediately went back to the Lord, and asked, "How are You going to do what You showed me? I'm not even the main speaker. I don't want to look like I'm trying to steal the show. There isn't even time for the words of knowledge."

As I was asking this question, I had a vision, which would give me the "wisdom of the Lord". I saw the day the stone was rolled away from Jesus' tomb—out from the cave came a brilliant blast of light and glory. I knew it was the resurrection. Then the verse came, "Jesus said to her, 'I am the resurrection and the life'" (John 11:25). Suddenly, I knew that there had been many suicides in that city and they were dealing with a spirit of death. I saw that the Lord wanted to roll back the stone and release resurrection power. Worship was still going on and I shared the vision with Patricia.

"You've got to share that."

"After I share, can I pray for a release of that?"

"Yes, break the spirit of death according to what you saw and then share your testimony." As I spoke out this word, the Lord said, "Call out the woman with cancer you saw in the vision this morning, and rebuke the spirit of death on her." Then the wave of the Spirit moved into several other healings. Patricia recognized the move of God's power and came running to the microphone. "You need to hear his testimony and then I'll have him pray for all wayward sons and daughters."

The whole thing unfolded like a television show. God did everything I'd seen in my vision. I gave the words of knowledge and the woman was healed of cancer. Hundreds of women were laid out under the power. Ten minutes turned into an hour and then Patricia got up. The power of God hit me and I knew what was coming. She said, "The Lord just spoke to me. We're going to take an offering and lay hands on this young man. He's going to the nations. He'll never return to secular work." God continued to orchestrate that meeting.

Not only did those people give a large offering—over 50 men and women committed to intercede for my marriage and ministry from that day forward. God supernaturally set it up and launched me in the ministry after my three months of preparation. I thank God that my wife and mother-in-law were in that service. If they weren't there and I had tried to tell them what happened they would have said, "No way, maybe when you're 30 or 35." But they both witnessed how the Lord put together the events of that meeting piece by piece; they were convinced that it was really God's timing.

Thank God that since that time Patricia and I have had a friendship and instrument that the Holy Spirit used to ordain me into the ministry, but the call came from God. I've also been ordained in Canada by my local church and through the Christian Minister's Association. In addition, for my U.S. ministry base, I've been recognized as a minister of the gospel through World Ministry Fellowship in Texas.

The Popcorn Anointing

It was weeks later before I understood that my launch into ministry was the fulfillment of the end-time army visitation, which I described in the beginning of this book.

Here's a quick bunny trail about what the Lord is going to do in the future. The way the Lord called me into the ministry is an example of what I call the "Popcorn Anointing". We see an example of this quick ministry launch in the book of Acts: "Now in the church... there were certain prophets and teachers... As they ministered to the Lord and fasted, the Holy Spirit said, 'Now separate to me Barnabas and Saul for the work to which I have called them'" (Acts 13:1-2).

The time has come when those who have remained faithful are going to be thrust into the harvest. This is God's sending time. Just as Paul was snatched out of the Arabian Desert, many will be brought out of their desert season into their giftings and anointing. This is the year of the Lord's glory. The gold (finances) is going to be released for end-time apostolic ministries, which will bring in the harvest. Scripture links the release of God's power with financial blessings: "With great power the apostles gave witness to the resurrection of the Lord Jesus and God poured rich blessings on them all" (Acts 4:33-35). In those days of the early church, not one of the believers was in need. Those who owned fields or houses sold them and brought the money to the apostles and the money was distributed to each one according to his need

First Road Trip

After Patricia called me into the ministry, I said, "OK God, I'm going to quit my job." Even though everyone had tried so hard to get me employed and I didn't have one speaking engagement yet, as an act of faith, I left my job for traveling ministry. I'd been saved four years. Nobody knew Todd Bentley and I was only 22 years old.

I remember my first road trip; Patricia invited me to William's Lake to be a part of her prophetic team. She said she couldn't pay me an honorarium and I'd have to pay my own way. She'd introduce me and let me prophesy and share my testimony.

In those first few weeks I said to God, "My rent is due. I have no money coming in but I'm going to go on this trip with my wife." Shonnah and I drove to the interior of British Columbia in my lemon-of-a-Mazda MVP van. The road trip was a nightmare; the radiator wouldn't hold water and we had to keep stopping. The five-hour drive took us seven or eight hours. I remember seeing Patricia and Ron's new red, air-conditioned van and asking, "God am I ever going to be there?"

Each night I was able to minister at the altars. Patricia also gave me an opportunity to preach on prophetic evangelism. One morning she announced, "OK, this morning Todd is going to prophesy to everyone whose last name starts with A-D and he has ten minutes to do it."

During that first traveling ministry opportunity, I continually purposed in my heart I was going to live by faith even though each day I was wondering how God was going to provide. In these meetings a woman had a vision and saw herself withdraw $500 from her ATM and give it to me. The day before I needed the rent, God gave it to me to the exact penny. I was so encouraged.

The next month I asked, "God how are You going to get it done?" Again, just before my rent was due, Greg Dennison came to my house. He was one of the men in Pat's first meeting who had committed to pray for me. He said, "Todd I had a vision a month ago and I saw myself writing out $500 post-dated checks. I want to be your first partner." He also became my first travel companion and disciple.

More Than Enough

The first few months of the ministry, when I prayed that God would provide finances, there was something inside of me that said I should never believe for more than I needed at the time. The devil would constantly remind me of struggling ministries and I thought, "Why should it be different for me?" These were Godly men who served the Lord. They had character and passion;

they had everything I wanted, but their churches didn't grow past 70 members.

I felt guilty for wanting to have enough to help the poor, to hire staff and to finance crusades. I was constantly under guilt and condemnation for having dreams of a big international ministry. "What if the Lord called me to only reach one?" I wondered. "Who am I to think I can reach 10,000? I'm always thinking about more than enough but I should just be satisfied with enough."

If anything happened that was good, I was afraid that it would slip away the next day. I felt unworthy of blessings—this mindset stemmed from the great lack I had experienced from childhood. Even in my ministry vision I had to have that spirit of poverty broken. I'd think about Billy Graham and Benny Hinn and wonder why I couldn't do that too? Then I started reading: "If you abide in Me, and My words abide in you, you will ask what you desire, and it shall be done for you. By this My Father is glorified, that you bear much fruit..." (John 15:7-8). I then realized—God doesn't just want me to bear fruit; He wants me to bear *much* fruit.

The story of Jesus feeding the 5,000 (John 6:1-14) also helped me. Think of it—that number just refers to men; it didn't include the many women and children who were also fed. And when everyone had eaten all they wanted, there were 12 full baskets *left over*. Hallelujah, there was more than enough! These scriptures became a foundation for my life and ministry. At first I thought God would never provide financially. Then at each new level I had to believe for more finances and I had to work it through in my spirit. I had to increase my level of faith that He could do it again and that I could trust Him with my future.

Hungry for Miracles

My hunger for a more powerful ministry in the area of miracles continued to grow. I read through the gospels and the book of Acts and said to myself, "This is what I want." I became convinced that in Jesus' ministry and in the early church, the way they brought in the harvest was with signs and wonders. I remember, at times, coming home from meetings and wondering, "God why did You heal this one and not that one?" In this season of pressing in for healing, I became quite frustrated that one deaf person would hear and six others wouldn't. I wasn't always moving in super faith. I remember times when I would lay hands on someone and wouldn't feel any anointing. In my mind I was thinking, "Are You even listening to my prayer God?" In my mind I was repenting of unbelief while out of my mouth was coming this great prayer of faith.

Many times when it seemed like the meeting wasn't lining up with my preaching and with my idea of what a healing service should look like, I would think, "Why is this so hard?" I would release a healing wave and everyone would just stand there with their eyes open and look at me. I would pray this mass prayer rebuking devils and sickness and pray for the healing presence. Then I'd look at the crowd and they would just stare. I would say, "do something you couldn't do—quickly!" People would just stand there and I would wonder if anyone was joining their faith with mine. I've been in meetings where I wondered if anyone was excited about what I was preaching. "If they are," I would think, "then how come they are not responding in faith?" I would come home from those meetings and think: "It's so much work to get someone healed. God, maybe we could just be a salvation ministry." But I couldn't ignore this compelling, burning hunger for more of the real gospel—the full gospel of power.

There were meetings where I preached faith, quoted scriptures and anointed people with oil in healing lines and I saw very few results. Certainly nothing you'd call miraculous. But, there was a violence in my spirit, to war and contend, "I'm not going to give up." I saw in scripture that "many died not yet receiving the promise" (Hebrews 11:39). I purposed in my heart to pray for the sick until I died, or until they did. I pushed past those first disappointing results and said, "I'll keep praying and God will do the rest."

Abbotsford Conference—August 1998

Even in those early days I didn't want to wait for churches to call me. I was "gung ho" to host my own crusades. For those of you who come to our conferences in Abbotsford today, you may find 2,000 to 3,000 people attending from all over the world—that's quite a jump from my first meeting of 25 people, mostly women, in a facility called the Abbotsford Revival Center. I can still hear the music—Clif Robertson singing "Poppa, poppa, pour it out, pour it out, pour it out," or, "Lord of the dance, You're the dancing Lord."

Even in our earliest meetings, God gave us favor. James, a local reporter from the Abbotsford News wrote an article called, **Revival Explores Range of Emotions...** "They shook and they lurched all over the floor," he wrote. Then he described our meetings as, "...an environment far removed from the staid pews of many Abbotsford churches" and reported that people would laugh hysterically, similar to how they did in the early days of the Toronto Blessing.

His article ends with this story:

Some who attended were members of the church, but there were also seekers–and skeptics, like Leslie Heppner. Heppner attended the meeting because her daughter Christina, who is involved in the church's ministry team, wanted evangelist Todd Bentley to pray about the problems her mother was having with her eyes.

Heppner was apprehensive and some of her suspicions were confirmed upon arriving. She sat with her arms folded and observed people breaking into hysterical laughter around her, some nearly collapsing to the floor.

"I wasn't very impressed at all when I walked in there," said Heppner, a Northview church member.

In spite of her misgivings, Heppner went to the front to be prayed over by Bentley. She said the young evangelist told her to let go of the guilt she was carrying. The message struck a chord with Heppner; who said she has felt a lot of guilt about her two divorces.

Heppner said she can't really explain what happened next, when she collapsed to the ground.

"At that time, it just really touched me and I started crying. I felt God did want me to let go of the guilt because it was out of my hands," she said.

Heppner will continue to worship at Northview but she has new-found respect for different worship preferences.

"I know I came out of there really believing the power of God touched me that night." She said.

Healing Angels, Visitation and Commission

I read and reread T.L. Osbourne's book, *Healing the Sick* and F.F. Bosworth's *Christ the Healer.* I preached the theology and principles of healing, read the healing scriptures and claimed them by faith. I confessed, "I am who

God says I am and I can do what God says I can do. I believe God's word." I prayed for the sick wherever I met them. I really wanted to see people healed. I just started laying hands on the sick on the basis of the authority that I saw in the bible. I believed it, so I started doing it. I didn't have a special visitation, anointing or commission, or special words from the prophets about healing.

I started preaching on every thing I saw in the bible that had to do with healing—the principles of faith, theology of healing, hindrances to healing and how to maintain your healing. I trusted that the Holy Sprit would confirm the word. I laid hands on and anointed the sick with oil. I believed God's promise in John 14:12 was for me: "Most assuredly, I say to you, he who believes in Me, the works that I do he will do also; and greater works than these he will do, because I go to My Father."

I copied the models of Oral Roberts, Benny Hinn and T. L. Osborne. Healing is for every believer because Romans 8:11 says that the same Spirit that raised Jesus from the dead lives in me and He's going to quicken and bring life to my mortal body through that Spirit. It's for me and for you.

I purposed that if I prayed for a thousand and no one got healed I would pray for another thousand. In those early days of warring and contending it seemed like I prayed for a thousand without anyone getting healed, but I just kept praying until something happened. Each time a miracle took place there was something new that happened in my spirit in the area of authority and faith. The testimony of what I saw, gave me the confidence that I needed to believe God would do it again. Each healing breakthrough spurred me on to want to see more.

In the beginning I had faith for backs, fibromyalgia and crooked spines. "Anyone got any pain in their body? Arthritis? Come forward now," I would say. At that time my faith level wasn't where it needed to be for the blind, deaf or crippled.

"Give Me the Deaf"

Eventually I said, "God I'm not satisfied with my level of healing. I want the deaf to hear." Since my Mother was deaf, I really wanted to damage the enemy's kingdom in this area. My area of crisis became my area of compassion.

I went hard after that anointing.

Everywhere I went I'd call the deaf forward and pray for them. I prayed for the deaf and I prayed for the deaf and I prayed for the deaf. For the longest time, when they left my meetings they were still deaf. I prayed for hundreds of deaf people and once in a while the deaf heard—partially. I saw results maybe two per cent of the time. I kept begging God, "Give me the deaf. Give me the deaf." Then, God gave me a key; He taught me about the deaf and dumb spirit. I saw it in Mark 9:25: "He rebuked the unclean spirit, saying to it, 'Deaf and dumb spirit, I command you, come out of him and enter him no more!'"

So, just like Jesus did, I began to command that spirit to "loose ears." The next time the deaf came I had a little more confidence and expectation. When a few deaf heard there was more confidence and expectation for next time. I learned that it was all about warring and contending. I used this principle in every major area where I wasn't seeing results. "OK God, I'm seeing breakthrough, but I'm not seeing breakthrough for tumors," I would say. In faith I would sow into praying for tumors until people were healed. Then I would move on to another type of sickness.

I discovered that healing comes in levels and that, as believers, we need to contend and break through one level until we get authority. As we agree with God and see several deaf ears or tumors healed, then our faith-level for that infirmity grows. The more people I prayed for, the more got healed. I prayed in faith regarding a particular illness until I received a breakthrough—the deaf, the blind and then those in wheelchairs. Now I'm contending for resurrections.

On the Road

As a result of my first meeting with Patricia in William's Lake, I received my second invitation, to Prince George Family Worship Center in British Columbia. In the first 18 months of ministry I went there six times. During this same time I also ministered in Mission, BC and the Yukon. These would be the first places where we saw demonstrations of God's healing anointing and glory moving through our traveling ministry.

Here are some reports of those early days:

Whitehorse, Yukon—January 1999

When I'd been in the ministry about six months I went to minister in Whitehorse, Yukon. Those were the early days when I would say, "God what am I doing here in minus 20 degree temperatures? I'm actually ice fishing with the pastors in my free time. No wonder all the Americans think it's only Eskimos and igloos here in Canada." I remember stepping outside and my nose hair would immediately crystallize. I prayed, "God, please don't send me here a lot or, if You do, please let it be in summer."

But there was a small group of people there hungry for revival. The first meetings were held in a Native Indian Hall. They called it the Potlatch House. People would come in wearing snow boots. Some even came from Alaska to visit the meetings. God gave us favor in these meetings when a news reporter from the Yukon News named Anne Pritchard came to the service—as a skeptic. Here is her article (with her summary of my testimony edited out):

Faith healer lays hands on Yukoners
by Anne Pritchard, News reporter

My hands ache. Constantly.
It feels as if knives are being stabbed into my wrist.
It's job-related, a result of banging out stories on a keyboard over the last 15 years.
It's a four-Tylenol-a-day pain in the...well, wrist.
So when I read about evangelist and faith healer Todd Bentley's "miracle, healing evangelism crusade," I thought I'd check it out.
I was interested anyway. I wanted to see if the guy was a shyster, a snake oil salesman.
You gotta wonder.
"Bring your lame, dumb and those with cancer and FAS - those with no hope of a medical cure," said Bentley's flyer, which was posted around Whitehorse.
In response, about 40 people—myself included—hit Mt. McIntyre's Potlach House on Friday night to hear Bentley preach - and maybe experience a miracle healing, or two.

The mood is upbeat. The crowd warms up singing songs of Christian faith. Then Bentley gives his own testimony to the crowd…

Finally the altar call! Most go up for healing.

Are they healed?

Sometimes there are healings on site and, at other times, healing will happen later, he says.

Sometimes people heal only to revert back to their original ailment, he adds.

"I will say that I have seen an incredible amount of people with bone injuries —a crooked spine straightened where God actually takes bones and realigns them."

Bentley claims recent miracles have involved eyesight and cancer.

He has prayed over folks at the Potlatch House, and laid hands on some.

Tonight, he started out offering to heal folks with arthritic pain.

About 30 of the 40 people in the crowd went barreling up to the front of the hall.

Bentley laughed, and called the rest up.

The crowd lined up, and Bentley walked to each one. Sometimes he touched their heads, at other times he just held his arms over the person and uttered a prayer.

Sometimes he did it solo, other times he asked someone for help.

And were they healed?

There's no way to tell, but everyone toppled, a— over teakettle, to the floor and lay there in a seeming euphoric mood - they appeared to be drunk.

Meanwhile, I'm hanging back watching the proceedings. I'm trying to keep an open mind, but this looks weird, people toppling over like tenpins at the hands of the young, stout earring-wearing preacher.

He sees me, eyes my wrist supports and starts urging me to the front of the room.

I think, 'What the hell,' and stride to the lineup.

He anoints my head with a golden oil (it looked like olive oil) and lays his chubby fingers on the top of my head.

I start to get dizzy, and am caught up in some sort of turbulent energy. It feels like the wind is blowing. Hard.

I feel like I'm starting to fall over. I start resisting, pitching forward to avoid hitting the floor like the rest.

Bentley starts to laugh, good naturedly—like he's seen it before.

Then I give up, collapsing like the others.
I feel woozy, like I've been drinking.
He leaves me there and then moves to the next person.
I feel peace, and euphoria.
And, you know, my wrists feel OK.
At least so far.
Bentley's healing crusade goes on until Thursday night.

Mission, BC—March/April 1999

My first experience with revival was within 10 months of being in the ministry. Patricia asked me to come in as a guest minister for one night at Mission Four Square Church. In the prayer service that evening the room smelled of refiner's fire and laundry soap. "But who can endure the day of His coming? And who can stand when He appears? For He is like a refiner's fire and like launderers' soap" (Mal. 3:2).

Patricia said "Something's up." During worship the air became thick with the dew of the Lord and people were saying, "I feel sticky." It was as if dew had fallen from heaven. The Holy Spirit said to me, "Todd you have not because you ask not. If I'm doing dental miracles in Toronto and Argentina I can give them here too." Moving by faith only, I told some stories and asked for dental miracles of glory and gold. That first service seven people received them. Patricia said "There's an unusual presence of the Lord, let's continue the services."

These dental miracles went on for a year in our ministry—signs of God's glory. During the Mission meetings, we packed this church out to overflowing; visitors would come into the meeting and see people with flashlights looking in other people's mouths during worship. The unsaved youth started to come in; then some started getting saved. We grew out of that facility and had to move to a larger church. This was truly the beginning of what revival might taste like.

Great Joy in the City
Mackenzie, B.C.—April 1999

Here's a report about this meeting:

Mackenzie experienced the reality of the scripture verse from Acts 8 as there was "Great Joy in the City." Evangelist Todd Bentley held meetings at Living Joy Christian Center, April 19-21. Unusual dental miracles took place, traces of "gold dust" could be seen on people's hands or face and people were healed of a variety of pain conditions and physical problems. The response was one of amazement and awe, and of course, joy. Fillings in people's teeth changed to silver or gold, and seemed to be highly polished—teeth even straightened. People with pain in their hips and pelvis received freedom from pain and could move in ways that were impossible before. Eyesight and hearing improved and people with asthma and respiratory problems reported great improvements. As a result of people experiencing the reality and power of God's love, many people acknowledged and accepted Jesus Christ as Savior and Lord. We continue to rejoice at God's goodness, His desire still is to heal the sick and the brokenhearted, and to bring liberty to the oppressed. In a world that is experiencing such strife, tragedy and senseless violence, hope can still be found in the reality of Jesus Christ.

Author unknown

Here are excerpts from an article by Peter T. Chattaway called *Gold Teeth Hard to Prove, Useful for Outreach*, May 1999:

The Great Physician may also be the Great Dentist. In the past two months, several dozen people have reported receiving gold fillings and similar miracles at churches and revival meetings throughout British Columbia.

They were having people come up to be prayed for, recalls Dorothy McKee, who says she received four gold teeth at the Mission Foursquare Church March 21. "My husband was checking people as they went up to the front, and he looked in my mouth, and voila, I already had them." Dental miracles have been reported around the world, most recently in Argentina, at various times over the years. The first instance of miraculous fillings in Canada took place March 3 at the Toronto Christian Fellowship. Within a week, over 300 people claimed to have received dental miracles there.

It took only a couple of weeks for churches in Langley and Mission to follow suit. Nine people reported receiving dental miracles at the Langley Vineyard's March 20 service; the next night, seven people reportedly received the same during Todd Bentley's revival service at the Mission Foursquare Church.

And the reports keep coming in.

We've had between 45 and 50 people who have reported some kind of dental miracles in their mouths, says Langley Vineyard pastor Jesse Padgett. Of those, he estimates about 15 to 20 have gone to the dentist for confirmation.

Bentley, an Abbotsford-based evangelist, says the Mission meeting marked the first time gold teeth have appeared at any of his meetings. Since then they've appeared in almost every meeting that I've done, he says, citing his recent rips to Mackenzie, Prince George and Portland, Oregon...

In addition to gold teeth, churchgoers also report gold dust and oil appearing on their hands. Paula Spurr, a musician and former deejay, says her hands began to sparkle during a 'God Rock' service led by Todd Bentley at Burnaby Christian Fellowship March 16.

"It was like Tinkerbell visited. Everyone's hands were shimmering a little bit.", she says. "It was funny, because that's not at all the kind of thing that I look for. I don't need bells or whistles to prove anything, but it happened anyway, so it was like a little present."

Phillip Wiebe, a philosophy professor at Trinity Western University, says the gold tooth phenomenon is not a new thing; he first heard stories of miraculous gold fillings coming out of California 35 years ago...

"And what meaning might such miracles have? For the person that would undergo this, it would be, I would think, wonderful and kind of reassuring, and it would make them think that 'God loves me, is thinking about me and cares about me,'" says Wiebe.

For everyone else, he suggests, signs such as these may be 'teasers' pointing people back to God. The Lord leaves these signs, here and there, that He's real, so that doubters like myself will have some obstacles and, maybe as a result of them, believe.

Mackenzie, B.C.—October 22-23, 1999

Here's the pastor's report:

Todd ministered this weekend to about 30 men. Almost every man was stretched out before the altar in a state of repentance. During ministry times, which usually happened before and after preaching, God displayed His love and power in a variety of ways. Some of the miracles that took place included a girl with a crooked spine becoming perfectly straight, shoulder problems instantly healed, people being freed of depression, fear and anger.

In April a man got saved while Todd was here, his wife was already a Christian. They have been going to her church and he has remained free of any desire for alcohol and has been growing in his relationship with God. This time their three sons were saved and they rejoiced in tears over the fact that the entire family was now saved.

A lady came to Tuesday's meeting intending to have Todd pray for her mother. Her mother had an asthma attack, and while being rushed to the hospital, had a heart attack in the ambulance. At the hospital doctors discovered a hole in one of the heart valves, and also that she had diabetes. She remained in a coma for six days, during which time they gave her insulin and waited for her to recover enough to do heart surgery.

During worship and ministry time the daughter had oil on her hands and as Todd was praying for people, he gave several words of knowledge, one of which was for people with diabetes. She felt a real peace and did not feel she had to go for prayer. The next day she found out that her mother had been released from the hospital, that there was no longer any trace of diabetes. The heart problem had improved so dramatically that it would be more dangerous to operate than to let it remain. She was even strong enough to walk about four blocks. Praise God, both the mother and the daughter gave God glory for this miracle.

Monday night during ministry two of the people on the worship team heard wonderful high harmony joining with them in singing—it turned out that nobody else was there singing with them, it was angels joining in. Awesome!

Throughout the men's conference and the open meetings there were times when the joy of the Lord would break out all over, and the Holy Ghost would minister divinely to people in different ways.

Andy Barnes, Pastor, Living Joy Christian Center

Prince George, British Columbia—January 2000

On my sixth visit to Prince George, about 18 months into my ministry, one of those weekend trips turned into 18 nights of gold and glory. We called it a "suddenly" of God. We were expecting a good time in God's presence and

He came and gave us a taste of revival.

We were recording a live worship CD and at one point the fragrance of the Lord filled the building. For about 45 minutes people smelled vanilla, cinnamon and roses. Psalm 45:8 refers to "the Lord's fragrant robes."

A deaf woman was healed. Diamond dust appeared on people's hands. The glory cloud came. The glory would still be in the church the next day. People fell out under the power in the parking lot or just walking into the building. The Evangelical Christian News reported on the meetings and people learned about it all over Canada.

Our worship leader, Clif Robertson, said that when people began to arrive at the building the presence of the Lord was already lingering there. People began to get drunk. I had planned to preach on the glory of God, but I didn't. Why should I preach on it when it was already there? Yes, people are hungry for the demonstration of the Spirit of God in power. But the most important thing is the presence; even if He didn't come with the miracles, we would just love His presence.

Prince George & Mackenzie

Here's Val Andres report:

During those early Prince George meetings Todd made several visits to a small northern community named Mackenzie. A native lady testified that she was healed of a back injury standing by herself at the altar. The next day her daughter, who was sixty miles away, called to tell her mom that she was healed at work of her back injury. It turns out that both healings happened at the same time, 11:00 o'clock. God is not limited to a building. Many people are going to be healed miles away.

In Prince George Todd was able to minister to two sets of young people in youth prison. Todd received words of knowledge and prophecy to speak into their lives. He was excited about reaching out to those in a lifestyle that he once lived.

The healing miracles in the meetings were not just physical; many were healed emotionally and delivered from demonic strongholds. The Spirit of the Lord moved for over two hours in deliverance one night. He who the

Son sets free is free indeed!

Todd believes that the healing anointing has come to another level. In the four weeks that he was on the road in October the healing testimonies seemed to be greater than at any other time. A man came out of a wheelchair, a man had a growth come off of his eye, and people reported hearing and seeing angels in services. October truly has been a month of harvest!

There were physical healings, spiritual conversions and people intoxicated with the wine of God, falling over and shaking, gold dust and dental miracles. Several would testify to feeling the Lord's presence in the parking lot and many were hit with the presence of the Lord before they even got in the sanctuary to take their seats before the meetings began.

Here's a healing testimony from that time:

Cancer Testimony

My name is Maureen. The doctor had told me that there were spots on my liver and they were cancerous. Last night I went to the Turning Point to receive prayer and during the evening started to feel a burning feeling in my side, and a feeling like something was squeezing me. Today I went to an appointment that was scheduled two weeks ago with the doctor; the appointment was to decide about surgery to remove part of my liver. They did another ultrasound and could not find the spots on my liver, only what they described as some fatty tissue, which could be controlled with a better diet. The doctor admits he can't understand it because this is the second time in two months things have disappeared from x-rays and ultrasounds. I understand it; it is a miracle from God.

I Need More!

Those meetings led to my first revival in British Columbia. Within nine months God was visiting our meetings regularly with the glory and the gold. There were extended meetings lasting several weeks. Each night people would receive gold crowns in their mouths and oil would manifest on people's hands like it happened in the healing revival of the 1950's. The presence of revival swept through our services—the fragrance of the Lord and the glory mist. It was in those early meetings that people began to see angels and receive healing in their

108

body. Christian News Week even did a report on this.

I distinctly remember one extraordinary and wonderful experience that happened in Fort St. John during that first year of ministry. After I prophesied over everyone in the service one night, at about one or two o'clock the morning, I returned to the place I was staying. I decided to worship the Lord for a while and give Him the glory for the meeting. I could sense His presence in the room. Then it was as if the door opened and someone walked into the room; I could suddenly smell the fragrances of the Lord. He fed me the fragrance from His hand. I remember the tears running down my cheeks as I smelled vanilla, cinnamon, roses and many other heavenly aromas. I thought to myself, I am so close to the Lord right now I can actually smell His fragrance.

God caused tremendous growth in the ministry through these early meetings as well as fresh encounters with the Lord, especially on the trips I took to the Yukon. I was crying out to God during this time, "Holy Spirit I want to see more healing, like in the days of the "Voice of Healing Revival." This powerful revival in the '50s birthed hundreds of healing evangelists. The following article excerpt describes the beginnings of that revival:

> "...there was a man by the name of Jack Moore in Shreveport Louisiana in 1946. This angel spoke to him and told him to begin to bring people together and so he brought Gordon Lindsay, A. A. Allen, William Branham, Oral Roberts, and Jack Coe... all together and they started the voice of healing... Five years later when the power hit (William Branham was commissioned in May 1946 but the corporate anointing began to take shape some years later), it hit the "Latter Rain" (movement) in '50 and '51.... (Eye of the Eagle II, Bob Jones and Keith Davis, 12/05/00).

Night after night in America tens of thousands would pack the tents of hundreds of evangelists, some well know and some not. The miracles in these meetings were as profound as miracles that some see today in Africa, India and other third world nations. Thousands were being saved. Some reports spoke of up to 100 people getting out of wheelchairs in one service. There were creative miracles; piles of discarded crutches lay at the altar, not just one or two here and there, but whole stacks.

What's A Healing Anointing?

After reading stories about the Voice of Healing Revival and other healing revivalists like Smith Wigglesworth, Maria Woodworth-Etter and Amy Semple McPherson, I was hungry to see miracles like that. When the Holy Spirit first started using me in healing I didn't know I had a healing mantle. I never heard God say I was a chosen vessel, that He wanted me to carry healing to the nations or that I had a special gift. I just believed what the bible said about preaching the gospel, healing the sick, cleansing the lepers and raising the dead. The bible says these signs will follow them who believe. He is Jehovah Rapha, the God who heals. I also realized, from scripture, that healing is part of the atonement.

I believed it was for me, and so, on the basis of faith in God's word, I just continued anointing people with oil and preaching God's truth about divine healing based on the principles of these six scriptures:

- John 14:12 – "He who believes me will do the works that I do and even greater works than these."
- Isaiah 53:5b – "…by his stripes we are healed."
- Psalm 103:3 – "…who forgives all your sins and heals all your diseases."
- Mark 16:18b – "…they will lay hands on the sick and they will recover."
- Romans 8:11 – "…the same spirit that raised Jesus from the dead lives in you…."
- Hebrews 13:8 – "Jesus Christ is the same yesterday, today and forever."

It was clear to me that healing is in me and every believer, but there's a difference between healing through faith in God's word and the gift of healing in I Corinthians 12:9: "…to another gifts of healing by that one Spirit."

While I was ministering in the Yukon, Canada I had a Holy Spirit visitation. "Do you want the healing anointing?" God asked me. I had just finished doing a healing crusade. I said, "God, what do You mean, do I want the healing anointing?" Then I remembered the story of Jack Coe, one of the most prominent healing ministers of the Voice of Healing revival. He once said to the Lord, "I'm not satisfied with the level of healing. How can I get more?" God said, "You need a healing anointing." Jack asked, "What have I been doing all this time?" God said that Jack had been healing by his faith and the faith of the people, which is good, but that He had an anointing for him so that it wouldn't matter whether people believed, are saved or have faith. God told him that there can be such an atmosphere and manifestation of His presence that whoever comes into His glory gets healed.

God was now asking me if I wanted that anointing so that it wouldn't be so much about whether people believe the principles of healing (although that's important). He was offering me an anointing, so that when I walked into a room people would be healed in an anointing that comes from His presence and the grace of the Holy Spirit. I said, "Oh, gosh, let me think about it." NOT! I said, "Yes, God I want it now." God continued, "The anointing is because of My presence; where My presence is, people are healed." I said, "God if I can get more of Your presence I know I can get more healings." Up until this time my goal was more knowledge, formulas, teaching principles and getting more faith.

I kept doing all the things that I did in the area of faith, healing lines and so on but at the same time I started operating in the dimension of gifting. It came into my life because I earnestly desired spiritual gifts. "Pursue love, and desire spiritual gifts...," scripture tells us in I Corinthians 14:1. God doesn't want you to desire something you can't have.

I continued to preach and teach the truth of divine healing. But when an anointing would come, people would get healed sitting in their seats. So that's how I began to understand the difference between the healing that comes by the faith principle and the healing that comes through sovereign atmosphere.

Whitehorse, Yukon—January, 2000

A highlight of this trip was to see a lady I'd visited in the hospital the last time I was in Whitehorse. At that time she was totally paralyzed from the waist down as a result of an incurable disease. Doctors, and her family, were basically waiting for her to die. After prayer, her legs received partial healing; she began to move them and regain some feeling. Now, she had her driver's license back and was even beginning to walk short distances with a cane.

Another highlight was being invited into the Catholic School to share my testimony with the grade 11 religious studies class. God moved and eight people prayed to receive Christ. There was such favor that they invited me back the next day to preach to grade 10. This time 24 students gave their hearts to the Lord.

In the evening service there was a new level of power. One man who was deaf had his hearing restored. Another man with a paralyzed leg, the result of a witchdoctor's curse in his homeland, was instantly healed. These meetings had such a level of God's presence that the demons would spontaneously cry out, throw some people on the floor and cause them to flail and thrash about.

When I left the Yukon I had no idea that the Lord would move me into a new season of healing, send me to Africa to get John G. Lake's anointing and show me a vision of the coming healing revival.

Chapter 12

A PROPHETIC JOURNEY

I longed to see the apostolic power return to the church. And I longed for an increase in my ministry. The Lord spoke to me about John G. Lake, so I began to study his life and how God used him. He had planted over 600 churches in South Africa.

He didn't just do miracles, signs and wonders but *lived in union*, in oneness and intimacy with the Lord. Experiments were done where diseases and bacteria were put on his hand and monitored under a microscope—they would dissolve or die. Lake carried an unusual anointing of the presence, the fire and the holiness of God. The anointing on his ministry was transferable and tangible. People would often open his newsletter and begin to speak in tongues or get healed because the anointing would be released through the letters that went out. When I read this, I got hungrier. I said, "God I want to see whole cities overcome by Your power and presence. I want more in the area of healing."

The Lord gave me a new commission. "Go to South Africa on a prophetic journey," He said. "I want you to go and get the anointing of John G. Lake." I said, "God I don't know anyone in South Africa." During that conversation with the Lord, I had an open vision and I saw the dates when I would go—March 10-27, 2000.

When the invitation came from a local pastor in Abbotsford, named Keith Abrahams, a prophet from South Africa, the dates matched exactly. He said to me, "Todd do you want to go and minister in South Africa if I arrange some meetings for you?" I thought back to my first year of marriage—Shonnah and I were in a service with a guest from Ghana, Africa and we were both overcome with weeping and intercession and felt like we would one day go to Africa.

The Great Cloud of Witnesses

Prior to going to South Africa the Holy Spirit gave me my first vision of the coming healing revival of signs and wonders. During worship in the local

Abbotsford Revival Center, I felt the Lord's presence surround me. My ears were opened and I heard the tongues of a great crowd. I looked around the sanctuary; there were fewer than 40 people and no one was speaking in tongues. I knew there was no way they could make this great noise. Then I knew it was the tongues of angels. I asked a woman beside me, "Jen, do you hear them? It sounds like angels." The room was filled with noise as if 70,000 people were praying in the Spirit. I felt waves of His glory and power come over me. I felt myself ascending. I was lifted into the Spirit like the apostle John who was caught up in the Spirit on the Lord's Day (Rev. 1:10).

I was standing on a football field in a stadium. I knew I was in a prophetic encounter. The stands were filled with angels, tens upon tens of thousands of angels. There was an immediate knowing that these angels were waiting to be released. They were cheering on the advancement of the kingdom in the modern day church. The church was the team on the field and the angels were about to be released onto a last-days generation to bring about the purposes of God. "Bless the Lord, you His angels, who excel in strength, who do His word, heeding the voice of His word. Bless the Lord, all you His hosts, you ministers of His, who do His pleasure" (Psalm 103:20).

A Vision of the Coming Healing Revival

The Lord showed me that during this upcoming healing revival, an anointing would be released greater than that of the Voice of Healing revival years ago.

God began to speak to me about the coming healing revival in Canada and beyond. Next, I was caught up in the Spirit over North America as if I was flying in an airplane. I saw many small rain clouds of healing and miracles. They were individually set up over many churches, cities, nations and ministries, pouring down healing rain. The rain clouds looked like those in the cartoons where they pour down upon one person and follow him wherever he goes.

I saw many small pools of water and I asked, "What are these?" The Holy Spirit said "I am releasing the pools of Bethesda. This is the release of John 5:1-4:

114

After this there was a feast of the Jews, and Jesus went up to Jerusalem. Now there is in Jerusalem by the Sheep Gate a pool, which is called in Hebrew, Bethesda, having five porches. In these lay a great multitude of sick people, blind, lame, paralyzed, waiting for the moving of the water. For an angel went down at a certain time into the pool and stirred up the water; then whoever stepped in first, after the stirring of the water, was made well of whatever disease he had.

In the vision, I saw the coming healing revival. I saw angels like the angel in John 5 who would be released upon this last days generation. I prayed it would be greater than the days of Alexander Dowie and John G. Lake. "Let there be whole cities and geographic locations touched by Your healing power."

The Transferable Tangible Healing Anointing

Then I saw many ministers, ministries and churches that are already flowing in this miracle, healing anointing, beginning to minister throughout North America. In my vision, as these ministers of healing finished ministering in one location and left, the healing miracle cloud remained upon that church or city, and continued to pour down healing rain.

It was a transferable, tangible anointing of healing being imparted to other ministries, churches and even cities. It spread like fire. Everybody who came in contact with the healing wave started to minister the power of God.

As in my vision, I believe that many places are going to receive such an outpouring of healing rain that pools of water are going to form, like modern-day pools of Bethesda. This outpouring of miracles, signs and wonders is a part of the apostolic move and will touch the four corners of the earth.

The Healing and Miracle Centers

The literal meaning of Bethesda is "the house of outpouring and grace". The grace of God will give us an outpouring of the rains of healing and miracles, until the power of God increases and we have a flood of miracle rain and many pools of healing. The pool of Bethesda was in a geographical place called

Solomon's Porch. The sick came from all over the nation. I believe these Pools of Bethesda the Lord showed me will be places of healing, miracles and revival in many geographical locations.

Once again great multitudes will come from all over the world to geographical healing centers, just like they came to Spokane in the early 1900's to receive from John Lake's ministry. In five short years of Lake's ministry, over 100,000 healings and miracles were documented. The Mayor of Spokane called the city the healthiest in America.

Who Is Going To Receive It?

There won't be just one pool of Bethesda or one Spokane, I believe, but over a hundred different cities that will be internationally known for the ministry of healing. The Holy Spirit spoke to me that these miracles and healings are for those churches and ministries that will fervently cry out for the rain, like Elijah on the mountain in I Kings 18:41-46:

> Then Elijah said to Ahab, "go up, eat and drink; for there is the sound of abundance of rain." So Ahab went up to eat and drink. And Elijah went up to the top of Carmel; then he bowed down on the ground, and put his face between his knees, and said to his servant, "Go up now, look toward the sea." So he went up and looked, and said, "there is nothing." And seven times he said, "go again." Then it came to pass the seventh time, that he said, "There is a cloud, as small as a man's hand, rising out of the sea!" So he said, "Go up, say to Ahab, 'Prepare your chariot, and go down before the rain stops you.'" Now it happened in the meantime that the sky became black with clouds and wind, and there was a heavy rain. So Ahab rode away and went to Jezreel. Then the hand of the Lord came upon Elijah; and he girded up his loins and ran ahead of Ahab to the entrance of Jezreel.

Elijah heard the sound of the abundance of rain. He knew in his spirit that the famine for Israel was over, and it was time for the rain to fall. In the same way, we know today in Church it's time for the Power of God. In I Kings 17:1 Elijah prophesied, "...As the Lord God of Israel lives, before whom I stand, there shall not be dew nor rain these years, except at my word." This scripture indicates that the rains would come according to Elijah's word. It's the same with the coming rains of healing. It will be at the word of the God's people, hungry for healing revival, in intercession and prophetic proclamation that the rains of miracles will fall. Though Elijah knew it was time for the rain to fall, he still prayed fervently on the mountain—he had to birth and call the rain forth. Though he saw nothing, he persisted in fervent prayer until the rain came.

If you are to be in the rain of healing and miracles moving across North America, you need to preach healing. And though you see nothing, preach healing and preach healing again. When you pray for the sick and nobody gets healed, pray again. Elijah persisted seven times and he saw nothing. When he finally saw the cloud, it was still only the size of a man's hand.

God's Promise to Fill Healing Rooms

In North America today, we have numerous healing room ministries— I know of over 60. We are getting ready for the power of God just like in II Kings 3:17-20:

> Thus says the Lord: 'Make this valley full of ditches.' For thus
> says the Lord: 'You shall not see wind, nor shall you see rain; yet
> that valley shall be filled with water. And this is a simple matter
> in the sight of the Lord...' Now it happened in the morning,
> when the grain offering was offered, that suddenly water came
> by way of Edom, and the land was filled with water.

God told them to prepare during the drought for the water, by digging ditches (water canals). As we prepare the containers for healing revival, then one day—it could be today or tomorrow—with no sign of wind nor rain, when it seems like we aren't getting the breakthrough we are looking for in healing, and we continue to persist in intercession, preaching and prayers for the sick—boom, the water canals will be full!

I hear the sound of the abundance of rain and I know in my spirit IT IS

TIME! Climb up on the mountain, call for the rain and call for the storm. When the rains first began to come in first Kings, the cloud was only the size of a man's fist, but it grew to the place where Elijah told Ahab to get his chariot and get going before the rain stopped him.

God spoke to my heart that there would be healings at first. Then the rain would become torrential and we'd move into creative miracles. Will your church be a pool of Bethesda for the sick and the lame? Well, then let it pour, for the Lord says that truly the people will come from miles around. There will be many cities like Spokane—this time not just with a man or a ministry—but whole cities under the anointing. People will be saying, "If I can get to that city I know I'll be healed."

Chapter 13

MY FIRST INTERNATIONAL TRIP

My first ministry opportunities were in British Columbia then in the Pacific Northwest. Then I started receiving speaking invitations each day and was booked six months in advance. I didn't have to say, "Who's got contacts?" It just happened.

It all started because I was beholding the face of God and the hand of God showed up. Intimacy, relationship and the anointing came out of spending time with God. The presence of God released the anointing.

After I received the vision of the coming healing revival I knew that my trip to South Africa would ignite something in my heart for the healing revival. This would be my first international meeting.

The night before I left for Africa to get the John G. Lake anointing I was at the house of one of Patricia King's intercessors. The phone rang and it was Patricia calling from England. When she found out I was there she said the Lord just gave her a word that I was going to South Africa to get the healing anointing of John Lake and that when I got it I was going to bring a healing revival to America. I hadn't shared any of that information with Patricia.

Durban, South Africa—March 2000

I believed that I would see great things in Africa and receive this anointing from the Lord. I went to Durban, South Africa with my friends Giovanni and Clif Robertson. Clif led worship at our meetings. When we got there, I told the pastor that I wanted to go to the inner city market place outside the church walls. I wanted to be in the ghetto with the drug addicts, gangs, the poor and the prostitutes. All I needed was a sound system in the streets.

One of the highlights—the pastor took me to Hawthorne, where there was a revival 20 years ago—now it was the darkest part of the city. He set up the sound system and I started preaching. "I came from Canada and have a testimony of the power of Jesus." After preaching, I challenged the people to come down and see the power of Jesus so they would know that the things I'd said about healing and changed lives are true. I laid hands on, and prayed for, over 1,000 people. It took hours.

Here is the on-site report of the day-to-day outpouring of God's power on that trip:

Over 800 Saved, Over 250 Recommitments
Durban Report

I'm going to concentrate this report on the open air preaching that I did. The others meetings were awesome too, but I love being out among the hurting people. There was no advertising for the open-air meetings that we did. We simply went to an area, mainly lower income dwellings, set up the sound equipment and began to play music. The flats (apartments) were arranged in such a way that, as the sound would go out, it would resonate between the buildings. Each area contained hundreds of people.

Different ones would share their testimony between songs, and then the message of salvation would be given. At first there would be 50-100 people come out to hear and see what was happening; but then as soon as people began to be touched by the Holy Spirit and be healed in their bodies, hundreds would appear. It didn't matter if it was sunny, cloudy or raining, the people came and waited, sometimes hours to be prayed for. One lady was set free from alcohol addiction. She came to the meeting drunk and went away a free woman. She came to other street meetings to give testimony of what God did for her.

Open Air at Hime Street (Wednesday)

We set up the equipment and began to worship God. We were in the midst of the projects known for the highest gang warfare and bloodshed. People were on the streets; some were hanging over their balconies listening to what was going on. Hundreds of people heard the message of salvation, healing and deliverance. Once the miracles began, people came from all over.

The crowd grew. People were healed of all kinds of sicknesses and diseases, the blind, deaf and crippled; devils were manifesting and being cast out—over a hundred people gave their hearts to the Lord. There was a man who had a stroke and could barely walk; he left that night carrying his cane! We ministered here in the street well into the evening.

Open Air at K1 Shopping Park (Thursday)

Today the people started coming when I began to preach. Some came right up to where we were, others stayed back; but when the miracles and healings began, they pressed in. Well over 50 souls were saved and many were healed by the power of God while hundreds of others looked on. Here are some healings that took place: a woman who was almost blind from cataracts also had an arm that was bent and frozen. She raised her arm above her head and she also began to see. Another had been involved in the occult and was set free. A woman who had painful leg problems began to jump up and down. You could see the joy on her face. A man whose facial skin was pulled toward the left and had numbness and paralysis was healed. A woman who could not see well enough to read began to read from the bible. Tears of joy filled her eyes as she thanked the Lord.

Open Air, Reger Road (Saturday)

It was raining, but we decided to go anyway. Hundreds came out after I preached. They stood in the rain waiting and listening as I ministered. Many were saved, healed or delivered. People fell under the power of the Holy Spirit and some landed in puddles. The people here are so hungry for the gospel that some would wait two hours to be prayed for. This day there were 44 saved. Those with impaired vision began to see clearly again. One man riddled with painful arthritis was healed. Many other healings took place as the people came with an expectant heart.

Open Air, Hime Street (Monday)

The people of this place requested that we come back again to minister. Many turned out again and were filled with the Holy Spirit. We went after those that didn't come. We became, not only fishers of men, but hunters of men, going out and bidding them to come. Some were saved or healed as we prayed in their homes, while others were saved behind buildings. Those that had been previously saved and set free were now also doing the work of the evangelist. So much happened, so many healings, so many salvations. God was in this place.

Return Visit to Hime Street (Tuesday)

It just keeps getting better. Hundreds of people listened as different ones gave testimony of the power of God in their lives. They came to receive Jesus as Savior, they came to be healed, and they came to be delivered from the oppression of the devil. One after another they kept coming. Some of the believers began to go after those that were standing around. There were those who came to receive Jesus and before anyone laid hands on them they would fall under the power. It is revival. The church here is stirred, excited and full of expectation of what the Lord is doing and what He is going to do.

The Barracks (Thursday)

This is old military housing that has been converted into homes. Hundreds came out to hear and see the gospel of Christ in signs and wonders. After a deaf mute heard and spoke and a deaf lady received her hearing, the people crowded around and came for their own miracle. Eighty three people gave their hearts to the Lord and many others were set free from addictions and sickness.

Open Air at the Flats (Saturday)

During another outreach at an apartment complex, I noticed that all the windows had bars on them. The pastor said that was because husbands and wives sometimes threw each other out the windows so the city put up bars. A small crowd heard the music and gathered to hear me preach. We started praying for the sick and many were healed.

About 20 gang members on the other side of the street saw people shaking and falling out under the power of God and began to mock us. I challenged them to come and be touched by God's power. I said, "If you believe that this isn't real then prove it by letting me pray for you. But I'm so confident that this is real that if I pray for you, you will shake and fall under the power like these other people. If it happens to you, then you need to give your life to Jesus. Are you up to the challenge?" We prayed for them, they all fell under

God's power and got saved. Many young people and gangster youth were on the ground crying—immediately after their salvation, they called for their buddies to be saved. Over 40 souls were birthed into God's Kingdom.

South Africa: In Summary

God poured out the power of Sozo (Salvation, healing and deliverance) in mighty measure while we were in South Africa. By the end of our visit, we were receiving invitations to return to this sunny country. We also learned that the King of the Zulu people wants us to come and minister to him and the Royal Family.

While on this trip, I didn't do anything special to get the John G. Lake anointing; I was just obedient. I went to South Africa and did what the Lord wanted me to do. On returning to North America, I also went to some places where John Lake ministered in the United States. After visiting the healing rooms in Spokane, I prayed at Lake's grave, asking God to give me what he had during his powerful healing ministry. "Release it again Lord, that whole cities will be healed."

Healing Wells Open in Albany, Oregon
July 17-19, 2000

When I came home from South Africa, the signs and wonders in my ministry began to increase. We began to have a growing sense of greater things yet to come. Within six months, our first visit to the Vineyard Christian Fellowship in Albany, Oregon would turn into a revival of healing that would attract international attention. Here's the pastor's report of our first week of meetings there:

As senior Pastor of the Vineyard Christian Fellowship in Albany, Oregon, from the church's founding days in 1994, I and my congregation have been contending for the release of the miracle healing anointing. I believed in my spirit that asking evangelist Todd Bentley to come for a series of meetings would result in a significant breakthrough. Through my years of ministry I have seen many healings and miracles, but only sporadically. However, this week was filled with continual waves of healings and miracles. As the testimonies continue to come in, we expect to find that about 200 people were healed.

For example, in the first five nights, ten deaf ears were opened and many back conditions were healed including curvature of the spine, herniated discs and whiplash. Four people testified that they have cancelled surgeries. After visiting her doctor, one lady testified to being healed of Hepatitis C. There have also been many testimonies of the healing of fibromyalgia and arthritis. Another lady, after a word of knowledge, was healed of a brain injury and memory loss.

A lady from Sweden, walking outside of the church with her husband, stopped out of curiosity. When someone told Todd she was deaf he went outside, laid hands on her and she was healed. Another remarkable story of a young lady's hips and shoulder healed, as well as a ganglia cyst on her wrist healed. She reported being pain free for the first time in months. A teenage girl with shifted hips from birth reported heat as her hips adjusted. She said that the constant head and neck pain were gone.

Another notable aspect of the meetings was the presence of God. The meetings started with a Toronto-like outpouring of joy and manifest glory of the Lord. About Wednesday the meetings seemed to amp up in the anointing even though many healings had already occurred the first two nights. As the week progressed, the presence of God has increased and many are now being healed in their seats or at the front. Before hands are even laid on them, many are falling under the power of the Holy Spirit. The meetings are lasting until 11:30 pm or 12:00 am and often people stumble out of the meetings still affected by the Holy Spirit.

We are planning to continue to have regular healing and renewal meetings and return visits from evangelist Todd Bentley.

Pastor Denny Cline

Denny invited me to come back as soon as possible, so I returned in August. I felt something was stirring. God ripped open the heavens; more Hepatitis C, food allergies, mental illness and vision problems were healed. There was also deep emotional healing as God bound up the broken hearted—people suffering from long standing trauma, nightmares, depression, torment and mental anguish. Some people were healed as they went, others didn't realize they were healed until they got a blood test back from the doctor a month later.

Albany Oregon—August 22-25, 2000

Here's another report by Pastor Denny Cline:

A young man after responding to another word of knowledge on anxiety and panic attacks was healed of a severe back and muscle condition that caused pain. He testified to feeling his back straighten out. Another lady reported that a serious car accident left her with a severe back condition that required her to make frequent visits to the chiropractor. She was healed in her seat. There were many other healings including a Baptist girl who was healed of a knee injury standing at the altar watching the power of God.

Not everything was that dramatic. However, there was great enthusiasm and the zeal for what God was about to do. Then came Alenna's miracle.

In one minute Alenna's eyesight was completely healed! At first, 68-year-old Alenna Nelson could see only 10-15 feet in front of her before everything went completely blurry. The next minute, Alenna, for the first time in years, could now see details on the leaves, painted on the wall, 60-70 feet away, in the very front of the church. Besides healing her eyes, God did so much more.

Yesterday afternoon, Alenna just wanted to go home. She was tired. Two doctor visits completely drained her and she couldn't face going to a long church meeting, even if it was for healing. But her daughter, who was unable to be there herself, had appealed to her to, "Please go to that meeting."

That day Alenna had actually been so tired that she had just wanted to go home. Her daughter persuaded her to stay for prayer. She responded to two altar calls—one for blindness, another for anxiety. Not only was she dramatically healed of near blindness, she was set free from a long-standing bondage.

These are her words: "I've suffered from anxiety for 20 years. My muscles are so tight they don't even relax when I sleep. But when I got up off the floor I felt the anxiety just disappear. It was gone." I just said, 'I'm going to do it by faith.' I just had the desire and so I went forward by faith. Now there's no anxiety and I can see all this detail."

And who was the channel for these miracles: it was 24-year-old Todd

125

Bentley. Only saved 6 years, Todd brought no college education or great cha-
risma, no backing from a huge denomination, or a life-long call—just a recent
call to go pray for the sick to be healed. As he puts it, "Preach the Gospel, pray
for the sick, cast out demons, raise the dead. I just went and did it," Todd
explains. "One minute I was an employee and the next, I'm doing nightly
healing meetings all over the U.S. and booked for a year solid." Todd, who is
now preaching all over the world, says that healing must always accompany
the gospel when it's preached because healing is part of the Gospel!"

I remember when God began to move in the Vineyard church in Albany, Oregon and I sensed for the first time we should do extended meetings. I thought to myself, "God, the Vineyard should be the last church where you would touch down like this for me." My style is not low key like you might find at most Vineyard churches. Although I do love the Vineyard beliefs and worship, my style isn't an exact fit—it's more loud, fiery and Pentecostal. So, at first, when I felt the Lord challenging me to stay for those extended meetings in January and February (and eventually trips back each month till May 2001) I said, "God, are you sure?" Pastor Denny had felt each time God moved the previous three visits (in July, August and November 2000) that we should stay. Little did I know it would be these meetings, and the publicity almost daily through the Elijah List, which would thrust our ministry to a new level. I remember thinking, "God, if this keeps going, should I stay for revival?" It was difficult to think of staying on, especially with my passion for ministry and crusades in developing nations and considering all the other meetings already on our schedule. I had to be willing to say "yes" and God rewarded us for it. Since those extended meetings, the ministry has now tripled in size and the healing power has increased in our meetings in America. These new blessings on our ministry, I believe, were largely because we broke through in those early weeks of the revival of healing in Albany.

Chapter 14

BACK TO AFRICA

I took my second international trip to Ghana and Nigeria, Africa in October of 2000. My team consisted of Shanee Clark, my disciple, and my friend Greg Dennison.

God opened up radio and TV for the preaching of the gospel as we entered this new country. We started the harvest right away. Three people in the studio got saved—the head of production, the studio manager and the Muslim DJ who interviewed me.

The radio station aired three separate radio programs throughout the central region of Ghana and within one day we ran into people in restaurants, market places and even several workers in our hotel who heard the radio. Four to five million people in this region alone had heard the gospel message I preached. It is impossible to document the thousands who have made a commitment to Christ through these broadcasts.

There has been a great outpouring of God's presence and power. Over 250 souls have been saved in the open-air services alone. We visited the local leper colony and 23 received Jesus; the remaining seven were already saved. As I prayed for them all I laid my hands right on the areas affected by their leprosy to show that they are accepted and loved.

In one open-air crusade well over a thousand heard the gospel. It seemed as if every person being prayed for was healed. People were set free from demons, addictions, deafness and vision impairments. As hundreds pressed in on us, healings happened so rapidly that it was difficult to keep track of them all.

The last evening of the crusade in Cape Coast I preached a new message God gave me called, "When the Holy Spirit Comes." There was a great manifestation of God's power at one point and I collapsed onto the stage. Many were healed and delivered. Another 37 souls came to Jesus bringing the total up to 287. During a second altar call for the baptism of the Holy Spirit, the people received the Spirit and spoke in tongues so easily.

El Nima, Ghana—October 25 to 27, 2000
Report by Greg Dennison:

This morning was the last of our crusades in this region. It was held in the old fishing village of El Nima. The supervisor of this area estimated the crowds at 5 to 10 thousand people. As Todd preached, over 350 additional souls responded to the call of the Gospel, bringing the total up to 637. Next

"If you want to receive Jesus, raise your hand."

Todd led them in a prayer for mass healing and miracles. Many hands went up to testify of being healed and the people wanted to come forward to give public testimony of the healing power of Jesus. Hundreds of people pressed in when the miracles began to happen and it was difficult to move. Some of the healings included vision impairments, deafness (including a boy who felt a deaf spirit come out of his ear), arthritis, and various long lasting pains (one lady with an illness testified that she was healed as she felt the fire of the Holy Ghost go through her body, healing a sickness she'd had for over 11 years). Another man came with an illness in his chest so severe it left him coughing blood and his body so weak he could barely walk to the crusade. He reported that as he came to the crusade the power of God fell on him and he was healed.

Kumasi Regional Crusade
Ghana, Africa—October 29 - 31st, 2000

We continued on to the city of Kumasi. God opened opportunities for me to preach at three different radio stations, which broadcast to five regions and millions of people. One of these stations broadcast two nights of the crusade live—the preaching, salvation calls, mass miracle prayer and testimonies of people who were healed.

Once again God confirmed the preaching of the gospel with salvation, healing and deliverance—a boy who had been deaf and mute for over 17 years started to hear and speak, a new convert was instantly set free from a continual shaking that had plagued him for over six years, the parents of a demon-possessed boy heard the radio broadcast and came from over 30 miles away. On the platform the boy shook violently and shrieked loudly as the afflicting spirits came out. He was also healed of a speech impediment.

The last evening of the crusade over 10 people were healed of vision impairments and blindness. One of them was a man who had not been able to read the bible for over 12 years. He joyfully read the bible from the platform.

One last great testimony of the manifestation of God's power came from a man who left his restaurant unattended to come to the crusade. He was the first to come forward for salvation. He told us that God had shown all three of us to him in a dream the day before we arrived. He saw Shanee holding a bag scattering seed. I placed a cross on his forehead and Greg hugged him and said, "happy birthday." When we showed up the next day, it was indeed his spiritual birthday.

There were 387 recorded commitments to Christ over the three evenings in Kumasi bringing the total to 1,024 souls in six nights.

Ghana, West Africa
(Accra Crusade) November 2-4, 2000

This was our last three-day crusade in Ghana. The first morning I appeared on "The Breakfast Show," the equivalent to the *Kathy & Regis* morning show; it's about all there is to watch in the mornings. This was followed by radio programming on the local stations. During our two-week stay in Ghana there were 23 TV commercials drawing people to the Accra crusades. These 90-second commercials showed me giving a vigorous call to come to the crusade while the location was flashed across the bottom of the screen. At the end of the commercials there was an explosion of the words, FIRE—FIRE—FIRE!

As we went about the city of Accra, people continually recognized me because of the TV and radio commercials and I constantly invited people to come to the crusades. There were 200 souls saved in the first two nights in Accra. Some of the instant miracles for these nights were as follows: a man healed of a blind eye, a girl healed of double vision, a man healed from a spine deformed for 10 years, a man 10-years blind in one eye healed and a man who had pain throughout his whole body was healed.

It was difficult to keep track of the healings because the people crowded around us and it seemed about 18 out of 20 people here were healed by God as we prayed.

To the Market

The next day I told the pastor:

"The power of God isn't just in the crusades. Take me to the biggest market. I want to go to where the people live and work."

"How about the fish market? It has 10,000 people."

"Great, bring the sound system."

This meeting was unadvertised and spontaneous. We set up right by the seashore. I started sharing my testimony. People all around me were busy, fishing and selling fish. When I said I would pray for the sick, hundreds pressed in. I gave an altar call and over 300 were saved. Then the miracles started happening—the blind, the deaf, and the crippled. People pressed in by the thousands and they had to sneak me into a cab and drive me out of there as people followed me down the street. All together over 637 people were saved. It was these meetings in Ghana that would birth in me the passion to do mass evangelism and reach nations through TV and radio broadcasts of the crusades.

The third night of the crusade was spectacular—God began to move even before I preached. Over 80 souls came to Jesus this night. I have lost count, but I believe this brings the total souls in Ghana to just over 1300. This is not even including those who received Jesus through the radio and TV programs.

The miracles were amazing to see: A deaf and dumb boy heard and spoke, a 30-year hip problem was healed; a deaf man was healed when a spirit came out; a growth on a woman's abdomen disappeared (she actually felt it go); a man, who normally used two walkers, was healed (he vowed to give both the walkers to the hospital) and a boy who was deaf and mute heard for the first time.

As often happens, God saved the best wine for last—people on this last night were healed and slain in the Spirit in greater numbers than any of the previous nights. Shanee and I then went on to Lagos, Nigeria, our first visit to this congested city of more than ten million.

Lagos, Nigeria—November 5-12, 2000

We were invited to The Redeemed Pentecostal Mission in Nigeria, Africa for a Signs and Wonders Crusade. I remember this event vividly because I found out that, at the same time, in this city, Reinhardt Bonke was hosting his historic Great Millennium Crusade. Over one million people came to each of his services and a total of over a million got saved.

I remember during the day the pastor saying, "We have to leave early to get back to your crusade, because they are going to shut down all the highways and most of the city buses are going to the other meeting." Here I am in the early days of my African ministry crying out to God: "Will I ever reach 50,000, let alone a million?" However, God came down with His power and numerous people received their salvation, breakthrough, healing and deliverance. I was pleased to know that God was with me as well as with Reinhardt that night!

Here is a letter that I received from the pastor in Nigeria:

Dear Rev Todd Bentley,

Glory be to God for the crusade. Testimonies are all over the city of Lagos, Nigeria about what God did through Fresh Fire Ministries. Attached is the list of some of the miracles recorded during the November Crusade in two locations. We are pleased to give you this reports of what happened during the your visit, Rev. Todd Bentley, to The Redeemed Pentecostal Mission Inc, Nigeria, Africa that presented the Signs and Wonders Crusade November 5th–12th, 2000. Some of those that received their miracles are as follows:

Two hundred and forty people received their salvation and another 140 came to the Lord in Itire, part of Lagos!! A three-year-old boy, deaf healed. A woman with paralyzed legs, healed and 10 people that are deaf and

A deaf mute receives his healing.

dumb, healed. Many people with Cataracts in the eyes, healed. Someone with Polio Myelitis and crippled legs for eight years started walking. An epileptic, delivered and healed. Twenty-five people with body pains, healed. A drug-addicted boy, delivered. Someone was delivered of demons and his swollen leg with water plus bacteria was released. A woman suffering from breast cancer—growths gone. Forty people that had waist pain, healed. Seven people with typhoid fever, healed; 14 people with intestinal disease, healed; eight people that had fibroid tumor saw them dissolve and 10 People were healed of malaria fever. A big lump in the breast was dissolved and healed and another crippled boy was healed. Two people with body growths--gone and eight people with eye problems, healed. A three-year-old boy, dumb, was healed and someone healed from unconsciousness. A serious hand injury was healed and a female lawyer who was bleeding for fourteen days—after prayers with Rev. Todd Bentley, the bleeding stopped instantly.

In another part of Lagos called Itire where you ministered for three days, Rev. Todd, this healing data was recorded: Six people that were deaf and dumb, healed; one person crippled healed; five people that had cancer, healed; four people that had fibroid, healed; 40 people with stomach pains, healed; a lunatic person, healed and 160 more people received salvation. The latest information from the ITIRE CHURCH LAGOS is that supernatural revival has broken out in that church and the whole area. Once again, we are so excited as God used you mightily for this Miracle, Signs and Wonders crusade with our church in Nigeria. We are looking forward to another bigger crusade which will be coming up March 2001 where you will draw a large crowd of 30,000- 40,000 with the power of the Holy Spirit.

Bishop John E. Amadi

Unbelief

I've got to admit that during those first few early African crusades I'd struggle with unbelief. I'd pray for someone and they would say they were healed and I wouldn't believe it. Often they wouldn't display huge emotion or shaking. Even though the miracles were before me I'd think, "It can't be that easy." When they told me, "I used to be paralyzed," I really wondered if they were. I had to wrestle through this. I finally asked myself, "Why would they lie to me?" If they lie it's between them and God. My job is just to pray for the sick and God's job is to do the rest.

Back to Albany

Every time I came back from Africa our miracles seemed to increase, so I was excited to return to Albany for my third visit in November 2000. God did it again. One of the first healings in these meetings came by a word of knowledge. A lady who had no eardrum, who had been deaf in one ear for 50 years, was healed. Then a woman who had been deaf in one ear for 41 years, also with no eardrum, came forward—two creative miracles back to back. By the end of the November meetings there were hundreds of healings again in Albany.

Here's an edited version of the healing report from Steve Shultz of the Elijah List:

No Eardrums?

"What is it about older people that are getting God's HEALING attention? I watched it again tonight. Oh, and teenagers too! It's as if God is making a point . . . as if He's saying, "I'm not done with the older generation—NOT EVEN CLOSE. At the same time, I'm just getting started with teens.

NO EAR DRUMS AND YET TONIGHT, THESE LADIES CAN HEAR! THIS IS MIRACULOUS! I've never seen anything like it—at least not for a few months: Viola is 86 years old and she hasn't heard out of one ear for 50 years! The doctors, because of a problem, removed Viola's eardrum in 1950! That's it. No hearing ever since—until a few hours ago. I was there. I saw it with my own eyes! Todd Bentley prayed a few simple prayers, and yelled Jesus' name into Viola's ears. "Jesus!" Todd yelled. After a few attempts, suddenly Viola is hearing sounds. Pretty soon, completely covering her one ear, she is able to repeat the new sounds she is hearing in her "dead" ear. Sounds that Todd is now whispering, "Father," "Father," Viola repeats. "Holy Spirit," Todd whispers. "Holy Spirit," Viola repeats. The congregation is getting loud and excited. "Jesus," Todd whispers again. "Jesus," Viola says back. Now the Albany congregation has gone wild! VERIFYING THE MIRACLE!

I go to Viola to talk to her because, if I'm going to write this to THE ELIJAH LIST, I'd better verify it. That's when I learn about 1950, the "mastoid" something and the surgery. Her friends who brought her are beaming. She can hear out of her "dead" ear—which is no longer dead!

Chapter 15

TOUCHED BY AN ANGEL

Years ago, Paul Cain and William Branham held powerful healing meetings in Grant's Pass, Oregon. A local businessman caught the healing vision and built a large, barn-like facility for these meetings. On December 5, 1950 William Branham dedicated this "tabernacle" to the Lord. At this time, during what is often referred to as The Voice of Healing Revival, Grant's Pass was one of many places holding healing meetings. However, because one man actually built a facility to host the great healing evangelists, more frequent meetings were held in one place and the Lord deposited a well of healing there.

December 5, 2000 was the 50-year anniversary of this dedication. Several prophecies were given that it was time to re-open the ancient healing wells of 50 years ago. On that occasion, I was ministering with Bob Jones, Paul Keith Davis, John Paul Jackson and Bobby Connor at the Eye of the Eagle Prophetic Conference in Grant's Pass. We were actually spiritually re-digging, trying to tap into, those ancient wells from the 1950's.

A Prophetic Sign

The pastor of the church in Grant's Pass, Oregon, Dale Howell and a mutual friend, John Macgirvin, hiked two hours back in the woods to fish in the Rogue River. John was sitting on a huge granite rock 15 feet above the river. The Lord said, "Reach into the crack in the rock." John dug in the sand and pulled out a silver Roosevelt dime. He held it up for Dale to see. "The Lord just told me to reach in the crack of the rock. Silver represents jubilee, 50 years." Dale said, "I can tell you what the year is on that dime." He was correct—1950.

The dime was minted the year God sent healing to the North West—50 years ago. The Lord told John that the dime was a sign that the healing revival of 50 years ago is going to start again and that the past revival was a tithe, a tenth, of the healing power that He was going to pour out. The coin symbolized The Voice of Healing revival, the first fruits of the coming healing revival. This sign confirmed the mandate of the conference and encouraged us to contend to open up the healing well.

Bringing the Angel

A man who was part of the healing rooms from Portland attended this conference in Grant's Pass. In the middle of the service he crouched by my chair and whispered, "I brought the healing angel from Portland, from John Lake's healing rooms. He's standing at the back of the tent." To be honest, I thought the guy was nuts. But, I turned around and there was the angel. I ran to the back of the tent and fell out under the power. John Paul Jackson laid hands on me and then I had an encounter with the angel. The presence of the angel knocked me out of my body. Then it was as if my spirit left my body and I was watching my body on the floor.

I walked around the tent in the spirit, knowing what infirmities people had. Then I began to wonder, "How am I going to get back in my body?" Eventually, I decided I would just go lie on myself. Prophetic experiences involve choices in the mind, so I had to purpose to enter in. I didn't know how to tell people what had happened—I thought they'd think I was nuts.

When I got up off the floor I didn't realize that I was being taken up a notch in the spirit. I just thought, "Wow, what a great service tonight. I had an encounter with an angel!" I began receiving more accurate words of knowledge and also discovered that I had received a gift of healing and of discernment. Today, there are times when I feel the angel's presence on my left side. When I touch someone with my left hand, I've been able to discern whether their sickness was a demon, disease, or a natural infirmity and what part of the body is affected by the sickness.

Boy Comes Out of a Coma

Right after that angelic visitation I had an extraordinary experience that led to a powerful healing. The next night, while praying, I went into a trance and a woman visited me. She shook me violently and said three times, "The headlines report, 'Boy Comes Out of a Coma.'" Then she went running out of the room. I asked the Lord, "What do you want me to do with this?" The Lord said, "There will be a man instructed to come tonight to take an anointing back to a boy who is in a coma in another city."

136

When I gave the word of knowledge I said, "There is a man here who was instructed to come tonight to take a anointing back to a boy who is in a coma." A man came running down the aisle and said, "You're not going to believe this but I was just at the hospital with a woman whose son is in a coma and she asked me to come tonight to stand in the gap, to get an anointing for that boy's healing." Later I heard the report that the boy was healed and got up from his hospital bed. Then the local newspaper ran a headline just as I had seen it in my vision.

Albany, Oregon—January 2001

Three weeks after the Grant's Pass angelic visitation, I came back to the Vineyard in Albany, Oregon for the fourth time. This would be the beginning of an extended revival of healing there. For months the church had been preparing for an open heaven through servant evangelism: giving out free gas vouchers and Cokes, handing hot dogs to the skateboarders and washing cars in the community. They did all this just to show the love of God to their community. I believe those acts really opened up the heavens because faith releases wonders and manifestations of God's power. Scripture tells us that faith works through love (Gal. 5:6). Blessing the city with loving acts, I believe, opened the heavens and invited God to give us an unprecedented miracle outpouring.

There was such a level of anointing for healing that we extended these meetings for weeks. People came from Canada, Europe, Asia, and other countries. There was representation from over 25 US states. Hundreds of pastors came. Night after night we packed out the church; sometimes people lined up hours before a meeting to get into the sanctuary. Some people even got healed in the parking lot.

There were profound demonstrations of miracles and healings each night—cancers, deafness, polio, various pains, and emotional maladies were healed. There were over 250 salvations, many rededications and water baptisms. Here are some reports:

by Steve Shultz, Publisher, The Elijah List

Todd's back in Albany, Oregon and as usual you never quite know what will happen. The first of the series of 17 nightly meetings began at the Albany Vineyard, Wednesday 1st-3rd. As Todd began to preach he was so overcome by the Spirit he was unable to speak. The presence of the Lord came into the room powerfully; some began to laugh, while others reported, "I've never felt such a presence of the fear of God. I wanted to dive under my chair."

After about 15 minutes of trying to get it together enough to preach, Todd and the podium went to the floor together. While he lay there, an angel of the Lord appeared to him with a large bucket of oil and told him to lay hands on anyone who wanted it. Still unable to speak, Todd wrote Pastor Denny a message relaying what he'd seen. He wrote later, the muteness was a prophetic sign, like Zechariah who was unable to speak before the birth of John the Baptist. But the birthing at this time is a new level of the supernatural.

The level of hunger at these meetings is wonderful, and nearly all went forward that night to receive from the Lord. Here are a few highlights of the meetings to give you an idea of what God is up to.

Prayer Cloths, Miracles and Other Testimonies . . .

Last August Todd anointed and prayed over prayer cloths for healing, and people sent them out all over the country.

Debbie sent one to her step-dad in California who had colon cancer. This week she received word there is no trace of cancer in his body. Her brother, who had cancer in his prostate and urinary tract as well as in his bones, also received a prayer cloth. He has been given a report from his doctor this week that he, too, is cancer free.

Twenty-five-year-old Adrianne had been an addict for ten years. She testified Friday night: "There hasn't been a day where I haven't craved drugs. I've been in and out of jail and prison for seven years. Pastor Denny prayed for me on Wednesday night; I haven't had any craving since. I have been clean and with the Lord for 104 days, but I still had cravings everyday until this past Wednesday. Thank you Jesus!

Phil, a young man with an incurable condition (and an unpronounce-able name), came for prayer. There was chronic pain in his knees for three years due to the disease. Todd laid hands on him and immediately the pain left, mobility returned, and he was able to run for the first time in two years.

Mary hit her nose in August resulting in continual headaches, and

138

impaired sense of smell. Her neck, back, and shoulders hurt all of the time. When she received prayer, she felt her nose reposition, her sinuses drain, and her sense of smell return. Also, she felt her back and hips reposition and the headache leave.

Stephanie responded to an altar call for lung conditions. As Todd laid hands on her, God showed him she had asthma and a lung infection, confirming her doctor's diagnoses made just that morning. After prayer, her breathing was totally free. She also was suffering with chronic back pain from three previous surgeries. The Lord removed the pain. She is now able to touch her toes and bend from side to side.

Spontaneously Healings Occur Throughout the Congregation

Todd had a word of knowledge about stomach problems. Delores, had stomach problems, felt "activity" in her stomach and then the pain left. Two weeks earlier she had injured herself falling on a cement floor and had been using a walker. The Lord touched that too, and she now walks without assistance.

As the Lord has declared His intention to increase the level of the supernatural we look forward, with great eagerness, for what's to come over these next 14 nights. WARNING! IF YOU SIMPLY WANT TO STAY SAFE AND COMFORTABLE KEEP AWAY FROM THESE MEETINGS!

Todd has been sent here to stir up the church to do the work of the ministry. These meetings are not just for watching—they are for equipping and activating, as well as healing and restoring. With the release of the new level of the supernatural, great blessing is coming to the church. But God is also bringing a release to GO OUT. Psalm 110:3 declares: "Your people shall be volunteers in the day of Your power."

Oregon Healing Meetings Become Healing Revival -- Horse-Feeding Trough Turned Into a Baptismal

This Thursday thru Saturday, Jan. 25th-27th, 2001, Healing meetings continue, led by the healing ministry of Bob Brasset from Victoria, B.C. Todd Bentley returns February 1 for more healing, signs and wonders meetings.

How fitting that—just as the Savior of the world was laid at His birth in a cattle's feeding trough, a manger—the newest births into the Kingdom of

God in Albany, Oregon are being laid in a horse feeding trough, dipped beneath the water in baptism and then raised to walk into their new LIFE.

So many baptisms have begun happening at the Albany Healing Revival, ON THE SPUR OF THE MOMENT, that a large horse watering trough has now been set up and remains in place, at the ready—as many are being healed, saved, and baptized—all in one night.

Is it a Salvation Revival—or is it a Healing Revival?

That answer to that question seems to be, "Yes, it is!" On Friday evening, a call was made for anyone who came prepared to be baptized. Only one came forward, but before he was baptized, more came forward and soon there were approximately 15 who came to be baptized, wearing only what they had on.

Later, while a group of teens (and there has been an amazing salvation move among the teens) was praying for a man in a wheelchair to be healed, suddenly a "SHRIEK!" came from the opposite side of the room. A young man had just gotten saved and the "crowd" attending to him shouted with delight as he was IMMEDIATELY BAPTIZED IN THE TROUGH—still wearing his previously-dry set of clothes—as the work of salvation in his life was made public!

Transferable Anointing—of Both Healing and Salvations

Already, at least three or four groups are reporting revival and healing outbreaks in their own spheres immediately upon returning home from Albany. In the last 17 weeks, some 25 states have been represented, as those eager to receive a healing touch have traveled to this small, previously "unknown" town of Albany. Just as was hoped by those who prayed this anointing in, the anointing IS transferable to other homes, churches, and home groups. One young man has taken to the streets and is seeing dramatic healing results in Gresham, Oregon.

Another group of teens have taken the anointing to their on-the-street ministry. But it's not just teens. One pastor is suddenly seeing revival break out in his church. He came for healing. He is now getting revival in his church.

The Origins of the Healing Revival

This healing movement—apparently launched when 25-year old Todd Bentley came to Albany, Oregon from Canada (at the invitation of Pastor Denny Cline who was introduced to Todd by Patricia King, also from Canada)—now continues even when Todd is not present. There is what is being called a "CORPORATE ANOINTING," according to Pastor Denny Cline. The anointing remains and other healing ministries are preparing to come and impart even more healing. Randy Clark is slated to come in May and other ministries are being scheduled.

Prophecy by Bobby Conner

The attention now being given to Albany—was first prophesied when Bobby Conner visited Vineyard Christian Fellowship of Albany, Oregon back in late 2000. Bobby prophesied that the Lord was going to put Albany on the "M-A-P," Which Bobby said stood for, "THE MASTER'S AWESOME POWER." (See http://www.elijahlist.com/words/display_word.html?ID=55 — released Sept 24, 2000)

So many healings were breaking out that, at the end of December, Todd Bentley decided to clear his schedule in January and hold healing meetings for 17 days straight. As each night progressed, the anointing seemed to build on the nights before.

The Albany Healing Revival Continues...
by Pastor Denny Cline

There have now been 91 first-time decisions to receive Christ as Lord and Savior, 50 recommitments with approximately 60 baptisms over the 18 nights including the last night after Todd left. We have already had people visit from over 25 states and six countries. Nearly a hundred pastors visited from all over the Northwest and around North America.

Every time we meet in consecutive meetings the power seems to increase as do the healings and miracles. These meetings are different than other renewal meetings. There is something fresh being imparted in healing, signs and wonders—as well as a tremendous deposit of fresh revelation that is coming from Todd Bentley's ministry.

We have contended as a congregation for the ministry of Jesus for five and one half years and have been to the brink of a revival-type outpouring at least four other times since our beginnings. But this is unique in the hunger that is being created in people as well as the fruit that is being produced. Not everyone is healed and not everyone is attracted to this type of atmosphere. There is a blend of the "fear of the Lord" with the joy of the Lord and the meetings go very long, sometimes for five hours. But our fellowship is committed to loving and caring for all who come, as best we can, with our present facility and core group's involvement.

The worship leader brought different worship groups from around the city to make it a corporate thing. They enlisted intercessors from all over so it would be a body of Christ move, not just a Vineyard move. We invited in other healing ministries so it was not a one-man show. It's more than a man having a gift. It's because of Jesus.

Let's believe that it can be transferable to a pastor or a prayer cloth. Pastors have hands laid on them and miracles break out when they go home. We mailed out over a thousand prayer cloths and three cases of terminal cancer were healed. The anointing is tangible and transferable. We want to see the demonstration of the Spirit of God in power.

Every night people bring the lost and some get saved. People were getting saved and then getting baptized immediately in their street clothes. We hit the street with prophetic evangelism and won backsliders to Christ. A 15-year-old prayed for someone whose back got healed. The body of Christ got excited. Once you taste this you need more. The presence of God was thick throughout the whole building.

Salvation and repentance, renewal, signs and wonders, they're all an expression of God's "dunamis" power. The church will be at least what we saw in the book of Acts and even more. The glory of the latter house will be greater than the glory of the former house. (Haggai 2:9)

This move is very much about teams, not superstars. It's about being in the presence of God, holiness, consecration and then releasing it to the people. I call it a God-consciousness. We need the gospel again with signs and wonders.

The Angel in Albany

In February I saw an angel, 20 feet tall, which stretched to the ceiling of the Albany auditorium. At the time, I didn't realize that this was the same angel I'd seen in Grant's Pass. The Spirit gave me a sign that this angelic visitation was real. A woman in the audience, Muffy Joe Howell, (the daughter of Dale Howell, the pastor from Grant's Pass) could also see the angel and when I asked her, she would describe the same vision I was seeing. She whispered, "Todd, there's a huge angel in the pulpit." Muffy had been crippled with an infirmity in her hips from birth. However, suddenly she screamed out, "The angel just touched me," and she was healed. Now I really knew God was up to something.

The audible voice of the Holy Spirit, which accompanied the angelic encounter, instructed me not to speak to the angel. (In subsequent encounters I also heard the audible inner voice of the Holy Spirit.) The angel had a key, just like a mayor holds the key to a city. Its commission was to turn this key over to pastors by imparting wisdom, authority, revelation and anointing so they could take healing back to their churches. The angel stayed in the pulpit and released a healing anointing while I prayed for over 30 pastors that night.

Healing Revival

I knew by the Spirit that the angel's name was Healing Revival. He was like the angel in John 5 that stirred the pool of Bethesda. "For an angel went down at a certain time into the pool and stirred up the water; then whoever stepped in first, after the stirring of the water, was made well of whatever disease he had" (John 5:4).

This angel was a prophetic sign that God is going to fulfill the vision of the coming healing revival I had received about a year before. I believe God sent the angel to Albany to establish healing revival and regional breakthrough. This angel is one of the many that I saw in a staduim in heaven waiting to be released to fulfill end-time purposes. Albany is just one of many cities and churches that will experience a great healing outpouring.

It was revealed to me that this angel is not an archangel, but ranks under them. He has authority to deal with powers but not principalities in the demonic realms. A power is a territorial spirit and it sets itself up over a city or region. "For we do not wrestle against flesh and blood, but against principalities, against powers…." (Eph. 6:12). A principality has a mandate over nations, just like the

Prince of Persia in Daniel 10:13.

In Albany, I saw the angel open up a pool on the floor about 30 feet by 30 feet. A portal opened in the heavens and a shaft of light came down. I was under the power of the Spirit and too inebriated to minister, so I called Denny to take over. He gave an invitation for the sick to come. The Lord told me to call the people up to be healed because the heavens were open. So many people came forward to get in the pool and to get ministry that it went on for a couple of hours; joy was also poured out and people were just scattered all over the floor. When people got near the pool they started falling down like dominoes, under the power, without anyone touching them.

One woman was healed from various injuries, including a fractured neck that caused other problems in her body. Another person reported that over 20 years of pain was healed, while a woman, whose breast cancer had spread to her ribs—it was so sensitive no one could touch her—was healed. This was one of the most unusual and spiritually intense atmospheres I'd seen.

Albany Report Continued
by Pastor Denny Cline

I would not usually include a Sunday morning service in a report, but there was such a carry over from the night before that this day is noteworthy. At times, over the last few weeks the spiritual battle for carrying on these meetings has been intense. Many have been hit with minor sicknesses, even Todd's children and wife, and some who have been battling serious illness for years took a turn for the worse. But in the midst of it all, God seems to be increasing the intensity of His presence and routing out the enemy. This morning the worship leader called up the sick to receive healing during the worship time. I sensed that some were still in their seats and were feeling symptoms like nausea and breathing difficulty. This was, to me, an indication that the enemy was on the run and people were about to get delivered. That is exactly what happened. Over the next half hour, many were set free in their emotions and their physical bodies as they received prayer from the ministry team.

144

My Mother Passes Away

In the midst of this dramatic move of God's presence and healing, my mom got pneumonia and died, February 2001. This was the last night of the Albany healing revival, which had lasted almost two months.

This was a real test for me. Each day people were being healed of stroke. Why not her? She had experienced a massive stroke in November 1999. I prayed for her and within two months she was walking and talking again. But she lived in an apartment by herself and she was depressed. She had a second stroke and came out of the coma to tell Shonnah that she didn't have the will to live. She was paralyzed on one side and had deteriorated to a place of complete incapacity. I had to decide whether to give in to confusion, discouragement and anger. Her death challenged what I preached. I finally decided I was going to push through. I went to my next meeting and said, "I'm going to go after this a whole lot more." I made a decision to press in and keep praying.

My mother's struggle with deafness was also like a signpost for me to really ask God for healing for the deaf. Consequently, one of the greatest anointings on our ministry today is for deaf ears. I've been in services where every deaf person began to hear. In one crusade in India, we actually witnessed 139 deaf mutes receive their hearing during six nights of meetings.

Chapter 16

SCOTLAND HERE I COME!

While I was still out on the floor in Albany, the Lord said, as a confirmation to me that this was an angel of healing revival, that He was going to give me the name of three revivals and the three revivalists that this angel had worked with. This word from the Lord would be a sign to ensure I would never doubt that He again is commissioning healing angels to stir up pools of healing revival in churches, cities and regions.

The first revivalist that the angel worked with was John Knox in Scotland. I said, "I've never heard of John Knox. Was there even a guy named John Knox? Who's he?" I found out he was considered the Martin Luther of Scotland. He was a great Scottish Reformer and the founder of Presbyterianism in Scotland. He overcame the religious spirit in the 1500's and birthed protestant Christianity out of the Catholic Church.

The second revivalist the angel visited was William Branham. The angel, who helped release healing revival through Branham, visited him in 1946. Revival history records that Branham's international miracle ministry, and the great American Healing Revival of 1947-1955, began with an angelic visitation. The angel told Branham: "If you will be sincere, and can get the people to believe you, nothing shall stand before your prayer, not even cancer." The angel also told Branham, an unknown preacher, that he would soon minister healing before crowded arenas of thousands. Branham received discernment of people's illnesses, thoughts, deeds and specific sins requiring repentance. Gordon Lindsay wrote in his 1952 biography of Rev. Branham's early life and ministry: "The story of the life of William Branham is so out of this world and beyond the ordinary that were there not available a host of infallible proofs which document and attest its authenticity, one might well be excused for considering it far-fetched and incredible." (G. Lindsay, 'William Branham - A man sent from God', pg. 9)

The third person the angel worked with was John G. Lake who ministered in the Pacific Northwest of the United States. He started healing rooms, which became wells of revival in Spokane and other parts of the Northwest region of America.

Vision of John Knox's Grave

Although I'd been to the places where John Lake and William Branham's healing ministries in the U.S. started, before this word from the Lord, I had never heard of John Knox, had never been to Scotland and had never particularly wanted to go. But seven days later I was in a church in Portland, Oregon and, during worship, was taken in a vision to Edinburgh, Scotland. I saw a castle and a moat. The Lord met me and we walked two hundred yards from the castle to the grave of John Knox. On the left hand side were three rocky outcroppings and beautiful rolling hills. I saw three specific sites: his grave and memorial, the castle and the rolling hills of Edinburgh. All these things went on during this prophetic vision.

Two days later I got an E-mail from a prophetess named Catherine Brown who lives in Scotland. She asked, "Hey Todd, are you coming to Scotland?" I said, "OK, I guess I am now. How about April?" Then the Lord said: "This is a sign to you that I am fulfilling the vision of the coming healing revival about the 100 healing pools of Bethesda." He said the anointing would be transferable and tangible. "I want you to take it all over the world. Every place you go I'm going to open up an increase in miracles, signs and wonders. It's not going to be just about what I do with you, it will be about transferring and releasing people into the ministry of healing."

That night in Albany the Lord asked me where I'd seen the angel before. I said, "God I've never seen him before."

"No, Todd, think about it."

I said, "I don't remember the angel."

"In your apartment three and one half years ago—remember that angelic visitation just a few weeks before I called you into the ministry? It was the same angel that you saw in Grant's Pass and Albany. That day in your apartment was when I commissioned you to take healing revival to the world. That's why I've done with you what I have so quickly, it's because of the angel that goes before you. This is your angel, the angel from John 5 (at the pool of Bethesda). Everywhere you go the angel goes. I want you to be a part of taking healing revival to the nations. I don't want you to have just a gift of healing. I want you to be a part of what has been prophesied, in breaking through and seeing the fulfillment of healing revival. I'm going to have over 100 healing centers. Albany is one of those pools. As a confirmation I took you to Scotland in a trance. Now I want you to get on an airplane and go find the grave of John Knox. Go to the sights that I showed you."

I toured five cities in Scotland and ended up in Edinburgh the last night of my ministry trip. I told the pastor that I wanted to go to John Knox's grave. I told him the story about the angel and then described the castle, moat, crag, the hills and the grave. When we got to the castle it was exactly like I'd seen it in my vision. I walked into the church called St. Giles. I actually showed the pastor where the plaque was and the memorial. Then I had a strong visitation of the Lord; the power of God fell on me for about four hours. When I returned from Scotland, I again saw an increase in signs and wonders.

Confirming Angel Sightings

Ever since my angelic experience in Albany, people I don't know, children and even warlocks have come to me in different services and described the angel. Countless times people tell me, "Todd there's an angel that follows you and I believe it is the mantle and anointing that was with William Branham."

This angel, at times, will visit in strength and authority and push back the demonic realm. When his presence is manifest in the meetings, as it's been over 25 times in two years, there's been an increase in accuracy of the word of knowledge.

Before you get into unbelief about my angel and say, "There's too much emphasis on this angel stuff," you need to understand that the angels are the ones who do the work of the ministry. I want to emphasize that our meetings are all about Jesus and His ministry and love for people. However, angels are real and they are sent on behalf of the saints to minister to people.

For example, angels ministered to Jesus when He came from the wilderness. "Then the devil left Him, and behold, angels came and ministered to Him" (Matthew 4:11). And all believers, including you, have an angel. "For He shall give His angels charge over you, to keep you in all your ways. In their hands they shall bear you up, lest you dash your foot against a stone" (Psalms 91:11). Also, scripture tells us that the "angel of the Lord encamps all around those who fear Him" (Psalms 34:7).

148

I believe in angelic ministry and angels who have different purposes and tasks. Angels are involved with so much of what goes on in the heavenly realm. I want to make it clear though, that Jesus is the one who does the healings, not the angel. The angels simply open up heaven and push back the warfare. They bind the devils of infirmity, they are aids of salvation and messengers, but the source of the healing is the Lord.

The Resurrection Angels

Some time after the Scotland trip, in January 2002, I was in Kelowna, BC, at a conference. Bob Jones called me to come up on the platform. "Son, I have a word for you. In 1975 I had a life and death experience. I hemorrhaged and died and was taken to heaven but couldn't enter. The Lord said He was sending me back to prepare the church for a harvest of a billion souls. When I returned to my body there were two angels speaking to each other. These were the resurrection angels speaking about the harvest and about me. Ever since that time these two angels have accompanied me and I have been used to raise the (spiritually) dead. The Lord has commissioned me to release these angels to you."

When Bob took my hands I trembled, shook and fell to the floor. I became light and weightless. The two angels lifted me toward heaven. I was not permitted to go in but suddenly, in this revelatory experience, I was on a brown horse in a harvest field of grain that went on farther than my eyes could see. Then I appeared before the stone that had been rolled away. I saw two angels sitting on the rock and they said to Mary, "The one you are seeking is not here." I felt the presence of Jesus who had risen from the dead. Then I knew I had received a true impartation of the Spirit that brings life from the dead and these two angels were part of it. I also knew that God would release power to me to raise the dead, those dead in spirit and even those dead in body. Bob said, "From this day forward, these angels will be a part of your ministry."

Chapter 17

TAKING HEALING REVIVAL TO THE NATIONS

As of today, I've traveled to over 30 countries throughout Asia, Europe, Africa, and South America. In the last five crusades over 100,000 have been saved. Today it's not unusual to preach to over 70,000 in a single service and have the crusades broadcast on the radio. The Lord has graciously brought me so far from those early days ministering to the youth in a church basement, or preaching to 50 or 100 people. And I never did make it to that bible school that my church had generously offered to send me to (Ha, Ha).

Our international headquarters are in Canada and we have offices in the United States and Africa. God has continued to give tremendous favor in these first five and a half years. I've preached the gospel with signs and wonders. The blind see, the deaf hear, the lame walk. Now our ministry emphasis is expanding to include humanitarian aid for the poor, mass feedings, building orphanages and sending containers of food into war-torn areas.

In this lengthy chapter you will read my personal ministry reports as well as many reports from various staff and team members written on location in many countries round the world. These reports document, not only our continued journey into the miraculous over during three different years of ministry, but also the amazing faithfulness, power and love of an awesome, supernatural God. Open your heart to the Holy Spirit and let Him impart to you faith and the tangible, transferable, healing anointing as you read.

PART I
HARVEST OF HEALING & MIRACLES

Masaka, Uganda—April 2001

Upon arrival in Entebbe, Uganda, we could feel the presence of the Lord. From the moment we touched down God began to pour out His anointing upon us. We were met on the tarmac by the pastors and then ushered into the VIP room where we cleared customs. Only the President and Cabinet have used this room. The Pastors had asked the government for special permission and received it. They had also asked for electricity at the crusade site for a good price and today they were told we could have it for free. God is good!

Once we cleared customs we were taken into the restaurant where they had set up for a press conference. Various newspaper reporters and photographers were waiting for an interview. The pastors, 100 of them working in unity, had done the groundwork, placing thousands of posters throughout the city. I saw one large banner across the street and I am sure there were more; they passed out thousands of leaflets, had press releases broadcast on a few radio stations, rented buses to bring in a thousand delegates from other cities, arranged meals and organized a Jesus march through the city of Masaka to announce the crusade. The crusade was to be held on the grounds of a golf course about 70 miles from Kampala. The pastors set up a large tent which was for leadership meetings during the day; in the evening it was reserved for those who are extremely sick or even dead.

After arriving, we noticed a newspaper headline that revealed the spiritual powers at work in the region. "Local Witchdoctor Stoned to Death," the headline announced. Apparently, the witchdoctor had run out of body parts for his traditional spells and summoned the powers of darkness, placed a curse and commanded a great accident on the highway. Fourteen people were killed when their van turned over. The witchdoctor was gathering these bodies. People were so enraged they stoned him to death on the streets.

We realized that the enemy was at work but that the Lord was too. We were about to see great destruction to the works of the enemy in Uganda—Jesus style—through miracles, healings and salvations.

First Evening Service

The crowd started with about 2,500 people and grew to between 3,000 or 4,000. After I shared my testimony we had an altar call and the hands shot up into the air. About 60 people gave their hearts to the Lord. Next, I loosed the anointing for corporate healing upon the crowd. The power of God fell and many were touched by the Holy Spirit. The miracles began. We do not have a total count on all who were healed but here are some specifics:

People who were completely blind had their sight restored and many deaf began to hear. A lady who had broken legs was healed; a woman whose uterus was out had it put back into place; a woman who had been in an accident could once again lift her arm; another person had a knee restored. Many who had tumors watched them disappear and cripples started walking without their canes.

Many who were oppressed by the devil were also set free—those tormented in their minds, demoniacs and others who thrashed wildly on the ground. One lady was carried to the platform; her demons were speaking, threatening to kill her. When she received prayer they began to scream, "We are leaving. We are leaving."

This was the first time that a crusade had been held in Masaka, and the first time for many of the Pastors to witness the power and demonstration of the Spirit. So many healings; so many miracles! After the meeting, we stopped in at a local radio station and were interviewed in a live broadcast about the crusade and the wonderful works of God. This was our first night, and we knew that greater things were ahead in the next few days.

Masaka Miracles Continue... 127 Souls saved
Thursday morning April 5

When we arrived at the crusade grounds there was already a large crowd of approximately a thousand people waiting in the tent. Anticipation was high; the people had come expecting to receive. The crowd was calling upon the Lord; the sound of their voices was intense. They had been there for hours waiting. Two national TV stations were present this morning to do a report on the meetings.

Just before I got up to address the crowd, a man came forward; it was obvious he was under some kind of demonic trance. Before he could do anything, he was seized by the power of the Holy Spirit. His body went as stiff as a board and he fell to the ground. The enemy was not happy with what was going on in the meetings!

After praying for the worship team, I began to pray for the crowd and to release miracles, rebuking spirits of pain, sickness and disease. Some of the

The testimony of a miracle.

miracles that took place were as follows: A man with a paralyzed arm was totally healed; another who could not bend his leg was jumping up and down and doing squats. A woman's vision was restored. Asthma and paralysis were healed as well as many other diseases. Many people who manifested demons were delivered.

Nine people gave their hearts to the Lord and then I shared on the power of the Holy Spirit. I ended my message with a call for those who wanted to know Him more. Hands went up all over the tent. Everyone stood to their feet as I prayed for the crowd and called upon the Holy Spirit. Approximately 200 came forward and as they received prayer they began to fall down under the anointing.

Thursday Evening—Outdoor Crusade

The crowd was larger tonight with an estimated attendance of 5,000. After sharing my message I gave an altar call for salvation. Many hands went up all over the crowd but only 45 came forward. The Pastor later explained that the reason why many don't come forward and why the crowd continues to grow after it gets dark is because many are either Muslim or Catholic. They do not want to be seen by anyone else.

There were many testimonies of healing tonight. We witnessed many cases of tumors disappearing, demonized people being set free and the healing of blindness, deafness as well as back, knee, arm and leg conditions.

A man who received Jesus as his Savior and had been deaf for six months was healed. A little girl who was partially paralyzed began walking. When a woman was hit with the power of God she began to vomit and was healed of from a tumor that she had for over 15 years. There was a girl who was taken

153

from the hospital and carried to the crusade. She had been bed ridden and couldn't even stand. Soon she began to stand by herself; then she walked off the platform.

No wonder the Bible simply says, "He healed them all."

So many were healed and so many received ministry that it was impossible to keep track of it all. After we prayed for the sick, another thirteen people came forward and received Jesus as their Savior.

Masaka Miracles Continue (490 Souls in Three Days) Hope Nursery & Primary School—Fri. April 6, 2001

About 600 children were present this morning and I shared what the Lord had shown me while I was in Moravian Falls concerning children, how He was going to use them powerfully in revival and healing. At the altar call 110 children came forward to receive the Lord. I didn't want the children to miss out on the open-air crusade meeting so we rented a bus to bring them.

Stella Marts Secondary School

This was a secular school with children ranging in age from 8 to 20. There were over 800 students there. The building was filled and hundreds were outside. After I finished sharing my testimony 150 young people came forward to receive Jesus.

Tent Meeting 11:30 a.m.

The tent was packed and the atmosphere electrified. Approximately 1,500 people were pressed in together and the presence of the Lord was thick. I

154

gave some words of knowledge and the people eagerly responded. The ushers brought many that were manifesting demons to the front. So many healings—kidneys, stomachs and backs and even cripples. One lady couldn't swallow and came to the meeting instead of going to the hospital—she was healed. Tumors disappeared, asthma and arthritis were healed, a deaf and dumb girl was set free and could both hear and speak. Seven more gave their hearts to the Lord with many that had their hands up still remaining in the crowd.

Open Air Crusade

On the third evening as I approached the platform I saw a local witchdoctor standing in the audience. He was dressed as a shaman, and had amulets and fetishes around his neck; his hair was dirty and dreadlocked and his robes were torn. He carried a large wooden staff with bones and other paraphernalia on the end. As my vehicle approached the platform, he began to challenge me and call on the power of darkness. He shook his stick wildly in the air, casting spells and incantations.

A holy anger rose in my spirit and I went to the platform. I took authority over the power of witchcraft and commanded in Jesus name, "You will not operate in witchcraft during this campaign." An angry cloud had already covered the grounds and it began to rain. He was enraged at me and continued to shake his rod. Then he left the crusade. God had given us a tremendous breakthrough. The sun came out again and we rejoiced.

Tonight's crowd totaled between 6,000 and 7,000, with 90 souls giving their lives to the Lord. I shared a message on covenant relationships and then called for the sick. Many were being touched in the crowd and those who were healed made their way forward to give testimony. Here are just a few of the miracles that took place:

Tumors disappeared—a lady was healed of a tumor she had for three years; another felt fire go through her back and her tumor dissolved. A doctor examined the woman and told her that the tumor in her spine was gone. Another lady who had lived with a swollen leg for four years was healed. Two young women, who were completely deaf, had their ears opened. People were healed of heart conditions, pain in their bodies, lung infections and many who were

155

demonized were set free.

The meeting was closed early tonight as the authorities were concerned for our safety. There had been some threats made by the Muslim community and the authorities were taking precautions.

Saturday Morning

The team and I went to a public school and I shared my testimony with over 250 young people; 48 souls came into the kingdom. After ministering at the school we drove to the crusade grounds where a tent was set up and people began to share testimonies of the healings the the night before. Someone who had TB for six years was healed and someone's withered hand was restored. Also, people with asthma, back problems, and demonic oppression were healed and set free.

I called out many words of knowledge. At the same time, I gave a salvation call and nine people came forward and gave their hearts to the Lord. One lady who came forward for salvation began to manifest demons, she went into a trance and when the demon was cast out she came into her right mind. There were so many more healings that took place—tumors, goiters, back and rib pain, hernias, lumps and more.

I shared a message on the anointing and afterwards approximately 2,000 people lined up to receive an impartation of the Holy Spirit. As the ministry team anointed them, the power fell and many collapsed, sometimes as many as four at a time. Bodies were everywhere.

After ministering at the tent, the team went to Kako Public School where over 800 students heard my testimony. Forty-two people gave their hearts to the Lord.

Evening Crusade

Upon returning to the crusade grounds, we found six to seven thousand people gathered together listening to the worship team. I was surprised to see the local witchdoctor on the platform with the pastors. I found out that when he was in a trance last night communicating with his demon spirit guide "a short, fat, white guy with a beard broke into his

156

trance and preached the gospel to him." He gave his life to Jesus because he knew the power was real. The pastors had already prayed with him and he had laid down the power of witchcraft. Now he was saved and in his right mind. I laid my hands on him and he fell out under the power and trembled.

Then the heavens opened and it started to pour... both in the natural and the spiritual. Hundreds fled in the pouring rain while others stayed to receive their miracles from the Lord. A lady who was paralyzed in her right leg, which was swollen to twice its normal size, was healed and she walked. Two deaf mutes began to hear and speak; several who were possessed by demons were set free. Vision impairment, tumors, stomach problems, and more were healed.

Sunday Evening ... Streams of Life Church, Kampala

When we arrived in the evening, there was a large crowd gathered outside in the parking area. The sound system was set on high and the choir was singing. Several blind had their vision restored and five deaf people began to hear. One woman, who was walking with crutches and wearing a cast, was totally healed. She threw aside her crutches and took off the cast. Many breathing conditions, fevers and more were healed, so many that it seemed that almost everyone that was prayed for received their miracle from God. This evening another 60 people gave their hearts to the Lord.

Monday

Today we visited four schools and had a great time. Another 830 people gave their hearts to the Lord today. At one school the children pressed into the team asking for blessings. We were overwhelmed by their hunger for a touch from God.

We returned to Streams of Life Church in the evening and another 80 people gave their lives to Christ. Once again the miracles began to happen. A young girl who was mute, never having spoken before, was healed. She began trying to repeat the words that were spoken to her. At first the words didn't sound very similar but soon she was able to repeat them exactly. The mother was ecstatic.

Another girl had sickle cell anemia and could not close her hand. After prayer she was opening and closing her hands with no problem. A man who was born blind, who had a white film over his eye, had the film begin to dissipate after prayer and he began to see. There were many possessed by demons that were set free.

This was our last night here in Uganda and we thank God that we could be a part of what He is doing in this country and the continent of Africa. This is only the beginning. With South Africa early last year and Nigeria and Ghana last fall we know that God has a plan for Fresh Fire Ministries in this continent. We thank God for the faithfulness of our partners who have helped us finance all our ministry in Africa.

Kenya Miracle Crusade—August 1 - 7, 2001

Before I even left for Kenya in August 2001, the Lord showed me someone I would pray for when I got there. I was speaking in Kelowna and the Lord took me to a Kenyan hospital where I prayed for a crippled man. When I came back into the service I yelled to my friend, "Hey Rob, remind me that when we get to Kenya we're supposed to go to the hospital to pray for this terminal guy and he'll be healed."

When we got to that hospital in Kenya, August 2001, the doctors and nurses went with me from room to room as the healings took place. I found the man the Lord had shown me earlier; he'd been bedridden for six months and was dying of AIDS. I prayed and fire went through him. He jumped out of bed and ran down the hallway yelling, "I'm healed, I'm healed." I turned to the doctor and asked, "What do you think of this?" He shrugged and said; "I guess we'll send him home."

In case you're having a hard time with the thought of me being sovereignly moved by the Holy Spirit to another place, I'll throw in a little teaching so you know it's biblical. First, the Lord can take your physical body someplace; this is called getting transported. This is what happened when Phillip finished ministering to the Ethiopian eunuch. "Now when they came up out of the water, the

158

Spirit of the Lord caught Philip away, so that the eunuch saw him no more; and he went on his way rejoicing," (Acts 8:39).

Also, this type of experience apparently happened a lot to Elijah because, in I Kings 18:11-12, Obadiah tells Elijah: "And now you say, 'Go, tell your master, "Elijah is here" '! And it shall come to pass, as soon as I am gone from you, that the Spirit of the LORD will carry you to a place I do not know; so when I go and tell Ahab, and he cannot find you, he will kill me."

The other way to travel is to be translated, that's where your spirit goes on a trip but your body stays home. Paul refers to this in II Corinthians 12:3-4, "And I know such a man—whether in the body or out of the body I do not know, God knows—how he was caught up into Paradise and heard inexpressible words, which it is not lawful for a man to utter."

Report #1

When my friend Rob Galbraith and I arrived in Kenya the nation really embraced us. National television commercials opened up the country for the preaching of the gospel.

The first night of a four-night crusade in Eldorate, about 4 hours from Nairobi, was a huge success. Around 10,000 people gathered for an open-air crusade in the "64 Stadium." The city had never hosted an event on this level. Over one hundred pastors worked together for the success of the crusade. After I gave my testimony and preached about the power of God to save, heal and deliver, nearly 1,500 souls were saved. I prayed a mass prayer of healing and deliverance and many were delivered from demons.

One lady who was carried to the platform, demonized and mute, was delivered, within moments, of severe pains in her body as well as several

159

demons. After the service she came running to me yelling in excitement because she had been set free from years of torment and sickness.

Many people were healed instantly by the power of God while standing in the field! Some testimonies of healing are as follows; a man who could barely stand or walk because of a dislocated knee for nearly a year and a half, felt the Lord heal his leg. This man was jumping up and down on the platform. Another girl who was deaf in one ear, heard for the first time. Another man com-pletely deaf for over 11 years began to hear. Many were healed instantly of what we would consider minor illnesses including ulcers, stomach conditions, years of migraines, back problems and all kinds of pain.

Open Air Market Crusade

We went to an area in the city where drug addicts and alcoholics gather along with many children who sniff gas. Nearly 1,000 people gathered after a time of spontaneous worship and preaching. Over 200 souls responded for salvation. The power of God came and one young man fell out on his face; this was the beginning of miracles.

In the park Rob and I had a healing line—here are a few reports of healing: one woman with a deaf ear heard; one lady whose neck would not move to the right or left was healed instantly; also, the same woman had not been able to see clearly for more than a few feet—she was healed of this eye condition too. One man with a paralyzed upper left side of his body and arm was healed and another man who could not bend his arms because of a condition in his joints and muscles was healed too. Many more were instantly healed of various torments and pains, including waist, ulcer, stomach and back conditions. Over 1,700 souls were saved and many people were healed in only two meetings that first day. GLORY, GLORY, GLORY!!!

Report #2

The second evening crusade did not come without much resistance. An African storm rolled in bringing a torrential downpour. We believed the crusade would be canceled, but when the pastor arrived that evening we were surprised to learn that nearly 11,000 people had assembled and though many had left, still thousands stood for hours in the rain and heard the gospel. Another 200-250 souls responded to the altar call for salvation, bringing the total in two days to over 1,950 souls.

The miracles continued; several demonized people were set free after being carried to the altar. During the preaching they fell out under the power manifesting violently in the crowd. One young woman was crippled with arthritis to the point where she was carried to the crusade and could not walk; after the devil was cast out, she began to walk.

Another woman had cancer for over eight years in the upper left side of her body and she could not raise her arm and had no mobility. Her body was rotten with cancer. The fire of God touched her, the cancer left and her arm was restored. One young man with a dislocated hand was healed and another woman was instantly delivered from the symptoms of typhoid fever. Many others were healed of all kinds of pain and sickness!

After the crusade we did a live national radio program to over eight million listeners. During the broadcast I laid hands on the two women interviewing me and they fell out under the power. Another radio broadcaster had to take over for them. Within moments of the radio program, phone calls of healing were already coming in and, by the next day, we began to hear reports of salvations. The manager of the station gave me another live national program the next day because of Gods power.

Report #3 & 4

The last two evenings the crowds swelled to between 20,000 and 30,000 people. In the final two nights of the crusade they broadcast live to over 8 million people. Many of the people that had already heard the national radio programs recorded the second day came to the crusade and testified to being saved and healed listening to the radio.

One woman who was bed-fast for over three months came to the crusade free from all of her drugs and completely healed. Another woman, Theresa, was healed of a dislocated knee while listening to the radio show. Three phone lines at the radio station were plugged with testimonies of healings and salvations.

The third evening over 1,500 people made commitments to Christ; the counselors worked for hours talking to the new believers. Members of the Eldorate Pastor's Fellowship are working together to disciple these precious souls.

On Sunday morning I preached in one of the local churches that nearly doubled in size because of the crusade. The pastor had to build more benches for the Sunday service to seat all the new believers!

As I began to preach Saturday evening, demon possessed people fell out under the power and were carried up onto the platform and delivered by the end of the message. The miracles that night were amazing. A man who suffered epilepsy since birth, who continually suffered from seizures, was delivered. Another man deaf and mute for over 28 years heard and spoke.

A three-year-old baby boy born deaf and lame was healed; his feet were twisted inward and he had never stood before, he stood that night for the first time! He also heard for the first time. Another deaf man began to hear and speak. A small baby, Steven, who was born completely blind, received his sight. Steven's mother praised the Lord for the miracle with tears running down her face. Maureen Mwbuaj received her hearing after being deaf for 10 years. Leuses's eyes were restored after being healed of blindness for three years. A woman with a tumor said that she was delivered from witchcraft. A demon-possessed woman said that a flash of light filled her soul as the demons left her.

Many individuals on Sunday evening were healed of growths and tumors. I called four individuals to the platform through a word of knowledge, and they all had tumors that dissolved after prayer—all four were instantly healed! Some of the people with tumors had them for over two years; one lady had one for 13 years. Another woman had already been to five hospitals and they could do nothing for her, but she was healed! A young girl named Lydia was instantly healed of a broken arm. Several paralyzed limbs were healed and ulcers of over 20 years, GONE! A man with a spinal cord injury for over seven years was completely healed.

On the final evenings of the crusade nearly 30,000 people filled the stadium; another 2,000 souls were saved. A reporter from Nairobi, with Miracle magazine, came to the crusade to do an interview for this national magazine. The pastors and the news report said that there had never been a crusade of this magnitude in this city before.

The Heavenly Vision
Atlanta, Georgia—August 2001

I was in a church meeting in Atlanta and I heard the Lord say, "Lay down on the pew." When I did, I felt myself ascending out of the building and propelled down a highway. I was flying down the highway without a vehicle. I passed over bridges, underpasses and signs. I was propelled onto the North Chattanooga highway. I ended up outside a large prison in Atlanta.

I went inside and walked the corridors until I came to the cell of a 22 year-old-man. I knew through a word of knowledge that he was in prison for crimes he committed before he was saved. I saw, in this vivid experience, every detail of this young man's appearance right down to the glasses he wore. I prophesied to him about God's call on his life as an evangelist and the revival that was coming to the prison. Then I was back in the church.

That evening as I ministered, I shared the experience and asked if it meant anything to anyone. One woman jumped up and said, "That's my friend's son. She was riding with me to the meeting tonight and received a phone call that there was an emergency and she needed to return home."

"Call that woman right now." She dialed the number and gave me the cell phone; over 1,000 people witnessed my conversation. "Do you have a son in a prison in Atlanta?" I asked, before describing him down to the glasses he wore. She said, "Yes." I then discerned witchcraft and prayed and rebuked a curse of death. This woman cried out in praise to God with me for His loving attention to her son in prison and for unveiling the darkness in her home. Suddenly, the situation in her home changed. "My 17- year-old son is a Satanist," she said. "He was trying to kill his father today." The phone call had diffused this crisis situation involving her second son. She got in her car and drove over an hour to the church to testify the word of knowledge was true.

Through prayer, the word of knowledge and revelation a crisis situation was averted.

The Miraculous
Ecuador & Peru—October 1-7, 2001

Report # 1

We had arrived in Ecuador, South America for a three-day crusade before heading to Lima, Peru. We would minister in a small Sports Stadium that holds 5,000 to 6,000. Pepsi Cola was sponsoring the event and now Pepsi wanted me to come and pray over their company here! I had already done a TV interview in the city of Quevedo and was hosting our crusade. During the interview the TV reporter asked me twice, "What is this energy I feel?" We told him it was the power of God and I prayed for him on TV. Then we went to do a radio program that reaches over 60 percent of the country.

This radio show has millions of listeners. The interviewer received Christ when I prayed for the sick over the radio, he said it was like Jesus walked into his body, and he felt the fire of God. He then testified to the listeners live on radio that he did not believe in Christ before and that now he does! The owners of the radio were listening to the broadcast and they called in. They said that they considered themselves very skeptical of God but the two of them said a strong new presence and fire came through radio and impacted them.

Within hours of being in the country and on the street having a coffee, the team and I were able to pray for three people to be healed and they were instantly healed and a man was saved. We called it the "Sidewalk Cafe Healings." One man fell under the power on the street!

Report # 2

Some say Quevdo, Ecuador is the poorest country in South America. Many in South America cannot afford wheelchairs and they don't go to doctors.

164

(Jim Drown, who is one of five team members in Ecuador, was healed of a tumor earlier this year in one of our meetings in Atlanta, Georgia. Jim says that since he was impacted by the ministry this year and has listened to almost all of our teaching tapes, he is "on fire more than ever," healing the sick and preaching the gospel!)

Within hours of being in the country, we stopped for coffee at a sidewalk cafe and in five minutes three people were healed. One man was saved and fell under the power in the street. We had many evangelism opportunities outside of the evening crusades. In a restaurant one evening all eight of the staff got saved.

We held an open-air crusade in the market where we were warned it was illegal to preach the gospel and that we could be arrested, jailed and fined!! We preached anyway. The crowd began small but quickly swelled to hundreds when the miracles began. One man who was totally blind received his sight. The deaf heard and nearly 9 out of 10 prayed for were instantly healed. Fifty more were saved on the street.

One highlight of the crusade in Ecuador was an invitation into a prison. The worst criminals were there. They put us in the main courtyard with the prisoners and locked the door. Armed guards with machine guns stood on the wall as we preached the gospel. Forty-nine prisoners, which we know of, made public commitments to Christ and we prayed for nearly 100 healings.

The harvest continued in the streets, prison, hotel lobbies and taxis. We saw hundreds of healings and souls saved in the evening crusades and were able to reach millions with the gospel through a radio broadcast. The preaching of the gospel was confirmed daily with signs and wonders including these specific individual healings in Quevdo:

One boy who was mute all his life spoke for the first time. I had the boy repeat English words instead of Spanish after his healing. My translator jokingly said the reason the boy didn't speak all these years is because he wanted to learn English. One crippled man on crutches was instantly healed; God did a creative miracle in his bones. One woman totally blind for over 20 years saw and another deaf and dumb boy heard and spoke. One evening seven deaf people heard in a single service. A man in that service who had not walked in years, walked home. The blind saw and the deaf heard, as the team and I prayed for the sick each night. One evening we prayed for over 1,500 sick people.

One last powerful testimony—a taxi driver, after dropping Ivan (my disciple) and me off at our hotel, turned to the pastor and asked, "What is the energy coming off those men? I feel something in the car." This man, backslidden for years, came back to Jesus!

Report # 3

In Lima, Peru we had open-air meetings from 1,000 to 2,000 people. The first service after I shared my testimony, over 150 people responded to receive Jesus! Every evening between 100 and 200 souls were saved in each service and nearly 80 people in a church meeting on Sunday night.

In these crusades God came in unusual power. We watched as, at the moment of salvation, many were instantly healed and filled with the Holy Ghost. This evening hundreds were filled with the Spirit without hands being laid on them. In the crowd the fire fell on hundreds of people and some began to shake, weep, scream, fall under the power and speak in tongues all over the park grounds.

Then the testimonies began! One woman, completely deaf and mute, heard and spoke for the first time. We wanted to verify the miracle so we asked if anyone knew the woman and a neighbor came forward and reported that this woman had always been deaf. This miracle and about 75 percent of all the healings took place en masse. A seven-year-old boy with a large hernia from birth was healed. Another woman, who could barely walk and had infections from 2 surgeries, was healed and could walk. In this one service God healed more than eight tumors. One lady with a tumor on her face showed us how it disappeared and another woman who had a visible tumor on her leg watched it dissolve. The Lord healed more than 50 deaf people and dissolved over 40 tumors. He healed pain and diseases in every service.

On the final day of meetings in Peru, we decided the ruling religious spirit and witchcraft needed to be broken so we had a "no holds barred" service. After prayer, hundreds of youth were laid out under the power, including children weeping, shaking, screaming and we saw nearly 500 baptized in the Holy Ghost at one time, all speaking in tongues. At least 1,000 people or more receive the spontaneous baptism in four days. In much of Peru and almost all of Ecuador the people have no experience with the river of God, renewal or revival. Most people don't even speak in tongues and have never seen the manifestations of the Spirit.

On the final evening the team and I got hammered in the Spirit and staggered around drunk on the platform. The pastors, worship team and hundreds of others in the crowd, who I taught to drink by faith, got drunk too. The crusade was so successful in these countries that we were asked to return to Lima, Peru the following spring and hold a large crusade in the stadium that holds up to 45,000.

Brandon Manitoba
October 10th-14th, 2001

After returning to North America, I went to minister in Manitoba—here is a report by someone from Brandon:

It was such a joy to have you ministering at the International Healing Conference October 10th-14th. We certainly enjoyed having Ivan Roman with us too. It was an incredible time in the Presence of the Lord. When you spoke on the deaf and dumb spirit nearly 100 people stood to testify of restored hearing, including me (Ramona). I had 25 percent permanent hearing loss and God healed it! He also healed my directional dyslexia after 59 years!

Andie Meyer, the young woman whose totally blind eye was healed, continues to astound her doctors. Her eye was shot out 7 years ago and she underwent surgery, and was given a cadaver cornea to try to save the eye. The surgery failed and the sight in her eye was 20/400, totally blind. When she went through the 'tunnel of fire' on Friday night, her sight was restored! Her Jewish doctor examined her the next day and wrote a note to Andie's father letting him know of the unexplained change. From 20/400 to 20/25! Not knowing what to do, he sent her to the University. Doctors there examined her thoroughly. It seems that she has a brand new eye, praise God! According to the doctor's report, they can find no sign of the injury or surgery!

Also, a woman at the healing Roundtable received a transfer of anointing (Yes, all saints can do this!) As a nurse, she was so concerned about all of the people she saw dying around her, she decided to do something about it. She went to work after the conference; when a baby was stillborn, and the doctors

167

could not resuscitate the infant after about 45 minutes of trying everything from the paddles, to injections, and bagging, they handed it off to the nurse to prepare the baby for the morgue. She took the child aside and, as compassion welled up in her, laid hands on it and, in the name of Jesus Christ, commanded a spirit of life to come in. The child was raised to Life! God is so Good!! This was not one of the traveling evangelists with a healing ministry, but a nurse who had faith imparted to her at the conference.

Ramona—Brandon, Manitoba

Tremendous Miracles and Healings
Ontario, Canada—November 14, 2001

Great news! My father made a decision for Christ in my meeting in Ontario tonight! I had been praying for my dad for several years asking, "Holy Spirit how can I reach him?" Since my dad was now unemployed after years of managing home hardware stores, I offered him a job in my ministry editing my tapes and videos. That way he would have to hear and watch the power of God and would be regularly exposed to the anointing. I claimed the promise in Malachi 4:6 that God would turn the hearts of the fathers to the children.

After a while I asked Dad to come on the road with me to a meeting in Ontario. That was where he had been raised and where he and my mom first met. After several nights in the meetings he was hearing and seeing the healing testimonies. I decided to pull him into the anointing and have him be a catcher. I started to lay hands on a woman and she manifested. She started screaming and writhing like a snake on the floor. I'll never forget the look of horror on my dad's face. It was like he was watching a scene from The Exorcist. Even though I thought that this power encounter would be hard to deny, I was still surprised when I gave the altar call that my dad put his hand up and walked down to the altar.

I was weeping inside and I remember feeling awkward in the moment. This situation was so unfamiliar. I thought, "Is this really happening? What's our relationship going to be like? What will happen tomorrow?" I was afraid and excited. To be honest, this was the first real emotional experience I had shared with my dad—ever. As we prayed the sinner's prayer, I wept. My lips quivered.

When I laid hands on him he fell under the power. I knew that this was the beginning of a powerful work of healing.

Later in the book my dad shares his testimony in detail.

Meetings in St. Catharines, Ontario

Praise the Lord! We have just finished four days of services with Todd Bentley. These days can best be described as miracle days. People with all kinds of sicknesses and infirmities were healed nightly. Here are just some of the miracles that occurred:

One man in our church whose heart was severely damaged (operating on only 1/3 of its capacity) was healed Sunday evening. One girl who was born totally blind in her right eye, started to see out of that eye for the first time after prayer on Tuesday night.

Many people were healed of ear conditions and degrees of deafness. One young lady received a tremendous deliverance after years of struggling. One could see the change on her countenance.

One pastor from Quebec, after attending these meetings, saw God move powerfully in healing and outpouring in his church. He called me and was so excited at what God had done. Even in our own church, the following Sunday, words of knowledge and healing occurred. One mother and daughter with stomach afflictions were set free and could eat anything with no reactions. People testified of major healing in their bodies—arms, legs, backs, knees, bladders, etc.

We witnessed major emotional healings of individuals suffering from traumas caused by accidents and abuse of different types. Todd preached one night on the different levels of anointing and gave a very good balance between faith and the sovereignty of God. Many of our people were touched and encouraged by this message.

I believe that Todd Bentley is a prototype of what God is about to release in the Body of Christ. Let the signs and wonders once again become evidenced in our lives! Then let's take it to the marketplace.

Ray Young—Pastor, The Father's House
St. Catharine's, Ontario

The last part of 2001 in Canada has taken us from Manitoba, Alberta and Ontario clear across the nation to several meetings in Newfoundland with testimonies of salvation and healing. There have been so many healings and tremendous testimonies of deliverances and emotional healings that I've included only a few below.

At the recent healing conference at the Toronto Airport Christian Fellowship (TACF) there were some 300 to 500 healings. In one day alone, as we were ministered, 70 people gave testimony of healings. A majority of these were testimonies of creative healings including a woman who had a severed retina reattached and her vision restored as well as several others who had partial paralysis or could not move their toes. One lady with Bels Palsy in her face was healed as the Holy Spirit created nerves. God also healed some 12 cases of nerve endings—severed or detached nerves. About 8 individuals received healing of vision impairment or partial blindness, including one woman who was completely blind in one eye since birth. In St. Catherines last week another woman blind from birth in one eye also received her sight. Several people removed their glasses and could see clearly; cataracts were healed and more. There have been several cases of deafness healed, including one man deaf in his right ear for over five years who had his healing begin as he was driving home from a meeting in New Market Ontario. When he began to hear he drove all the way back to the meeting and said, "I am beginning to understand in my deaf ear." Four days later he testified again about his hearing.

On the Saturday night in Toronto the Holy Spirit fell on a woman with Multiple Sclerosis. She stood, walked to the platform and testified that she had not walked like this in 11 years: "The circulation is flowing again in my legs." One man testified that the cysts in his kidneys were removed and another man had a tumor disappear in his ear. God also did a powerful creative miracle for a man from Manitoba who had internal injuries years ago that damaged his stomach and digestive system. He responded to a word of knowledge and within a week I received a testimony that his organs and stomach were healed. For the first time in more than 14 years, he ate his wife's apple pie. Yummy!

PART II

HEALING & MIRACLE HARVEST GROWS

Battling for Miracles
Newfoundland, Canada—January 10, 2002

The meetings in Newfoundland got off to a slow start. It was the first time that I'd done meetings in that part of eastern Canada and when I preached it felt like my words were bouncing off the walls. I didn't sense a strong anointing for healing, let alone faith that something was going to happen. I was feeling a little discouraged because the meetings were smaller than I had expected.

Also, my mother's family is from Newfoundland and many of my uncles and other family were in the meetings. They were from a Salvation Army background and I was concerned that if any manifestations happened it would scare them away. But God gave tremendous miracles and testimonies anyway and, as difficult as it was to minister, we saw several breakthroughs.

Each evening we pressed in for detailed words of knowledge. I believe that the prophetic ministry and revelation is important to break the religious stronghold. In Springdale, a community of only 3,500, the church exploded on the Sunday morning after I received an angelic visitation in the pastor's office. I released a prophetic word for the church and prophesied most of the morning to the rest of the congregation. Then it happened— one young man was taken into a vision of Jesus and individuals were running around the sanctuary like they were in a marathon. Some people began prophesying, others experienced drunkenness in the Holy Spirit and one elder, who was pinned to the floor for over 2 hours, received a creative miracle. The doctors planned to surgically repair crushed bone and cartilage that completely blocked his nostril. It was healed when an intense burning passed through his sinus cavity. One man, who used pain medication everyday for two years, testified that his hips and sciatic condition were healed. On the Sunday evening I was overcome in the pulpit with the drunkenness of the Spirit and laughter. That led into a fire tunnel that laid out 90 percent of the people in the service. Yes Lord!

Miracles in Newfoundland
Newfoundland, Canada—January 10, 2002

It was our privilege to host Todd Bentley and Ivan Roman during their meetings in Newfoundland. Truly God did marvelous things among us.

In the meetings at Springdale, Todd struggled to operate under the open heaven he is used to. It seems he came up against the religious spirit like he never did before. While the word he shared was awesome, Todd found it difficult to move in and get responses to his words of knowledge. We did, though, have a number of notable miracles for which we give God the glory.

An injury to a church elder over thirty years ago resulted in one of his nostrils being completely blocked. As he lay on the floor, unable to move because of the "weight of His presence," his nose began to burn to the point of being uncomfortable. When he finally got up he could breathe normally.

A young woman with hearing problems in one of her ears responded to a word of knowledge. She said she felt a "pop" and miraculously can now hear in that ear. One man had muscle damage in his calf muscle and had circulation problems. He has been healed. He testified and jumped up and down in a service something he could not do before.

One young woman responded to a word concerning damage to the rotator cuff in her right shoulder. Not only did God heal her so she could use her arm and move like she could three years ago, but God also exposed the injury and the hurts associated to it. She is healed!

An elder's wife was healed of back and neck pain from an injury she received in a car accident six years ago. After a word of knowledge and prayer, she went around for several days with "a heat glow" around her head. After taking many pain tablets a day for six years, she now has no pain and no medication.

During Todd's meetings in a neighboring town, miracles happened even between meetings. While four friends were having tea, the Spirit began to manifest. One person had an egg-sized lump disappear from her calf muscle, another had a small lump vanish from her thigh, and yet another had her shoulder and arm muscles healed. They even witnessed gold dust.

The highlight of the meetings in Springdale was on Sunday morning *when Todd shared the prophetic word on the Book of Remembrance and the Book of the Future. He also gave a prophetic word to the church. Todd said this was a new season; the religious spirit was about to be defeated in Springdale and Newfoundland and that we had been given the Gideon anointing to see this accomplished, an anointing of revival. On Saturday night Todd had an angelic visitation in my office. The angel "Harvest" brought with him an anointing for revival and harvest. With a great fervour, Todd encouraged us to break out of the winepress, and move into our destiny.*

The meetings concluded in Springdale on Sunday night with Todd becoming drunk in the Spirit and the whole congregation participating in a time of rejoicing and joy as we moved through a "fire tunnel."

Dave Mercer

Fighting Dark Powers
Reinosa, Mexico—February 2002

The first of two nights in Reinosa, Mexico was difficult, however, God gave us several key miracles and over 100 salvations. That evening in my hotel I felt spiritual backlash. We discovered that the local witchdoctors covenanted together to release the power of witchcraft against the meetings.

At 2:30 a.m. I saw the form of a woman and I felt her presence at the foot of my bed. She had astral projected there. I knew the power of witchcraft was being released against us. I took authority in the Spirit over its power. "Every curse, spell and sorcery you will not prevail against me and this campaign. Greater is He that is in me than he that is in the world. I will go forth in His power and prevail."

Breaking the Power of Witchcraft

The Holy Spirit spoke to me and told me about these witches who had gathered. The next evening at the crusade I said, "A witch came to my hotel room last night to challenge the power of God. I know there are many witches and warlocks in this meeting. I'm going to confront you and the power of witchcraft now." I took authority over the atmosphere and climate of the room in Jesus name. I broke and rebuked its power and commanded every devil associated with witchcraft to let go.

Individuals were thrown two rows back. Twenty-eight people writhed like snakes on the floor. The team carried these manifesting people to the altar. One woman, with blood in her mouth, began screaming and shrieking. Another young woman, who had been set free from demons, looked to her left and saw a grotesque demon step out of a local witch. She fainted. When she regained consciousness she said she wanted to know Jesus.

God gave us an open heaven and miracles began to take place. The local town cripple, paralyzed from the waist down for 11 years, bedridden for two years was there in her wheelchair. She was in such chronic pain she could not even hug her children. The Lord healed her and she pushed her wheel chair out of the meetings.

That day we had an open heaven of miracles and over 200 people got saved.

The Miraculous in Calcutta, India—March, 2002

I went to Calcutta with our team member Ivan, my father Dave and our associate Jeff Vosgien. We didn't take a full team this time because of the danger. India is unlike any place I had preached the gospel. We ministered in a village just outside of the main city of over 15 million. The Indian government opposes Christianity and we had to come into the country as visiting our friend Dr. X. We cannot hold public meetings or meetings in the market like we do in other countries. The Hindus actually held a festival to oppose our coming.

The Hindu chants and prayers could be heard day and night over the loud speakers throughout the village, idols were on the roadside everywhere and the spiritual oppression was great. But we held on to God's word in Isaiah 60:2 which says that when "darkness shall cover the earth, and deep darkness the people; ...the Lord will arise over you, and His glory will be seen upon you."

The Christians and missionaries who were there for the healing impartation face beatings and sometimes even daily threats on their lives. Recently, three foreign missionaries were burned. Many new converts are chased down and threatened, made to deny Christ or persecuted in other ways. Also, the common deception that Jesus is just one of many Gods, makes it difficult to have large meetings and harvest here. However, we will have victory.

We stayed on a large compound patrolled by armed security. People were hungry for the power of God. Some of the pastors and evangelists attending the conference traveled five days from Nepal and the Himalayan mountains; some even walked three days to catch a bus for a two-day ride just to be there. In the first morning session, 145-150 responded to the altar call after I made it clear that they would need to forsake all other Gods, religions and idols. Most of the converts were children (aged 5-15), school teachers and a few villagers.

The Miracles Begin

Soon the Lord began to hear testimonies of miracles. One pastor's wife was healed of a tumor on her left side when a word of knowledge was given. A man and a woman, who were new converts, were both healed of deafness. This man's wife, who wore a brace around her back and hips and could barely stand from the constant pain, was healed as well. One man with TB was blind in his right eye. He gave his life to Christ and God opened his vision more. There were many other healings as well.

Harvest

After three days in India we began to overcoming the resistance to the meetings and the number of salvations reached 706. The new converts were followed up and discipled by the team in India and bibles were distributed. Most of the converts were Hindu and Muslim and face daily persecutions, threats and even violence for their commitment to Christ.

As I preached the gospel nightly, we told them that a commitment to Christ means the forsaking of all other gods and idols. Many began removing idols and making steps to be delivered. One young woman, after receiving her eyesight, ripped off her bandage on her wrists; it was a fetish that carried a curse, even though it was supposed to protect her husband.

More Miracles Deaf and Mute

Hundreds pressed in nightly to be healed and many fell under the power, including hundreds of young children; it was precious to see them receive. The miracles were straight out of the bible and created a stir throughout the village. The first miracle happened to a local man, widely known in his village as a deaf-mute—he heard and spoke. The second healing was a Muslim woman, also deaf and mute. She was 16 years old and already married. God healed her and she wept with tears of joy on the platform. Then three deaf mutes, all siblings, began to receive their healing and speak. A woman paralyzed on one leg for over eight years, testified of her healing and the healing of another sickness. An evangelist's wife from Nepal gave a testimony of a tumor of four years dissolved at the moment I spoke the word of knowledge. Just then she had a visitation from the Lord in which He told her she was also being healed of other infirmities.

Blind and More Souls

The miracles continued as another woman, blind in an eye for over 25 years, begins to see! After the third service, over 400 came into the kingdom; we also saw over 306 salvations the previous two days. Thank you Jesus. On the third day the healings continued as three more deaf heard. God also healed three crippled legs and knees that could not bend or walk properly for between 8 and 10 years.

The Team

Jeff, Ivan and Dave were used mightily. God also used my dad to open deaf ears even though, ironically, he was trained to do sign language with deaf mutes years ago! When a demon growled at him, my dad roared back, "Every devil go," and the man was set free. Ivan prayer for a young woman that was in constant pain and she received a partial healing. Then

176

the Lord told Ivan to ask her what it would take for her to follow Jesus and she said, "I want to be healed and then I serve Jesus". Bam... under the power, up and healed! Jeff prayed for an elderly lady who could not bend her left knee for 20 years. After prayer—BAM—healed, kicking and running across the altar.

Miracles happen nightly here in India! In a few nights, we witnessed 19 deaf mutes hear and speak. Over nine completely blind people were healed and more received healing of their partial blindness. Cripples began to walk and many healings of various sicknesses occurred. We prayed for hundreds nightly, one by one.

More Souls

In five days, over 900 people prayed to receive Jesus. The resistance to the gospel was strong in India. The Muslim and Hindu faiths are pre-dominate—many come just to receive healing and believe they can have Jesus and their gods too. Every night we made it clear in the altar call that turning to Christ involves forsaking all. We also explained what it would cost to be a Christian because many face persecution for deciding to follow Christ. Many people who want to be saved are afraid of the radical Hindus and Muslims.

The first breakthrough came Saturday morning. I was led by the Spirit to preach on demons. In the service, Ivan had a vision of one of the Hindu gods; Jeff and Dave saw a large demon. That night, a woman violently manifested a demon; we were told it is the most powerful spirit in the Hindu culture. After two hours, she was finally set free. This woman was married to a Christian. With the help of her two Hindu brothers, she had even physically beaten her husband because of his faith. That night she and her daughter got saved.

Incredible Baptism of the Holy Ghost Service!

Saturday afternoon, at a meeting attended by 116 leaders, pastors and evangelists, I preached on the Holy Ghost and power. The power of

God fell and the pastor and I began to shake and jump up and down under God's fire like pogo sticks.

The Holy Spirit seemed to be rushing or, as someone said, "Swirling in from the roof like a small tornado." At the beginning of the service we heard a sound like a generator—then it hit. People fell out of their chairs and began literally rolling across the floor for a few minutes. One wave of the Spirit after another rolled in—leaders became drunk in the spirit and many started to laugh. I could not preach on the baptism because it was already taking place. Fifty to sixty individuals responded to a call for the infilling of the Holy Spirit. As God's Spirit rolled in, a roar-like sound ascended to heaven and row upon row of people were whacked onto the floor.

People assembled on the side of the road outside, I imagine it was like the day of Pentecost. Some Indian leaders who received the baptism of the Holy Spirit and the gift of tongues were even heard speaking in English... and we understood it! Many others were taken into visions. One woman came running to the altar saying, "I see the fire of God." An hour and half later the visitation lifted after several received deliverance from devils. One woman hissed like a snake. Even her tongue made snake-like manifestations until she was set free!

Miracles Continue
By Jeff Vosgien

Here are a few great testimonies from the last two days; one young child about five years old had a crippled left limb from birth. She could not even raise her arm. When we prayed, her arm was immediately healed and she raised her arm several times. You should have seen her father's face! Another amazing miracle was a 19- year-old deaf and mute girl who received her hearing and spoke for the first time after her healing! We could not get her to stop yelling; she kept on trying to speak all the new sounds she heard. After the miracle, they both made decisions for Christ! Two young children who were crippled received healing; one began to use his legs and walked for the first time. Another, who was in a sitting position, rose up by himself and stood. He was excited about walking; his healing was progressive. Another great mira-

cle was the three- year-old girl with blindness from birth and another man completely blind from birth who both began to see. The man saw a little at first and then, as the healing progressed, he could even see my hand waving. He screamed with joy when he saw the camera flash. Praise God!

Easter Resurrection Celebration
San Jose California—April 1, 2002

by Senior Pastor Greg Babish, Celebration Community Church

Glorious Resurrection celebration weekend, beloved Revivalists! As the Jewish community sings the Passover song, "Dayenu (It Would Have Been Enough)," we acknowledge that our gracious Lord of Glory keeps on sending us His best ... keeps on pouring out His River ... keeps on revealing triumphant, conquering, victorious Christ in us .. and keeps on releasing grace for grace!

And now God has sent beloved, prophetic, healing evangelist Todd Bentley back to the San Francisco Bay Area. Last night, Thursday, March 28th, he began an Easter weekend of POWER-filled meetings. Discerning regional spiritual warfare, 26-year-old Todd Bentley identified the constricting, choking, suffocating python spirit (of cursing/witchcraft/divination) over our entire area - and went right after it. Breaking the assignment of death and rebuking the python spirit and all its effects.

He absolutely nailed it for so many of us who had been wondering WHAT was wrong with us! That spirit that had been trying to slowly squeeze the life of the Spirit out of us was broken; we were given a supernatural, divine strength to overcome. Todd called for the angels to minister to us as angels strengthened our Lord Jesus on earth.

Todd obviously really loves releasing the anointing that heals and teaching the revelation of our Kingdom authority... biblically-sound, experiential Christianity in the fullness of the manifestation of God's Presence.

As he said, "Do you know who you are? Do you know what you have? Do you know how to give it away? God wants to move us into the authority of the rule and reign of JESUS! Don't be a victim of circumstances, your feelings, or what anybody else says! Occupy, seize by force and militantly POSSESS THE LAND! Make it happen! As Caleb says in Numbers 13, we are

`WELL ABLE' to overcome; we're not grasshoppers! (Prov. 23:7) Most of us are satisfied, apathetic and afraid to press in—this hinders the manifestation of the life of God. `WELL ABLE' means in the Hebrew 'to have power; have the capacity to have success; could and can.' This scripture emphasizes that we can have as much of God as we want now instead of waiting for Heaven. Todd made the important point that Christianity is not centered on the past or the future. God is here and now. We won't need healing in Heaven. Healing is for NOW!

Todd Bentley inspired us with his flamboyant fun, his wild testimony, and his attitude: "I'm gonna have the fullness of what You say I can have, Lord!" This lines up with the apostle John's prayer: "Beloved, I pray that you may prosper in all things and be in health, just as your sould prospers." (3 John 2)

God's Power Touches Mwanza, Tanzania
Estimated Attendance of 25,000 First Night—Over 500 Saved
By Brian Hill

Welcome to Mwanza

Our 39-member Fresh Fire team arrived in Mwanza to a spectacular welcome. A huge gathering of over 200 pastors, church officials, along with others greeted Todd and the team warmly. Todd was given an ambassador's welcome with a garland of flowers placed around his neck. Later, we were told that no other "westerner" had ever received such a tremendous greeting. After a short press conference, the team was loaded up into passenger vans and Land Rovers. The crusade was now officially "in country."

Severe Poverty, Great Unity

The infrastructure of Mwanza is in shambles. Poverty and squalor reign supreme over these beautiful people. Many of our team members were heartbroken at the living conditions (or lack of) that prevailed. After an arduous trek over terribly rutted dirt roads, dodging other cars, carts, people on heavily laden bicycles and countless pedestrians, our team arrived at the Hotel Tilapia; a veritable palace compared to what we had just witnessed. Humbled

180

by the experience, our hearts were being prepared for our commission.

The following day, Todd met with the council of church leaders. They informed him that an incredible 80 percent of the churches in Mwanza had gathered to support Fresh Fire's crusade! One idea that gained great momentum was to rent large trucks or buses to pick up as many crippled and sick people as possible and bring them to the Crusade. As the crusade budget had already being taxed heavily by ongoing expenses, many of the leaders and later team members, donated their own money to rent over three large buses for the entire time of the crusade! The local church contingent gave us more incredible news. They had canvassed the area with posters, calendars, radio announcements, etc. In some of the radio spots, it was being announced that although AIDS does not have a cure, Jesus could cure anything!

As a 'grand finale', they informed us that the High Commissioner of Tanzania was coming to personally open the Crusade with a speech. With his arrival, representatives of all the media, including national television, would be attending. This would, in fact, give national attention to the event!

Child crippled from birth WALKS!

During Todd's leaders meeting, a small group of Fresh Fire Ministry team members visited a local orphanage. Numerous children gave their hearts to Jesus and several received healing in their body. After prayer, one child, crippled from birth, rose from his chair and began to walk shakily on his own! Other children—blind, deaf and dumb—began to see, hear and speak!

Gift Shop Deliverance

While they were in the hotel gift shop, team members prayed with a Muslim man who wanted to give his heart to Jesus. As they did so, he began to writhe around and hiss, like a snake. They commanded the demon to leave and the man was delivered and saved! During the days before the crusades started, the team went into the market to do the works of Jesus. People were saved and healed everywhere we went. In one home for street kids, over 30 children and two staff members prayed to receive Jesus into their hearts!

Prison Warden Set Free

We also visited the largest prison (2,200 inmates) in Mwanza. The top officials of the prison, including the Chief Warden who was also in charge of six other prisons in the region, greeted us. We were given the opportunity to offer prayer to the staff members. Before she even left the states, a member of the team, Pastor BB Rail had a Word of Knowledge regarding someone in the government that had a disabled child. At first no one responded but then the Director called up one of the women guards into the room. The team member prayed for the woman, who received it well. Then BB asked if any one wanted to receive the gift of Salvation. Again, no one moved. Then, unexpectedly, the Chief Warden stood up from his desk and announced that he would accept this gift. One of the officials standing behind the Director looked shocked as his superior prayed the Prayer of Faith! Upon receiving his salvation, the Director said, "I feel happy." He grinned widely as he shook the hands of numerous team members.

Healing and Salvations in the Hospital

Other Fresh Fire Ministry teams went out to the AIC Health Center and to the open markets on the street. At the AIC, the team reported 3 salvations and 10 healings. Of the saved, the first woman was delivered from hearing voices and being tormented with continual nightmares. With the aid and confirmation from a local pastor and the interpreter, the woman said she felt something leave her body and now felt happy and peaceful! A man with an IV in his arm was healed of malaria then asked for salvation. The man was visibly strengthened and was beaming with joy as the team left his bedside. A Muslim man gave his heart to Jesus and then was healed of chronic stomach pains. A child of about four or five years old, had malaria and over 80 different parasites in her body. When the team arrived, she was unresponsive, almost catatonic. After receiving prayer, she was smiling and happy. Flora, another patient, received salvation and was healed of malaria and migraines. Several of the women on the team were in tears of joy, reporting that her face was actually glowing when they left.

Street Ministry Miracles

Next, we took God's power to the street, where we saw many miracles and salvations. Here's one notable story: A Muslim man had injured his leg in an

182

auto accident and the other leg was crippled from polio. He received prayer and the injured leg regained its strength. As a result of his healing, he gave his life to Christ! The team discovered that the area that they had chosen to minister in was about 85 percent Muslim.

The Crusade Begins
First Night: 25,000 Estimated Attendance–Over 500 Saved!

I have never experienced such a joyful time in worship as I did this evening (and I'm on a worship team!). Though a video camera and all the gear that goes with it encumbered me, I couldn't stand still. The choirs from Uganda and Tanzania were awesome. The crowd danced and sang with all their heart.

The High Commissioner of Tanzanian government arrived shortly before the last choir was up on stage. He joined in the praise heartily. Afterwards, he addressed the crowd, giving his endorsement to Fresh Fire Ministries and encouraged the people to heed the evangelist's words. He then proceeded to give a gospel message of his own, and challenging people to repent for their lack of commitment to following God.

Salvations and Healings

Rather than going into preaching, Todd launched straight into releasing a wave of healing over the crowd. He also gave an altar call in quick succession. About 270 people surged forward to receive salvation. Hundreds more were waving their hands to signify that they had also received healing or salvation but the crowd up front was so tight that they were unable to press forward. A few people, healed in the crowd, were able

The crowd worshipped and sang.

183

to come to the stage and testify:

Eight or nine deaf people received either partial or full restoration of their hearing. A young crippled girl pressed towards the stage, waving her crutches over her head in victory. She had been in the middle of the crowd and was healed in the first wave of healing. The crowd went wild! Another woman began to receive her sight. A man with a skin disease that inhibited his movement was able to bend and jump easily. Several demons manifested in people and the team joined in to cast them out and deliver their hosts. One woman was very violent as she spat and raged, writhing like a snake on the stage. She was set free and began to rejoice and praise God.

The Fresh Fire Ministry teams continued after the power was shut off around 7:00 PM. Many more testimonies will be forthcoming in the days to come as the leaders gather information from their respective teams. This has been a fantastic day!

Fishing For Souls at the Docks

The next day got off to a great start as teams gathered for intercessory prayer and worship. We have been meeting in a small open-air restaurant in the hotel complex that is right on Lake Victoria. It is also a favorite place for local fishermen who paddle their small boats into the cove to drop lines for Tilapia, a local fish. This setting seems prophetically appropriate for our work here.

After prayer, we loaded into our sturdy vans and bounced and careened our way to one of the open markets of Mwanza. This one is on the lake where local fishermen and cargo boats full of grain and other produce come to sell their goods. Mid-morning is a busy time for the market and people filled the streets.

Today, Todd conducted the open-air meeting in a highly concentrated Muslim fishing village. Local pastors and Christians from Uganda came along as interpreters and musicians. As they began to play lively Swahili music, a crowd of about 500 or so gathered. Todd was introduced and he began to preach. The atmosphere was heavy with unbelief or fear, so Todd continued encouraging the crowd to give their hearts to Jesus and to also meet the challenge to come up for God's healing. By the time the meeting was over, we had around 150 saved souls and several healings of damaged bodies and many opened ears!

184

Night 2 of The Crusade
50,000 Attendance/ 700-800 Saved / Numerous Healings

The word had obviously been spreading throughout this city of over 1 million that something very unusual was happening. This night, the crowd swelled to approximately 50,000 people. An air of anticipation grew as the worship teams danced and sang jubilantly.

Confronting the Powers of Witchcraft

When Todd came up, he immediately attacked the powers of witchcraft and sorcery. The previous night, we found out that curses had been placed against us. Blood and animal parts were found on the stage that morning, which is evidence of the evil that oppresses this area. Todd, through a word of knowledge, began to fast and pray, starting the previous night, to get a breakthrough against the local powers.

Todd gave an altar call for those who wanted deliverance from witchcraft, including witchdoctors who desired to give up their occult practices. The front area, roped off for ministry, was soon filled to overflowing. In that altar call alone, around 400 people got saved! When Todd led them through a salvation prayer, many people began to manifest violent demonic activity. Prayer teams to help deliver them from their torment immediately encircled these people. Approximately 40 demonized people were delivered.

One woman was extremely violent and thrashed about for about 45 minutes while the team prayed over her. When she was brought to the stage, she tried to attack Todd! After more lengthy deliverance, she was restored to her right mind and gave the following testimony: A witchdoctor had blown powder in her face and up her nose, which caused her to lose her sense of smell and hearing. Also, she said it felt like a knife was constantly being driven into her back. When she was delivered, her hearing and sense of smell returned. The back pain was gone as well.

Miracles Increase

That night hundreds of people were healed in a mass wave of healing. Here are a few of the testimonies:

A three-year-old boy, called up by a Word of Knowledge, had never walked in his life and also had malaria. He received dramatic healing and ran back and forth across the stage several times!

A man with a paralyzed right leg was healed after I grabbed his leg, and cast out the demon oppressing him. A woman, with a tumor protruding from her stomach, received healing. The tumor shriveled up and disappeared! Several crippled people were able to walk on their own. A woman with polio was able to stand straight for the first time in years! Several deaf/mutes were healed. This brings that count up to well over 12 so far! A woman with a stunted leg gave her life to Jesus as she watched her leg grow!

Hundreds of others were healed of various pains and sickness but were unable to get to the altar and testify because of the crowds pressing in for healing! An estimated 700 - 800 souls were brought into the Kingdom by the end of the night!

Fresh Fire Ministry Team - Street Reports

Reports from the Fresh Fire Ministry teams are now flowing in fast. In addition to what has already been reported, there have been at least 300 more salvations through street ministry, visits to hospitals, orphanages and schools, ministry in the crusade crowds and one-on-one encounters throughout the day! The reports of healings are incredible: two people with AIDS freed from chronic pain; 28 deaf ears opened; 21 blind eyes healed; 15-20 cripples healed; 15 tumors either shrunk or disappeared; 12 demonized people set free; 8-15 people with various lung diseases healed; 12 wombs restored and too many general healings to mention!

Crusade Night 3 - At Least 700 Saved - Healings Abound

We are now at the halfway mark of the crusade, with only 2 more nights to go. The crowd has consistently been around 30,000 - 50,000 people. It is hard to get a solid count, as there is a constant ebb and flow of people coming and going.

Todd shared his testimony with the people. It was much like what many in the crowd were dealing with in their own lives. When Todd gave the altar call, hundreds of hands went up all over the field. They began streaming down towards the altar until there was no more room. Still hundreds in the crowd waved their hands as they gave their lives to Jesus.

186

As has happened in all the previous nights, when the prayer of salvation is shared, dozens of people begin manifesting demons fighting to keep their hosts in bondage. A special tent was dedicated to delivering these people, but the numbers were so many that some were dealt with right in front of the stage.

Spontaneous healings also took place all over the field. Here are a few: a woman, crippled for over a year received healing and walked on her own; dozens of deaf ears were opened; numerous blind eyes were restored and a woman was healed of a tumor on her stomach, the size of a baby's head!

Here are some more notable healings:

• People witnessed their tumors disappear during the mass healing wave.
• A thyroid goiter shrank to half its size.
• A woman's stunted leg grew 2".
• A baby, paralyzed in her legs and blind from birth, received both her sight and strength to her limbs!
• Another girl of about 4 years old was deaf from birth. When she got healed, she began to cry and tug at her ears.
• Many people, crippled from disease or injury received healing and regained use of their body.
• an eight-year-old boy, demonized so badly that 6 grown men couldn't hold him. Though he didn't speak English, a voice erupted from the boy, growling, "Who are you!" at one of the Fresh Fire Ministry team members. Eventually he was delivered and later testified on stage that something was strangling him.

The current tally of salvations exceeds 2600. The healings are innumerable!

Intercessors and Pastors

We drove up into the hilltops where a small group of local Christians had been fasting and praying for over 10 days, interceding for the Crusade and the people of Mwanza. These dedicated souls were gathered in a tiny room at the back of an orphanage for children whose parents had died of the AIDS virus. We blessed and prayed for the intercessors as well as the children gathered in the front yard.

For three days, Todd met with about 500 Pastors and Church leaders from all over the region. He taught and exhorting them about the Elijah Anointing; the transferable gift of healings, signs and wonders. On the last day, he preached out of Matthew 10: Preach the Gospel, Heal the Sick, Cleanse the Leper, Raise the Dead, Cast out Devils. He ended the conference by laying hands on each and every person, transferring the Healing anointing to them all.

Crusade Night 4
Still 30,000 – 50,000 Attending / Over 1000 Saved This Night!

As with the previous nights, the crowd surged like the ocean tide. At all times there were at least 30,000 people in the field but when word spread about a particularly spectacular healing or deliverance, the people would come running off the streets to see what was happening, driving up the attendance to around 50,000!

Salvation = Healing

Todd opened the evening by teaching the people how to receive God's miracles and healings. He explained how, in scripture, the word for salvation speaks of healing of the spirit, soul and body. "If you can ask Jesus for a healing, why can't you receive everything else that He has?" During the call for salvation, demons began manifesting and the ushers started carrying people out of the crowd and into the deliverance tent as the demons caused their hosts to thrash about violently. At least 1,000 people prayed "the sinner's prayer" in that moment.

The miracles come forth!

Soon, people began coming forward with testimonies of healing. In just a few moments, there was the testimonies of a blind eye, a deaf ear and a tumor all being healed! Other miracles that were testified to on stage were:

- A man with a tumor for 15 years – the tumor disappeared!
- A young man, deaf in his left ear for 3 years, received his hearing.

- A woman with a tumor for 28 years – healed!
- A man with chronic back pain, unable to work for 5 years – healed and jumping around!
- A man, deaf in his right ear for 25 years, was healed instantly!
- A woman who went blind in one eye, a month ago – received her sight!
- A woman deaf for 30 years – instantly healed!
- Another woman with 2 tumors in her abdomen for 2 years – again they had disappeared after prayer!
- Twin boys mute and deaf from birth – speak and hear for the first time in their lives!
- A young boy, afflicted with AIDS, showing classic symptoms (nausea, lack of appetite, weakness) was prayed for at the crusade two days earlier. He was brought forward by a relative (both his parents had already died of AIDS) and testified that the boy was now eating and regaining his strength! After more prayer, Todd instructed the woman, who brought the boy, to take him to a doctor for testing.

Tonight the count is approximately: 8 tumors, 2 blind eyes, 7 deaf ears, 3 mutes, 1 AIDS victim, 1000+ salvations – and many, many more that went undocumented – **ALL IN ONE NIGHT!**

5 Days Total Attendance Over 210,000 Over 5000 Salvations Countless Healings, Miracles and Deliverances

Sunday Morning Services

On Sunday morning, the Fresh Fire Ministry teams ministered in ap-

189

proximately 20 churches throughout Mwanza. In those services more salvations and healings continued. In one service, Todd and Dave prayed for Mary, a paralyzed woman. Todd prayed over her, cast out some demons, and Mary was set free. She was able to get up and walk on her own!

Final Night of Crusade
50,000 Attendance/ 1500 Salvations / Pentecostal Fire / Incredible Miracles—the Best Wine of the Party

God always seems to leave the best for last. The final night of the Crusade was no exception. The attendance was high, approximating 50,000 people. Todd preached on salvation and being filled with the Holy Spirit. At the altar call, over a thousand people surged forward and half that many waved their hands from the crowd behind the roped partition. The estimated number of salvations for Night 5 was approximately 1500!

When Todd prayed with the crowd for the Holy Ghost Baptism, thousands more were filled and speaking in tongues! As with all the previous nights, when people began to press in to God, the demons came out of the woodwork! At least 16 people were rushed to the special deliverance tent for intense prayer and another 10 demoniacs were set free right in front of the platform.

Miracles upon miracles

When the Holy Spirit fell on the ripened field of souls, the manifested power of God blazed forth! There were so many healings and other miracles that it became difficult to keep track of them all. The following is a partial list:

- 32 tumors healed and disappeared!
- 18 cases of deafness – healed and hearing!
- Several mutes – healed and speaking!
- Several cases of partial blindness – healed and seeing!
- One man was paralyzed for 2 years, unable to walk. After receiving prayer, he stood on his own and jumped around on the platform!
- A woman, near the front of the crowd, was suffering horribly from AIDS. She couldn't move and could barely breathe. Some of the

Fresh Fire Ministry Team members prayed for her and she was able to stand up and climb the stairs to the platform. She testified that her breathing was easy and she felt strength coming back into her body!
*   • Another man had been insane, not knowing right from wrong. He said he would eat garbage from the street, not realizing what he was doing. In the past, he had spent some time in American hospitals but was not cured of his condition. After receiving the Holy Spirit, this man came into his right mind! He stated that he was going to start living a normal life and was hoping to find a job soon.*

Summary of Miracles During the 5 Day Crusade (approximations only):

*   • Salvations: 5000*
*   • Deliverance: 100*
*   • Tumors: 60*
*   • Deaf and/or Mute: 80*
*   • Blind Eyes: 25*
*   • Paralytics & Cripples: 25*
*   • AIDS (obvious symptoms reduced or eliminated): 4*
*   • Various other healings: Too many to count!!!*

Tanzania Highlight: Invading the Fish Market

Here is my (Todd) most fond memory of Mawanza. I said, "Let's go to the market place." The police said that the Muslims were enraged and had killed Christians in the past. The police recommended against it. The local pastors said it would be better if we just stuck with the campaign in the evening and not go to the markets.

I asked, "What would Jesus do?" I decided to take our team to the heart of the Muslim district to present the gospel with signs and wonders. I knew that this would shock these precious Muslim people.

We set up at the local fish market; hundreds were there and the local leaders gathered. Wearing their white robes and religious head covers they crossed their arms, seeming to issue an angry challenge, as if to say, "Who do you think you are coming into this area proclaiming Jesus?" There was an angry stir in the air.

We preached the gospel with boldness. There was urgency—we must snatch a few from the fire. I shared my testimony, one hundred and fifty seven Muslims pressed in to know Jesus. But there was a confrontation in the spirit, a wall of resistance, the greater core of the audience continued to mock and scoff. I knew we needed a power encounter. The Lord gave me a download of faith so I issued a challenge, "The first person who steps onto this platform will be healed right now, whether blind, deaf, crippled, whatever the infirmity. If not, we will discontinue our campaign. We will turn our backs on God, say the bible isn't true and my team and I will go home. If the first person isn't healed then everything I've preached in this city is a lie."

The Muslims were confused; they murmured angrily. They were caught off guard over my boldness. No one moved. I issued the same challenge a second and third time. "Bring me a sick person. Why am I so bold? I challenge you today. If my God doesn't heal the first one here, everything I have preached is not true." Finally, three people came forward. One blind, one crippled and one deaf. As the Lord sovereignly performed these miracles my team all breathed a big sigh of relief. (Oh ye of little faith!) The heavens opened; there was a shift in the Spirit. We were shaken to the core and spoke the word of God with boldness. Our team prayed for over an hour for many others to be saved and healed. In this city we preached to over 210,000 in five days.

A New Kind of Power Evangelism
South Korea—August 8-30, 2002

After training, equipping and teaching on the prophetic, how to hear God's voice and prophecy we released over 1,000 Koreans to prophesy over one another for over 30 minutes. I said, "If it can work in the church, Why not in the market?" "For you can all prophesy one by one, that all may learn and all may be encouraged" (I Corinthians 14:30-31).

"Take this outside the walls of the church to the market place."

Hundreds converge on the food courts at the mall. We hung up a sign that advertised "Free Spiritual Readings" and set up six tables, with two people and a translator at each. We gave prophetic words over the lost for two hours, while hundreds of others went throughout the mall praying and gathering more unbelievers. There were 174 souls saved in two hours. Several of them were Buddhists.

The prophetic anointing carries in it the power to convict, convince and reveal. Even if the word is "Jesus loves you!" delivered under the Spirit of prophecy, it reveals God. Hearing God is as easy as Psalm 139:17-18: "How precious also are Your thoughts to me, O God! How great is the sum of them! If I should count them, they would be more in number than the sand."

All you have to do is ask God for one of His thoughts for a person. You may just have a mental picture. Sometimes you may not understand what God is showing you, but the person will.

Most times we cannot operate in the gifts of the Spirit in the market place because we turn it off outside the four walls of the church. We need an increased prophetic awareness. Let's start asking God for words in unusual places, especially restaurants.

God wants us to make ourselves available to Him. It's time for the Samaritan-well anointing. In John 4:5-42 Jesus shared a word of knowledge with a Gentile woman about her many husbands and her response was, "Come, see a Man who told me all things that I ever did. Could this be the Christ? Then they went out of the city and came to Him." The whole city came because one woman received a word from God.

Power Evangelism Strategies

Christians need to invade the world with God's power. We need to try prophetic, dream interpretation or "free prayer" booths in flea markets, malls, coffee shops or juice bars. God is going to anoint street preaching again, like in the old- time revivals. Servant evangelism is powerful too—acts of love carry power!

God can use anybody. I was teaching on prophetic evangelism once and a business man and his wife decided to make themselves available, gather some prophetic people and go to the market for 10 days. They set up a booth offering Free Spiritual Readings. After each prophetic word they offered salvation and 650 souls came to Jesus. Its time to take it to the markets—that's where Jesus had some of his greatest miracles and healings.

Over 5,575 People Come to Jesus
Peru and Ecuador, October 2-11, 2002

Most of the 24 team members who came with us on this trip had never been overseas or seen the type of miracles that they witnessed. One pastor from the Midwest said, "I saw more genuine miracles than expected; when one says the word 'miracle' it can be used pretty loosely."

There were over 80 deaf mutes healed and some 20 cases of blindness, over 40 lame and crippled healed, tumors and more. There was deliverance from demons and the sick on beds and mats were carried into the stadium. There were sick people everywhere carried in from hospitals with the nursing staff and the IV still in their arms. Hundreds of crippled bodies, sick children with deformed heads, exposed sores, growths and wheelchairs covered the crusade grounds each night in both Ecuador and Peru.

The crusades, held in two sports stadiums, were put together over a six month period by hundreds of volunteers, more than 600 pastors, over 500 counselors and several full-time coordinators. As always, our partners and intercessors made this crusade a success—their prayers and financial support helped us reach over 45,000 people in the crusades alone.

Headline news footage of the event was on the number one rated TV show, "Video Control" in Ecuador. During the interview on the show the

194

host returned to God after being backslidden for two years. He even added to the interview, preached and gave a prayer for salvation. This TV show is like "Much Music" in Canada and "MTV" in the USA that reaches mostly teens and people in their early twenties.

Crusade and Team Highlights

The first day in Lima, Peru the FFM team went into the local prison. Most of the prisoners had committed rapes and murder and were young men in their early twenties. Over twenty souls were saved. One couple on our team, unknown to us at the time, was told by a guard they'd not get out alive

unless they paid about $50. Of course, when we found out the ministry reimbursed them!

The first night at the crusade grounds was a little overwhelming for some on the team. The platform was set up in the middle of a housing neighborhood and there was traffic all around, a few thousand gathered on the grounds and the sick were everywhere. The team didn't know they would step nightly into the masses to pray for thousands. Demons threw people on the ground. One woman wailed, kicked and screamed through her deliverance and another, after two days of manifestations, coughed hers out. A teenage boy paralyzed from the waist down from a car accident was healed on the spot as I called out a word of knowledge.

What really undid the FFM team was the outreach to the hospitals. When they prayed for one, hundreds of others would crowd around for prayer. There were nights they pushed and pulled at our clothes by the hundreds and it was necessary to push our way out of the service or back to the platform

The people are so hungry and desperate each night. Some live on only a hundred dollars a month and are sick and crippled with no means of medical assistance. Relatives were weeping as their loved one on a stretcher is prayed for or cried tears of joy when cancer was healed.

One night a dying woman was carried into a crusade service on her hospital bed. She received prayer, sat up and said, "The pain is leaving my body and the fluid in my lungs just emptied." Her breathing was restored and strength began to return to her body. The daughter pressed through the crowd with tears in her eyes and helped her mom try to stand up out of the hospital bed.

I remember the first night of the crusade in Chicayo, Peru, I saw Jesus in a vision step into the cripple section. When I prayed for mass healing, instantly six or seven, who could not walk, walked for the first time in years. Jesus did it! We took crutches, walkers and canes up on the platform when we could each night and waved them in the air in the devil's face. "Jesus Is the Same Today, Yesterday And Forever." God used the team and they saw blind eyes and deaf ears open almost every night. We encouraged them to keep a nightly journal and E-mail what they could of how God used them. My heart is to impart, train and see others do the ministry of Jesus.

One other favorite miracle was of a mother and her seven or eight-year-old daughter—both had tumors in their bodies. During the mass prayer from the platform, where hundreds of healings happened, with no hands laid on them, she and her daughter were both healed when they felt fire go through their bodies.

Some nights there would be 20 deaf mutes healed in a service. Sometimes Jesus touched them in the crowd, other times we would pray for them on the platform. I can still remember the precious children saying "hello" or "mama" for the first time. I just about weep writing about it now.

In the final service after I preached, "What kind of Jesus do you have?" over 1,400 responded to the altar call. The last night together the team shared how excited they were to bring this fire back to their churches and that their faith level was increased to believe all things are possible. Others are already praying about how they can come to India or one of our upcoming missions trips in 2003.

Hundreds were saved each night. On one other occasion over 1,300 responded to the gospel call. We saw over 5,575 souls saved and many more than this healed. The Holy Spirit still confirms the gospel with signs and wonders!

Jinga, Uganda
November 2002

Even though it had been sunny all day, the first evening of the crusade, at 3:45 a dark black cloud poured rain. We'd been expecting 50,000 people that evening. Only 8,000 showed up and when I gave an altar call, only 76 got saved. I was discouraged and I was feeling discouraged for the team we'd brought.

Early the next morning the team prayed and the skies were blue. That afternoon when we got to the crusade at 3:45 the clouds rolled in and it rained. The attendance was about the same as the night before. Usually we can expect growth of 10,000 each night. That evening during the altar call 100 got saved and the Lord did bless us with some creative miracles.

I don't remember doing a mass crusade with only 176 people saved in two nights. I was used to seeing that many saved in the open-air markets. I wondered if this was the kind of witchcraft I'd faced in Uganda two years before, when a witchdoctor chanted on the other side of the river. Those practicing witchcraft have power over the weather and accidents.

That night at the crusade we had several amazing miracles. During the mass prayer I said, "If you're being healed come to the altar." The first miracle testimony was a man who had had a massive growth over his male extremities. This affected his relationship with his wife and she was getting ready to leave him. During the prayer his tumor shrank. He was ecstatic. The next miracle was a woman who had visible breast cancer—skin and tissue had eaten away the breast. She was totally healed; a new layer of skin appeared. The third miracle was a woman who had breast cancer for three years and had tried all avenues to get healed—multiple trips to witch doctors and soothsayers. Many people in Africa go to witchdoctors like we go to doctors. Finally, after trying everything, they surgically removed her breast. She was known as "the woman with one breast." This woman had a new breast grow out during the mass prayer!

On Sunday afternoon, busloads of people came to Lake Victoria, near where the Nile River begins. The team and I baptized over 400 people in one hour! This was so special because I got to baptize my dad!

"Holy Spirit why are you healing all these reproductive organs?" I asked. "I want to open the womb of the church," responded the Spirit, "and begin healing its reproductive function and the breasts that nurture. It was a sign of the birth of the coming harvest."

The next day the skies were blue. The Holy Spirit told me, "Fast today for the Spirit of Elijah so you can overcome the spirit of witchcraft working against the crusade." I fasted all day and at 3:45 p.m. the sky was still clear. At the crusade, the crowds swelled to 20,000 or 25,000. When I arrived at the crusade grounds at 5:15, I thought I'd gotten the breakthrough: "Praise God, we've made it."

All the talk of the town during the day had been, "Let's go see the power the white man possesses that even breasts grow in the meetings." Soothsayers and witch doctors were there because of the creative miracles. The Holy Spirit had told me to give an altar call for witchdoctors, anyone who had practiced it or come under the power of its curse.

When I got on the stage at 5:30 p.m., I grabbed the microphone and it started raining on me. Thousands of people ran for the exits. It was pandemonium. I said, "Today in prayer the Holy Spirit told me He wants to break the power of witchcraft. If you're a witch doctor, a soothsayer or practice witchcraft or come under the power of witchcraft come to the altars now." Eighteen hundred people responded.

I prayed for the Holy Spirit to come and rebuked the power of witchcraft, "Devil let go of the people now in Jesus name." Nothing happened.

I just went after it again. I said, "In the name of Jesus, power of witchcraft let the people go." Nothing happened. I prayed the third time. "I command every devil of witchcraft and sorcery to let go of the people now in Jesus name. In that moment it was like something snapped in the Spirit. Hundreds were thrown to the ground in one swoop. There were violent demonic manifestations—foaming at the mouth, vomiting, writhing, contorting, rolling and slithering in the mud—but simultaneously, in the heavens above, the rain cloud split in two and rolled away.

The sky became blue and there was a double rainbow. Hundreds were being delivered. The ministry teams were throwing people up on the muddy platform. I could barely move. Team members were running everywhere; three hundred were carried into the deliverance tent and our Ugandan team ministered to them. The rest lay on the grass down front where they experienced sovereign deliverance.

Then the testimonies came. A woman paralyzed in the neck and one paralyzed from the waist down were healed; several people also testified of being healed of insanity and madness. We went on to great victory. For the next few days the skies were clear and the crowds swelled to 60,000. About 34,000 people made life commitments to Christ during our ministry in Uganda. Truly, the Lord had revealed Himself to us as healer, deliverer and mighty warrior.

Bombay, India—December 2002
by Pastor BB Rail, Fairfield, Iowa

Millions of gods occupy the hearts of the people of India; hence India itself has many faces. Multitudes of people, pressed together, overcrowd the streets and market places. Hoards of vehicles dart unpredictably from the left to the right side of the road. Small black and yellow taxis aggressively swarm like bumblebees through bumper-to-bumper traffic. Everyone honks in agreement with the sign on all the trucks: "Horn OK Please." Pedestrians appear to be fair game.

The local authorities did not allow the word "miracles" to be used in advertising the services. Instead, colorful flyers invited people to come to a "Jesus Festival", and experience the peace and love of the Christmas Season. Christmas trees, tinsel, ornaments, even frosty the snowman, did not distract us from focusing on the harvest!

God immediately revealed His nature as "the Lord who heals you" in the very first service by causing tumors, growths and cysts to instantly dissolve. The conservative crowd, predominately Roman Catholic and Hindu, stood in amazement and grew each night as God faithfully confirmed His healing Word with accompanying signs and wonders. Armed guards became so overwhelmed seeing the miracles, many requested prayer and some were born again! Faith among the people rose to such a high level that on the last night a young girl, paralyzed from polio, spontaneously began walking. Everyone cheered as we all watched her "staggering run" through the crowd!

**No need for these crutches any more.
Praise the Lord!**

The people are unbelievably kind, grateful, and humble. Many of the ladies who had been healed were so thankful they began bowing down and wanted to kiss my feet. We made sure they understood Jesus alone was their Healer and to worship only Him!

A final highlight before leaving Bombay was a visit to St. Lawrence's private school. They gave us VIP hospitality. The students were captivated by Todd's personal testimony and allowed us to pray for each one of them. Approximately 1000 were born again that morning, bringing our harvest total to 4,525 as we departed for Goa.

Goa, India

Our arrival in Goa, India was like stepping into another world. We were met at the airport with flower leis, fresh coconut milk, and a group of students playing Christmas songs. Were we really still in India? Clear air, white beaches, and tropical landscapes dotted with plantation type homes.

Expectations were high as we headed off to the "festival" grounds. God did not disappoint us. Once again, as He demonstrated His power over sin and sickness, the crowds doubled each night! The Lord had put in my heart that the Church was like the lame man outside the gate named Beautiful. Just as that man received a miracle, the Church would be filled with the power of God and rise up. Many cripples received healing that night; it was as though Goa would be the Gateway for God's healing revival!

As in Bombay, many blind, deaf and dumb were healed. There was such an explosion of joy the musicians could not hold back from playing. With each healing report, the music would explode and everyone would begin shouting and dancing before the Lord. Fortunately, the platform was of solid construction. The hunger of the crowd for salvation and prayer was of such a magnitude, the people all but trampled on another to come towards the front. Desperate for Jesus, unlike anything we see in North America. Meetings for pastors and leaders were held during the day. Todd gave me one of the morning sessions in which I shared my healing testimony and the Lord healed many backs. It is quite difficult to ad-equately report all the wondrous events that we witnessed.

A typical altar call. "You must forsake all other gods."

We left India with a conservative count of ministering to a total of 16,450 persons, of which 10, 825 were born again and placed in Churches. One hundred and thirty-nine deaf and dumb were healed, 11 blind eyes opened and eight cripples began to walk. A medical doctor on the platform verified all healing.

Goa, India—December 2002

After ministering in Goa, India I awoke at 2:00 a.m.—a demon, 14 feet tall, manifesting as a menacing black shadow stood at the end of my bed. Chills went through my body. The whole hotel room was dark but the demon was even darker than the night. The room had turned chilly. I yelled, "In the name of Jesus, devil, go." After I blurted out this command, the spirit left my room.

I found out later that the spirit went to the room of three other staff members and tried to take their lives. My dad was struck blind: "I was bumping into dressers. I couldn't find the phone; I panicked, my heart started fluttering. I'd only been saved about 14 months. I really thought I was going to die but after several minutes it left."

It went to the room of my mission's director, John Macgirvin. The shadow passed his door three times and then came in. "I felt like I was drowning in fluid in my lungs. I tried to pound on the wall to get Dave's attention, but I couldn't. I couldn't even breathe. I finally staggered to the bathroom and expelled some clear liquid. I couldn't speak; I could only rebuke it in my mind." Jim Drown, my South American coordinator also felt the dark presence enter his room.

Here's another India report from a former doubting Thomas:

Over 10,825 souls saved, 139 deaf healed and countless other healings and miracles—December 8-19, 2002
Pastor Ken Greter, Abbotsford City Fellowship, BC, Canada

A team of seven from the USA and Canada embarked on a trip of a lifetime to Southern India December 8-19 2002. This was undoubtedly the

most profound evangelistic crusade I ever had the privilege of being part of. Quite frankly, my heart was somewhat skeptical regarding the testimonies I had heard from Fresh Fire team members involving miracles that were just like in Bible days. Well I am here to testify that with my very own eyes I saw the most amazing miracles, signs and wonders in India. I turned from a "doubting Thomas" to an "authentic, Holy Ghost Bible-believing believer!"

In all of my 22 plus years in pastoring, my Christian walk has never been so shaken to the core like it has been as a result of this crusade. I believe that every pastor needs to experience for himself the same miracles Jesus performed while on the earth. Jesus truly is the same yesterday, today and forever! I can hardly wait to go on the next overseas crusade, where souls will be saved, pastors and leaders will be encouraged during the teaching sessions, and numerous signs and wonders will take place!

PART III
A GREAT HEALING & MIRACLE HARVEST

Goma, Democratic Republic of Congo
Congo Report #1—March 1-10, 2003

I have never been so overwhelmed. We have just arrived in the city of Goma, Democratic Republic of Congo, a border town of about 500,000 on the Rwanda border. In 2001 a volcanic disaster destroyed or damaged more than 50 percent of the entire city. Volcanic rock and ash some 10 feet high buried and crushed churches, schools, homes and businesses. The twisted metal wreckage of half buried vehicles sticks out from the hardened lava. Hundreds died and tens of thousands are still homeless.

A building almost buried in hardened lava.

One young woman shared her story of how her father, who is a pastor, cannot enter Congo to be home with his family. The rebel government here calls him an exile. Her home was half destroyed in the volcano and she has now taken 50 other people into her home because their homes were completely destroyed. They have nowhere to live and nothing to eat.

Another story I will never forgot is, how 75-100 Christians gathered into a catholic church when the volcano first erupted, to pray for God to have mercy. They were all buried alive in the church.

People here are totally desperate. After years of civil war the country is split into three pieces. A natural disaster destroyed what was already desperate lives coping with hunger and third world conditions. Thousands of children are without education. They can not afford the 5 dollars a month for school and thousands more are without the basic school supplies for an education.

As we crossed the Rwanda, Congo border we were welcomed with a band and Jesus parade. As we traveled through the ruined city, in the midst of volcanic boulders, ash and destruction the city stopped. There were traffic jams and shouting and dancing in the streets. Jesus came to town! I knew in my heart God would give Goma beauty for ashes and the oil of joy for mourning.

Isaiah 61:4 "and they shall rebuild the old ruins, they shall rise up the former desolations, and they shall repair the ruined cities, the desolations of many generations."

Since the devastation in 2001, promise after promise of humanitarian aid and relief efforts have been pledged. However, the people have seen very little relief. I was asked to meet with the president of this region of Congo and pray. There are now three governments and they are still trying to sign a peace process and build one unified government. Fresh Fire Ministries said, "We will help." Even today we will take food to 2,500 families in a refugee camp for those left homeless after the volcanic eruption.

There are more than 12,000 people hungry and living in conditions so inhumane that our animals live better. I saw homes that were nothing more than plastic tarps, sticks and mud. We told the president Fresh Fire wants to build an orphanage, put roofs on churches, feed the poor and

Over 12,000 people live in shelters like these since the volcano destroyed their town.

204

send a 40-foot container of cranberries and school supplies for the children.

Shonnah, the FFM team of 16 and I were broken, so overwhelmed with the need that we were speechless. I was so impacted that for a week after I would break down and cry. I have never wept so much. I am weeping even now.

As our team and 7 truck loads of food made our way towards the refugee camp, the children ran to the roads with their buckets in their hands or whatever they could find to hold food. It was heard among the hungry crowd, "We aren't going to get the food and eat tonight even though we see the trucks of food!" Corrupt pastors and thieves have taken the food from the people so many times before, these people wept saying "will we really eat?" We all distributed the food to the families.

James 1:27, "Pure and undefiled religion before God and the Father is this: to visit orphans and widows in their trouble, and to keep oneself unspotted from the world."

Years of civil war and the Rwanda genocide of the 90's has left thousands of children without families. Many lost their homes and families in the volcanic disaster of 2001, thousands more are without education, and even in some desperate cases, food.

Jane's Orphanage

Shonnah, the team and I, were taken to an orphanage. A woman, named Jane and her husband, have such a heart for theses children to feed

them, clothe them and house them. She has opened up her home to receive the children even though she gets no assistance from the government. They house over 125 children and over 325 children are expected to eat there.

Jane's orphanage

205

The kitchen facilities for over 300 children

The facilities are terrible; the boys sleep in no more than what I would call a rented old barn, without windows or insulation. The beds are so full; they sleep sometimes eight to a bed. I saw faces of these children broken and many maimed from the civil war. I saw children with scars across their foreheads hacked open by machetes and children without hands, arms, or fingers.

I said, "How do we feed these people?" And the woman said, "There are times when we can't even get food from the city to this rural area. One, the roads are buried in molten rock, and two, we have no truck to transport food."

I saw the kitchen in nothing more than a 6 by 6 foot shed. One huge cooking cauldron (pot) and the firewood stacked in the corner. As I walked through the orphanage I saw no toys, and when we brought out biscuits, the children were so desperate; they stepped on, pushed and screamed at each other.

Today, Fresh Fire bought one truckload of corn, rice, beans; a 3-week supply. There is no government aid, no ministry support, nothing. We need to do more. Fresh Fire Ministries has committed to building 1 new orphanage facility and providing food for the orphans. We can also purchase 1 boys dormitory, that they rent right now, and the money they save on rent can help to feed the children. We can do all this now for $3,000, what a North American family might spend on a vacation!

God has given us tremendous opportunity in Congo. We were asked to meet and pray with the general of the entire rebel army. There are more than 80,000 soldiers. They have asked us to train evangelists in the military so they can better evangelize the army. They have also asked us to build a church on the military base.

FFM has opened a pilot office in Goma and taken staff from our office in Uganda, Africa to work with the government in Congo. The advisor to the president, a born again spirit filled Colonel, aids and administrates leadership of each project.

206

Will you partner with Fresh Fire Ministries and give a special gift today for humanitarian aid in Congo? Help us now to build orphanages, send school supplies, repair churches and do more to feed the hungry, build a military church, and show this city there is somebody who does care. Psalms 41:1, "How blessed is he who considers the helpless; The Lord will deliver him in a day of trouble."

Congo Report #2
The First Miracle Crusade Night

A small Fresh Fire team of 17 drove four hours through Rwanda over the border to Congo. This would be another life changing experience for both the staff, and those who had never been a part of a mission's team in Africa.

It was hot; the air in the city was still filled with volcanic poison and pollution. The poverty and desperation here was the worst that I have seen yet in any country in Africa. Over 200 hundred churches worked together with our Fresh Fire Ministries crusade team based in Uganda to host this five night miracle campaign. The first evening, a small group of 20-25 thousand people gathered, Baptists, Anglicans, Pentecostals, revival churches, Protestants, and unbelievers came to hear the word and to be healed.

The Crowd Grows, Miracles and Healings Begin

Over the next five days the crowd swelled to over 60, 000. Each night thousands were saved, each day people would testify to being healed the evening before while listening on radio.

Each night the crusade was broadcast live to those living in Congo, and parts of Rwanda. One night I asked how many people here tonight got saved on the radio at home last night; 100 plus hands went up. Each night, there were healings, miracles, and even signs and wonders in the heavens above. The first evening a deaf school of 32 lined up on the platform, each was prayed for and 26 deaf and dumb heard and spoke in that one wave.

The Crusade is Disrupted by Witch Doctors

After two days of breakthrough, the third evening I noticed the crowd had dropped by several thousand. There was a report in the city that day that during the third evening of the crusade local witch doctors had planned a violent confrontation.

Then the rains came and during that meeting once again we offered fervent intercession and petitions up before God. "God break the power of witchcraft, we rebuke the rains, pray for heaven to open." In that instant not only did the rain cease, but the temperature of the wind changed.

Tonight six or seven people were cast to the ground simultaneously under demonic influence, each one was carried on to the platform, devils were cast out in Jesus' name, some screamed, shook, and even spewed spit from the mouth, we believe that these ones were sent by the witch doctor to disrupt the meetings.

The Crowd Grows Again

The next day the crowd swelled and the report of the local Congolese was "we saw with our own eyes, they broke the power of the witch doctor."

Each night the Fresh Fire Ministries team would wade their way out into thousands who had made their way forward for prayer. When the miracles broke loose, a

Notice the volcano in the background still belching smoke.

208

press of people ran up to the front. People were grabbing, pushing and shouting. A Fresh Fire security detail, a gift of troops from the president himself, had to break up several fights.

Each night the Fresh Fire Ministries team, even ones that have never prayed for the sick, shared testimonies of the deaf that heard, and the blind that saw. When the team would return to the hotel they would share testimony of what took place that evening. Two nights the team agreed that it was as if every single person they prayed for was healed. Each night there were testimonies of tumors healed, various pain, sickness, TB and paralysis healed.

Cripples are Healed

One night two cripples were placed on the platform, one boy whose legs were twisted from birth, received prayer. My wife heard the Lord whisper to her, "Pick him up." His legs straightened and he began to walk! Within moments the crowd screamed and cheered again as the second cripple stood and walked twice across the platform.

Sunday morning each team member was given an opportunity to preach in their own church service. Each team member shared testimonies of healings in their service and testimonies of salvation. One pastor, during the evening Sunday crusade service, testified, "I now know this anointing is not just upon Todd Bentley, it is a transferable, tangible healing anointing." When my dad and John Macgirvin, the Mission's coordinator, preached at a church on Sunday, they prayed for one cripple, his legs straightened out and he danced around the church. Dave gave several words of knowledge, even calling out first and last African names! Whew!

The Pastors' Conference

The pastors' conference, consisting of 1,500 to 2,000 pastors, leaders, evangelists, and ministry workers, gathered each day. Each service built until the anointing service took place, teaching on soaking, the healing anointing, spirit of revival, holiness and repentance. In one service Pastor Ken, Mission's Director, gave an alter call to repent of sexual sin, more than half of the people came forward to get their life right with God. In the final service, more than 1,800 leaders stood shoulder to shoulder in the hot sun in a line one mile long winding down the streets of the city to receive a fresh touch from God.

Fresh Fire Ministries' Commitment to the Congo

Fresh Fire Ministry's commitment to a lasting impact in this city is to build a church, equip an evangelist in the military, put roofs on churches destroyed in the volcano, build an orphanage, build a school, and ship one full container, 40 by 40 feet, of food and school supplies for the children.

We taught the pastors that the greatest miracle is salvation. We will keep a Fresh Fire Ministry's pilot office open there to oversee and administrate ongoing relief work in the city. God has called us this year to nourish the whole man. To feed the hungry, visit the widow and orphan, clothe the naked, deliver the oppressed, cast out devils and love the brokenhearted.

If God has moved your heart to help in the Congo make a donation today, humanitarian aid Congo call: 1-866-853-9041. Or send your check to Fresh Fire Ministries, PO Box 2525, Abbotsford, BC, Canada V2T 6R3.

Revival in the Land
Congo Report #3
by Pastor Ken Greter, Abbotsford City Fellowship

"The Spirit of the Sovereign Lord is on us, because the Lord has anointed us to bestow on 'Goma' a crown of beauty instead of ashes" (Isaiah 61:1,3b).

As I sit here, I wonder if it's really possible to give an accurate description of the devastation that we saw while in Goma, a city of about 450,000 situated near the Rwanda border. This city was once a tourist hot spot for people from all over the world, but due to a massive volcanic explosion that occurred over a year ago, Goma now lies in ashes.

For approximately three days during the eruption of Mount Nyirracongo, tons and tons of volcanic lava spread like a black blanket covering a huge section of the city and brought it to an absolute stand still. Gerald

210

Mwebe, our African co-coordinator, wept when he first came into the city to prepare for the Fresh Fire crusade. I now have a bit of an understanding how Nehemiah felt when he was told the wall of Jerusalem was broken down and that the gates were burned.

The evidence of destruction brought about by this volcanic eruption could still be seen everywhere. Entire downtown sections were completely wiped out; 20-foot steel telephone poles were partially immersed in 6 feet of hardened lava rock; churches, homes and schools were completely demolished. Understandably, because of the magnitude of this catastrophic event, thousands and thousands of people were left homeless, and many, even to this day, are living in some of the most deplorable conditions imaginable.

Todd and Shonnah knew that the Holy Spirit had brought them to Goma for such a time as this and the entire Fresh Fire Ministry's team, consisting of 17 from US and Canada, were ready to roll up their sleeves and begin the long process of restoring beauty from the ashes of total devastation.

Due to the physical, economical and psychological impact of the recent civil war and continuing tensions, Congolese pastors and Christian leaders were in desperate need for encouragement.

We arrived in Goma, Congo on March 3rd. Multitudes of people greeted our arrival with cheering, whistling and singing. We were escorted through the downtown with a first-class parade and then rushed into a building where the media was waiting to interview Todd.

Right from the start, Todd and Shonnah wanted to visit some of the most devastated areas and help out in humanitarian efforts. Contacts were made immediately and in short order seven truckloads of food items were purchased, filled and ready for distribution. The Congolese pastors took us to a camp of 12,000 displaced individuals living in conditions that the average American would consider inadequate even for animals.

We formed a convoy consisting of pastors, military personnel and the media, with seven trucks loaded with beans, corn, soap

Getting ready to distribute food at the displacement camp.

211

and other necessary staples. Upon arrival, children everywhere were shouting and raising their hands, ecstatic that the trucks had finally arrived to fill their empty tummies. The interpreters were telling us that the kids were screaming; "Now we don't have to go hungry any-more."

Enough food was given to this camp to feed them all for approximately two months. If there was ever a time that I've seen the fulfillment of James 1:27—'Pure and undefiled religion (is) to visit orphans and widows in their trouble...' this was the day.

During the week Todd and Shonnah were inundated with interviews with governors, colonels, presidents and pastors. Talk about favor! In most places we went, there was total security protection guaranteed; what a relief this was as tensions between governments and the different military factions were still at an all time high.

The morning meetings were scheduled for pastors and Christian leaders, with over 2,000 registered for the sessions. After some initial resistance, one morning Todd delivered a message with great fervor entitled, "The Fear of God, The Ministry to the Poor and God's Mercy". The pastors were riveted to their seats, their hearts were deeply touched and the place was blown wide open. We concluded the final morning by lining up all of the registrants outside the church building to receive Holy Ghost impartation from Todd and the Fresh Fire Ministry staff.

On the first evening of the crusade we saw crowds of up to 25,000 eager to hear "the man of God from Canada" share about his past background. A bizarre and humorous rumor that circulated for a short time was that Todd was a professional wrestler. Many of the team got a kick out of this and for a while Todd was subjected to some good-natured ribbing.

As is common in many cities in Africa, the people are steeped in magic and witchcraft is widely practiced. The city of Goma was no exception. Word reached us through the interpreters that the "man of God from Canada" was a challenge to the Witchdoctors and that a war was brewing.

Apparently, the witch doctors were trying to shut down the meetings by sending out curses and by subtly planting some of their cohorts in the crowds. For a brief time it appeared that they were succeeding as rains fell on two different nights, causing somewhat of a damper on the attendance. But glory to God, during the Saturday evening crusade, Todd began to operate under what I call a "breaker anointing" and after the altar call was given, hundreds responded. It was then that Todd went after the spirits of witchcraft

212

and oppression.

We were now in the pouring rain, which had held off until after the altar call. Next, five women, tormented by demons, were carried onto the platform where their bodies twisted and contorted in a manner not possible for a normal person. Oh thank God for the blood of Jesus! One by one their bodies and minds were set free from the demonic strongholds and they were gloriously filled with the Holy Spirit. We found out that these witches had hid in the crowd every night. However, the Holy Spirit exposed and set them free. Truly this was like an 'Elijah and the prophets of Baal' confrontation.

The final evening of the crusade was a surprise to everyone. The pastors estimated that between 60,000 and 70,000 people crammed into the soccer stadium ready to hear the Word of God. As a result of these five nights of crusades, over 15,000 souls came to Jesus. This figure did not include those making decisions for Christ as a result of radio broadcasts. An awesome harvest! Also, hundreds received the Baptism of the Holy Spirit, the lame began to walk and the blind received their sight.

On Sunday morning many of the team members preached in the churches, and reports came back to us once again of numerous salvations and healings. One Fresh Fire team that preached in a Methodist church was able to pray for the pastor and his wife; this couple was gloriously baptized in the Holy Spirit!

Revival Among the Pygmies

One highlight of these meetings was when a group of tribal pygmies walked 60 kilometers from the jungle to attend the crusade, dance for the team and bring gifts. These four-feet tall, full-grown adults are considered to

To offer perspective of the pygmy's height, John Macgirvin, our Mission's Director (standing behind) is 5'6".

be the lowest of the low in their society and, in fact, there is even a common belief among some Africans that the Pygmies don't even have souls. We've heard reports of recent inhumane acts against these people including murder and even cannibalism.

One African woman has been so touched by God's love for these people that she provides them with food and disciples them. She is called 'Mother Mary' by the Pygmy tribes she has adopted. Mother Mary has been spreading the gospel for several years to this people group, traveling as many as 50 kilometers one way to reach their villages with the gospel of Jesus Christ.

The pygmies live in the jungle and by faith and they sometimes survive days at times without food. Their testimonies of God's miraculous power of provision are right out of the bible. Here's one example: once they were out of food for eight days and the Lord instructed them to eat dirt. As they did, it had the taste of corn and beans in their mouths.

When they arrived at our hotel, they sang a special song to us called "Jesus is My Winner-Man." These people had more heart, soul and fire as they danced and praised the Lord, than just about everyone else. At the conclusion of their song, Jim Drown invited them to pray for the Fresh Fire team. There was not a dry eye among us as these precious Pygmies laid hands on each Fresh Fire participant blessing us with the power of the Holy Spirit. The other Africans at the hotel were shocked that we would even allow the pygmies to touch us.

Up to this point, Mother Mary has led more than 900 of these Pygmies to Jesus, and she believes that this is just the beginning of what God wants to do among the Pygmy people. Hallelujah! People from every tribe, tongue and nation will be found in the Kingdom of Jesus Christ.

Miracles in the Open Air Market in Rwanda

We were all deeply impacted during the last leg of the journey as we left Goma and came into Kigali, Rwanda. Todd spontaneously decided to have an open-air crusade in a busy section of the city. We connected with one of the local churches in Kigali, and after a sound system and speakers were set up, Todd blasted away with his testimony. In no time at all, hundreds began to crowd in to hear Todd's story about how Jesus set him free from drugs and a wild lifestyle, and when the altar call was given, dozens came forward to receive Jesus. Miracles began to take place all around us as the Fresh Fire team prayed for people in the crowd.

The harvest was so ripe; it was like the fish were literally flying into the

214

boat. Altogether, between the cities of Goma and Kigali, we recorded 15,277 souls coming into the Kingdom of God. What we experienced in this open-air market was just the first fruits of a much bigger harvest that Fresh Fire believes to reap as we go back in September 2003 to hold a crusade in Kigali, Rwanda and Kisingani, Congo.

Remembering the Poor

Last but not least, Todd and Shonnah along with the Fresh Fire team were taken to a very special place that brought tears to everyone's eyes. An African lady by the name of Jane, along with her husband, both ex-government employees, have answered an amazing call to feed and disciple 125 orphans, permanently residing in some makeshift shelters (how's that for a contradiction in terms?) As many as 200 more orphans are fed daily by their ministry, with no government aid. As many as six to eight children sleep in one bed.

I had never seen so many children with hands and fingers chopped off by machetes. Huge scars could be seen on dozens of children criss-crossing their faces and bodies. These children are the victims of a brutal civil war in which over a million people were killed. Shonnah was overwhelmed and in tears—totally speechless. She absolutely fell in love with this couple and with the orphans.

We thank God that we were able to quickly gather together a small truckload of food and goods for this precious orphanage. Todd pledged in his heart to go back to the Fresh Fire partners in US and Canada, and to share the vision of providing another building for this orphanage and to assist in the establishment of a regular feeding program. Todd also felt impressed by the Holy Spirit to raise funds in order to put some roofs on some of the churches in Goma, and to build a school in order to facilitate the education of under-privileged children. Plans have already begun in conjunction with other ministries to send a 40-foot container loaded with cranberry sauce, and school supplies to help with the children's education and physical well-being. What a massive project! We serve a mighty big God!

Many of the Fresh Fire team members shared with us that they had never experienced miracles of this caliber in their entire Christian life. It was almost as if we were living 'smack-dab' in the middle of the book of Acts. Who

215

says God doesn't perform miracles today? Jesus is the same yesterday, today and forever. If you need convincing, plan to come on a trip with Todd and Shonnah for a future crusade and watch and see with your very own eyes. To God be the glory!

Greater Battles, Greater Victories
Lilongwe, Malawi, June 4-7, 2003

"... For dominion belongs to the Lord and he rules over the nations" (Psalm 22:28).

This was one of the most amazing mission's trips I have ever experienced, as over 90 people from Canada, USA, South Africa, Austria and Australia joined with Shonnah and me to feed the poor and to live out Matthew 10:8, "...heal the sick, raise the dead, cleanse the lepers, drive out demons."

I knew that this long awaited Malawi crusade was going to "go over the top," because of the constant opposition before we arrived. Just days before the crusade was to begin, Gerald Mwebe, our African Coordinator, sent an urgent request telling us that the Malawian health department would deny Canadian entry into their country because of the fear of SARS (Severe Acute Respiratory Syndrome). However, we praise God because Gerald was able to convince them that if we would get a medical checkup indicating negativity to SARS, we could come. All 24 Canadians scrambled and were able to get these reports just in time. Other complications among team members included stolen laptops, accidents, stolen vehicles and delayed flights.

It was only later on in the crusade that we learned from a local pastor that this region is a paradise for witchcraft and most North American evangelists go to Blantyre, a neighboring large city where the churches are much bigger and the crusades larger. Having 2,500 in our evening crusade would be considered a great success.

The opening night about 2,500 attended. The local pastors were very encouraged by the turnout as they repeatedly told us Lilongwe was a

216

preacher's graveyard. Approximately 500 responded to the altar call. I knew in my spirit we needed a breakthrough so I invited all team members to fast over the next few days.

The second night of the crusade the attendance was higher. Before preaching the Holy Spirit told me to call forward those who had made blood covenants to witch doctors. Over 400 responded to the call. In addition, hundreds of children received the baptism in the Holy Spirit, with the evidence of speaking in tongues. Children could literally be seen all over the crusade grounds, totally intoxicated with the wine of the Spirit. That night there were over 1,000 salvations recorded.

These Signs Shall Follow Them That Believe

It was an honor for Fresh Fire Ministries to partner with Rolland and Heidi Baker of Iris Ministries on this trip. We engaged in the largest feeding program either ministry has ever attempted. The Holy Spirit has given Iris Ministries tremendous favor in the nation of Mozambique and the surrounding countries in Africa. Through the generous contributions from those who have given toward the Malawi Outreach and Humanitarian program, FFM was able to donate a 2003 flatbed large truck to Rolland and Heidi's ministry. This truck was put to constant use while we were in Malawi, including hauling generators and sound systems for the open-air market meetings, carrying local worship teams around, and as a pulpit for preaching.

The Lord promised a great harvest if we would preach the Gospel and feed the poor in Malawi. This nation was just coming out of a severe famine due to drought during the last couple of years. The 90 members of our group were divided into eight teams. Every day they fed the poor and preached the gospel. Even after the first day of the outreaches, team captains came back ecstatic with reports of the blind seeing, the crippled walking, the deaf hearing, and the sick recovering.

Every day, teams were sent out to local villages, hospitals, and other remote areas, where miracles and healings took place, and where thousands upon thousands of bags of maize and beans were distributed to the poor.

At the hospitals we distributed the maize and beans to everyone, including the patients, who are required to provide their own food during their stays. The main building at one hospital had four floors, and of course no elevator. Thanks to our huge team of 90, we were able to form a line winding all the way up the staircase and pass bags to the top floors.

In many cases, food was given to the local leaders of the camps or village in order to ensure everyone received their fair portions. In fact, in a number of situations, potential riots began to brew during the feeding process, forcing us to solicit the efforts of the local Malawian police authorities for assistance.

There are few things in the world that are more satisfying than having the privilege of providing precious souls with both the natural and the spiritual Bread of Life. We were excited to be able to feed hundreds of Muslims as well and were able to plant the seed of the Gospel into their hearts.

On one of the morning outreaches, as the Gospel message was preached and the salvation invitation was given, nearly 30 village chiefs came forward to accept Jesus. Another 500 from the crowd responded. Revival had come to the land.

At every crusade I host, I encourage the locals to bring the dead so we can pray for a resurrection. During one hospital outreach, a handful of team members sneaked into the holding room of the morgue. Although there was no resurrection, I know many more opportunities will be waiting in the future, and yes, the dead will be raised in Jesus' name.

A Young Girl Healed of Polio

A young girl stricken with polio received Jesus into her heart, and immediately burst into a big smile. When a team member prayed for her she felt the power of God hit her body and experienced circulation for the first time in two years. What an awesome sight as she left the hospital totally healed, carrying bagged food on top of her head that had been donated by FFM partners.

Refugee Camp Hears the Gospel

Dzaleka, a refuge camp of 20,000 people who have fled civil wars and other catastrophes in their homelands—Somalia, Burundi, Congo, Rwanda and Malawi. After preaching, hundreds of children got born again. But, many adults in the crowd were very skeptical. By the unction of the Holy

This was our largest undertaking. We un-loaded several thousand bags to prepare for distribution at the refugee camp.

Spirit, I invited those who needed a miracle to come forward and assured the crowd they would witness the power of God. A number of deaf and dumb mutes came forward, and when the first miracle took place the crowd

surged forward, almost suffocating some of the team members.

Immediately after we prayed for the sick, we distributed bags of beans and rice. What a blessing it is to fulfill the Matthew 25 mandate of Jesus-"feed the poor, clothe the naked, visit the sick and imprisoned.

The Orphanage

Several team members visited an orphanage and prayed for Tullie, a 14 year old boy with a blind left eye. They witnessed a progressive healing—he could see "men like trees walking." After continuing in prayer, Tullie was able to identify a small piece of candy, and said, "I see a sweet." He immediately began to cry, which caused all of the team members to break out in tears of joy as well. The supervisor of the orphanage said Tullie had been thrown into the city dump at six months old and his eye was pierced. Imagine not having sight in one eye for 13 and a half years. What an amazing miracle!

Confronting the Powers of Darkness

Though we were met with much resistance at the evening crusade, (some of the stage and platform collapsed, injuring people) Friday night was truly the breakthrough we were looking for. Over 3,700 came forward for salvation and the baptism of the Holy Spirit. Lilongwe had never experienced anything like this before.

Before I could direct the new converts to a special area for further prayer and follow up, a back-lash of demonic power erupted. Those who were demonized began manifesting and creating commotion in the crowd. Over one dozen demonized people, mostly women, were hurled onto the stage where they writhed around like snakes, screaming and flailing in every direction. I prayed for a woman, commanding the evil spirit to loose its hold on her body and mind. The evil spirit defied me, spit and cursed me. I actually felt an evil substance, like poison, shooting up my arm. Thank God for the blood of Jesus and His resurrection authority. By the end of the evening, all of the demonized were no longer victims but victors, all because of Jesus.

One of the more outstanding miracles was a local witch doctor who heard the radio broadcast of the crusade, and responded to the altar call. He also received a physical miracle in his body—oh yes, truly, greater is He that is in us, than he who is in the world.

Jesus Appears In the Crowd

Saturday was the final night of the crusade, and again, approximately 2,200 received Jesus in their hearts. I will never forget what happened. I saw an open vision of Jesus, clothed in a scarlet robe, walking among the new believers. Wherever Jesus was standing, dozens of people in that area fell under the power of the Holy Spirit. The presence of God came as a glory cloud and hovered over the crusade grounds. Truly Malawi will never be the same.

Creative Miracles

Every evening the team prayed for the sick and cast out devils. During one of the evening crusades, a number of team members witnessed a creative miracle as a 18 year old team member laid hands on a little baby's head, commanding the healing virtue of Jesus to flow into the body. The baby had what is called water on the brain. His head was noticeably enlarged. Instantly, the head began to shrink back to normal size, to the amazement of the parents. To God be the glory! He does all things well.

Malawi, as well as many other African countries, is plagued with AIDS. At the crusades, I invited those afflicted with AIDS to come unashamedly and receive forgiveness and cleansing. Three different individuals (one who was listening at home on the radio) were tested by their doctors who pronounced them totally healed of this dreaded virus. AIDS can be beaten!

Hotel Supervisor Healed

At the hotel where we were staying, the grounds supervisor desperately wanted to attend the crusade meetings, but was unable to because of his conflicting work schedule. He was experiencing excruciating back pains, and during one of the evenings, was taken to the hospital hoping that some medication would alleviate the pain. However, nothing seemed to help.

He was taken back to the hotel lobby and heard the crusade over the radio. At the exact time he entered the lobby, I asked for those who needed healing to put their hand on the radio as a point of contact. He immediately felt the power of God surge through his back. There was no small stir among the staff in the lobby that evening as he shared his testimony again and again.

Is it true? Is Jesus the same yesterday, today and forever? A little child, paralyzed from birth received a miracle and began to walk for the first time. As in scripture, we were starting to see the sick "walking and leaping and praising God" (Acts 3:8).

I know that reading a big list of statistics can be boring, but remember that every number represents a person loved and touched by Jesus, a person whose life will never be the same! Here are the final totals from Malawi:

- Over 10,000 responded to the call of salvation
- Thousands received baptism in the Holy spirit
- 124 Blind received sight
- 18 Healed of HIV (AIDS)
- 61 Healed from dreaded Malaria
- Over 120 deaf and/or mute heard
- 11 People healed from tumors
- 52 Healed of the "killer" Tuberculosis
- And many more miracles and healings

A Team Member Shares

Perhaps these numbers seem distant or unfathomable. I hope that in the following accounts you can hear the heartbeat behind the multitudes…and see how God touched thousands…one precious life at a time. Here are a few accounts from my trip to Malawi.

God's Love for Muslims

One afternoon, we were at a school preaching and praying for the sick. The Lord whispered to me, "A 14-year-old girl is here who is Muslim and afraid of receiving Jesus because her family will persecute her."

Looking around at the beaming smiles and hungry hearts, I was a bit alarmed at how I would find this girl in the circle of faces. Holy Spirit highlighted one bright shining girl named Roshan. I asked her if she was Muslim. She said yes and told me that she was orphaned years ago and had to stay in the care of her very harsh, very Muslim (Sik) grandma. Holy Spirit warned me, that Roshan was afraid to talk to me in the crowds for fear that her peers would squeal to her Grandma, and she would face painful repercussions. So I smuggled her on the ministry bus!

She was desperate for Jesus but petrified at the costly persecution facing her if she chose Jesus. Suddenly my leaders announced that we were leaving. A decision had to be made. Roshan decided that she wanted to accept Jesus. So we prayed together and then she had to leave. Holding her hand through the window, I pleaded with her to come to the crusade that night. We drove off, tears streaming down my checks. I was devastated at the thought of what awaited her at home.

Hours later, we arrived at the crusade; at least 50,000 people blanketed the fields. Roshan was waiting for me as I stepped off our bus! She brought her aunt and two little cousins (all Sik Muslims!) who wanted to be healed from their full-blown AIDS. Her aunt's right eye was blind because of the HIV virus. We preached the gospel to them and they accepted Jesus. Then we asked the Lord to heal her AIDS and fully restore her sight as an indication that the virus had left her body! We prayed fervently and nothing happened. My heart sank, and the crusade started so we were whisked to the stage.

On my knees, crying out to God for wisdom of what to do, I just worshipped Him. Then the Lord dropped one word into my spirit, "prostitute!" This aunt definitely did not appear to be a prostitute; she was conservatively dressed in nice clothes. "Uh oh! Help God." I wavered, trying to decide whether or not to risk losing the relationship by offending her. Finally I asked her the question and learned her story.

Her husband had sold her into prostitution before he died! This trade was the only way she could support her family. Now both of her daughters had AIDS! After wrestling through worries about how she could ever take care of her family financially, she finally repented of prostitution and decided not to go back to this life of sin. We prayed and her sight was fully restored! Can you believe the kindness of God? Here was a partially blind, Muslim prostitute with AIDS and her two sick children not even looking for Jesus when He looked at the devastation the enemy wreaked in their lives and healed her!

Three Blind Women

One afternoon in a village, I was praying for a 90-year old lady whose skin was weathered and cracked, and who was about 90 percent blind in both eyes. She loved Jesus desperately.

With fiery faith, I prayed for her for awhile and nothing happened.

Distraught and desperate, I started crying. Immediately, the Lord reminded me of the account in the gospels when He spit in the dirt, made mud, and used it as salve to heal a blind man.

"If you want to see healing, this is what You do. Why not today? Why not now?" So, I took some dirt, spit in it, made some mud and gently put it on her eyes. Seconds later, she started jumping up and down screaming, "Hallelujah! Hallelujah!" She could see!

Immediately, another lady with one blind eye approached us. In order to prove to the village that this was about Jehovah Rapha—not our American team—I had the 90-year old lady pray for the next blind lady and she received her sight!

Then another woman with only partial sight in both eyes approached the three of us. I wanted the saints to be encouraged to pray for each other after we left, so we all prayed...she too was healed!

Shara Pradhan, Kansas City, MO

Johannesburg, South Africa
June 8-10, 2003

Johannesburg is a big modern city, a total change from Malawi, which was years behind. At night we ministered in church in a rough part of the city and during the day we did outreaches.

After a meeting one night I told the pastors to take us to the street children. Unemployment is so high (over 50 percent) that many children and adults live on the streets. It was about midnight when some team members bought food at a local grocery store, started making sandwiches and passing out food. Tthe rest of the team just loved on the children and prayed for them. It was early morning before we returned exhausted to our hotel room.

There is continuing white/black tension in South Africa. We went to minister in a park where whites would never go. Even the pastors had never done anything like this before. The park was a high crime place—stabbings, shootings, car jackings and drug dealing. Apparently, no insurance company would cover vehicles in that area.

While we were evangelizing there a crippled woman was miraculously healed. This woman was carted by her husband on something like a skateboard—a piece of wood on four lopsided wheels with a rope handle. She was completely healed and walked two blocks with the team. Many were saved and healed in that street outreach.

Open Market Ministry

Another day, during an open market ministry, 150 people were saved. These outreaches are my favorite. We chose a desperate, dark area of the city and set up a small sound system in the busiest area. Music always draws a crowd of people. So one of the worship leaders from church started off by singing and dancing to some upbeat worship songs. I preached, gave an altar call

Daytime outreach in the market place.

and we all prayed for the sick. During two of these open-airs, the blind saw, the deaf heard and the lame were healed!

Several weeks after returning from Malawi and Johannesburg, I was ministering in Kansas City when I asked several team members in the audience to share about the trip. I jumped for joy on the platform when I heard the following report which had just come in by e-mail:

Tuberculosis Ward Emptied In Malawi!
June 22, 2003

Oh hallelujah!!! I just got word from Malawi of an incredible report and had to tell you right away!

Two weeks ago while in Malawi, Iris Ministries partnered with Fresh Fire Ministries to hold open-air meetings in the city of Lilongwe, Malawi for 4 evenings. I was in charge of organizing outreaches to take place during the day in which the Gospel was preached and food was distributed in each of 7 locations. One of these locations was a "hospital" with very poor humanitarian and sanitary conditions. Many of the patients in this particular hospital had to sleep on the floor and we found many desperate people there. We distributed food to every patient and every member of the hospital staff. This brought much joy and word of what we were doing spread throughout the city.

We also went through the entire hospital and prayed for every patient to be healed. Well, I've just received word that within 24 hours all the patients in the tuberculosis ward were healed and discharged from the TB ward!! All of them! There were over 65 patients in this ward, many of them on oxygen and in advanced stages of tuberculosis! Not one patient remained in the hospital!

More and more reports are coming in from people in Lilongwe, Malawi about how they were healed. God is so amazing! God is so good! There are many other testimonies...the next one I will send is regarding the salvation of 30 village chiefs!

Linda Pallone, Iris Ministries

I know that after reading these tremendous reports of revival, healing and harvest that you are no longer satisfied with the normal Christian life; there is a hunger in your heart to say, "God I want this anointing to come upon my life."

My purpose for sharing so many healing testimonies isn't just so you hear my story, but, so you understand that Jesus is the same yesterday, today and forever. I am just one of many first fruits of the promised healing revival the Holy Spirit has spoken about through many prophetic voices. A revival generation is still rising up as a healing army to the nations. My life is just one of many divine sign posts pointing to the greatest times in church history yet to come.

Chapter 18

DAD'S STORY

This is my dad's chance to tell his story. If you remember, our relationship wasn't very strong as I was growing up. Well, God is very gracious and this story has a very happy ending. If you've been to any of my meetings since September 2001 you've seen my dad ministering right along side me. But I'll let him talk now.

Sitting on the stairs in the church, I had no idea what to do. Everyone was worshipping and praying. This was totally foreign to me. I was at my first conference with Todd and I wondered, "Why am I here? What are all these people doing?" They were singing and dancing and praising the Lord. This was not something I was used to seeing. This was not like anywhere I had ever been before. The hairs on my arms were standing up; a cold chill entered my body. "What was this?" I had no explanation. "Was this my first experience of Jesus?" It was September 19, 2001 and from that day on my life would never be the same again. But I didn't know that yet. My name is David Paul Bentley and this is my testimony:

I was born in Toronto, Ontario Canada in 1956. I had a 13-year-old brother and a 6-year-old sister. Both my parents worked but they still struggled financially. Even through it was hard they tried to keep us all feed and clothed.

In Toronto there was an outbreak of Tuberculosis. At this time a lot of people were isolated for signs of TB. My parents were both hospitalized for about two years. When I was about five-years-old my father passed away with tuberculosis. My mother couldn't care for us all. Much to her dismay she sent my sister and me to live with her sister on a farm outside of Toronto that was called Lang Staff.

As a five-year-old who had just lost his father, to now be taken from his mother was excruciating. This was something I will never forget. I ended up living with my aunt and uncle for about four years. My uncle was an alcoholic. He had his own family, two boys and one girl to take care of. There was not a lot of food there and they lived off of the land. He was not a nice man and treated me like an outsider. I was the youngest one living on the farm. It was too far to go to school so I never attended.

When I was about nine years old my mother remarried a man in Nappanee, Ontario. He already had children. They sent for my sister and me. There were two girls and one boy and the youngest was 14-years-old. His name was Jimmy and he was deaf and dumb. This was going to be even harder than normal. How do we communicate? We didn't get along at first but a while later I started to learn sign language to communicate with my stepbrother. (I didn't know that this would come in handy years later when I pray for the deaf.)

Summer was over and it was time to start school. I was nine and going to school for the first time. They decided to start me in grade one. I was in class with five, six and seven year olds. Because of my size and age I became a bully, showing off, fighting, and getting into trouble. That was my way of getting attention. This only lasted for a year then they transferred me.

They decided to put me into classes with kids my own age and size. But I continued to fight. Learning was not a priority for me. I had to show these kids that I was tough. I would find the biggest kids and start a fight. I was transferred from one grade to the next even though I was failing classes. I was getting too old for primary or middle school so they put me into high school. It was going to be tough now there were so many kids there. How was I going to be the bully? I tried to get into fights on a daily basis. One day I broke a student's leg. We were fighting in the hall and I threw him down a flight of stairs.

I'd had a couple of warnings about fighting so I was suspended for two weeks. I didn't bother telling my parents. I had a friend living on a reserve and he didn't go to school so we started hanging out. We got a hold of a bootlegger and started drinking wine every day. Then we started smoking so each day I took a few of my parent's cigarettes. It didn't take long until I got caught. My stepfather thought he would fix me and make me smoke a cigar. He didn't know that I had smoked them before. My friend and I would steal them from the drug store a couple times a week.

We started hanging out back of the bars and watched for people to put beer or anything of value in their cars. Then we'd take it. Drinking, drugs, and stealing had become our daily activities. Being drunk and stoned made that two weeks go by fast. I went back to school and within two days I got a broken arm in a fight. Even with a broken arm I was still fighting. In gym class one day the teacher grabbed me from behind. I reflexively turned around and hit him in the nose with my cast. His nose broke.

I was black listed from all schools in Ontario. My life as a 15-year-old changed fast. Now I had all day every day to do what I wanted. My friend and I started drinking more and smoking more just to stay high. It was taking more and more just to get where we were the day before. Soon we were trying other ways to get high, we started inhaling everything we could find, it didn't matter what it was—glues, stolen gas from cars or lawn mowers, Cutex etc. This was a new high.

One day three of us were in my stepfather's shed. We were all sniffing and drinking wine. One of my friends, Gary, said he had enough, that he was going to go home and commit suicide. We thought he was joking. About ten minutes later we heard a big bang. We ran to his house, but it was too late. He was lying on his back porch where he had shot himself in the head with his dad's shotgun.

This incident didn't have an effect on my behavior. By this time I was willing to try anything and everything. I was sent to a physiologist but he just said I was an angry young man. At 16 I was well known by all the police. I was always in trouble. They decided to take me for a day stay at the Kingston Prison, as they did with a lot of kids who were in trouble. This is one of the most dangerous prisons in Canada.

That was a day that I would not soon forget. Now this tough kid didn't look so tough. Unfortunately, my behavior didn't truly change. I didn't want to go back to that place so I got a job in a bowling alley to get money so I wouldn't have to steal my cigarettes, liquor and drugs. This lasted for a while but I decided it was time to leave this small town where everyone knew what every one else was doing. My brother was trying to be helpful and said I could move in with him. He tried to get me in school in Toronto but couldn't. I ended up getting a couple of different jobs. One was stocking shelves in a gas station. I was able to do this and still do drugs and booze daily. In Toronto there were even more kinds to try.

I started hanging out with my cousin. He was the leader of the Toronto Hell's Angles. There I tried marijuana and acid. I would get it from my cousin and even sell it to the people I worked with. Now my newest thing was pot and acid and alcohol. At nights I baby-sat my niece and drank vodka from the cupboard. Then I'd fill the bottle with water. I thought I was being very sneaky but my sister-in-law figured it out.

At 17 I wanted away from my brother so a friend and I rented a place together. Now no one could tell me what to do. I went to the bars with my cousin and that started a new downward spiral. I got myself some false ID and started hanging out at the bars all the time. This would be where you could find me every day after work. On the weekends I would be there all day until I was so drunk they would kick me out. I started drinking beer for breakfast.

I met a girl who worked next to where I worked so we met daily at the bar. We stayed there until closing time every night. We started hanging out together all day and night. About a year later she became pregnant. What to do? We took a holiday together to British Columbia to visit my brother. I fell in love with BC so we decided we would stay. We never went back to Ontario, not even to get our belongings. We married and settled in. This was hard for me as I liked being a single man, but I knew I had to take care of her and the baby that was soon to come.

I got a job in the mill. She thought this would give me a break from drinking for at least 8 hours a day. I just had to learn how to hide my addictions. I hid my beer and pot in the garage where no one went but me. On my way home from work I couldn't pass the bar without stopping. Most of my drinking was hidden.

On January 10, 1976, Todd David Bentley was born. Now my life had changed, married and a new son—I was just 19. Now it was time to grow up fast. My job at a mill enabled me to take care of the family financially.

My wife was slowly losing her hearing. We couldn't communicate. Things went from bad to worse and we fought constantly. This gave me an excuse to even drink more. I stopped coming home and started hanging out in bars more and more. Soon we were separated.

Todd was now about five years old. We only got together on weekends but not for long periods of time. Todd and his mother moved to Newfoundland where he began school. When he and his mother moved back to BC I had already moved to Alberta with Darcia (who has been my wife for the last 20 years). During these years of living apart, Todd and I would not see each other for long periods at a time. This was not what I had wanted but divorces bring a lot of painful baggage. Through these years I still drank and did drugs daily. Todd and I were not as close as I had hoped and he had been told things about me that weren't true. This talk kept us apart even more.

As a rebellious young man he started getting in to trouble—stealing, setting fires, etc. until he was sent to jail. I thought that would straighten him out. But little did I know he was a lot like me! He was doing drugs and drinking, all the

230

things I hoped he never would.

When he got out of jail we tried to get him back into school but that didn't work. I would see him just hanging uptown doing his thing. I told him if he was going to do drugs he should do them with me. At this time it seemed like a good idea. This would keep him from getting in to bad drugs on the street. We did drugs and drank together. This seemed to be an every day event. I now became my own son's drug dealer and bootlegger.

He was getting so carried away with drugs he had lost all the jobs I got him. Now he was stealing my drugs and he had overdosed several times. He progressed to street drugs. We talked about it but that did no good. After his third or fourth drug overdose he just disappeared, all his belongings, everything we had given him in his apartment was gone. Even the furniture that was not his was gone.

I'd pretty much given up hope for him. Darcia and I figured the next time we heard anything about him it would be from the morgue or a prison. A year passed and he phoned me to say that he was reborn. Well I thought he was high, plus I didn't know what it meant to be reborn. He tried to explain it to me but I didn't believe.

The next time he phoned he told us he was getting married. This was not what I expected to hear. I still didn't believe he had turned his life around. I told him we couldn't make the wedding but we would set up a honeymoon for them. I really didn't think he would get married, but he did. When Todd came to the island he had the most beautiful wife, Shonnah. We all spent a week together, the first time in years.

Todd started telling us about God. This was not the Todd I knew! At this time I told him I was not at all interested in, "his new God thing." Well Todd soon started a Ministry called Fresh Fire and he kept telling me about it. He sent me some tapes of his meetings. I watched with disbelieve—people screaming, falling (pushed?) over and supposedly being healed. "What kind of scam is this?" I wondered. I thought he was in some kind of a cult. But, I had to admit he was doing great. This God thing had made him a happier person. I still didn't believe it, but if it made him happy that was great. Todd went on to have three children, which made me a proud grandpa. For many years Todd tried to teach me more about God but I didn't think that was me.

At age 45 it had been almost 30 years that I had been drinking, doing drugs and smoking cigarettes. I hadn't cut back over the years; in fact I did more than ever. I would still have my beer for breakfast, pot and beer at lunch; I was drinking about a dozen beers a day, and smoking more than a pack of cigarettes. For many years I thought I was getting away with all this. I was fooling my self thinking that Darcia didn't know what was going on. She knew, but she also knew that the more she tried to stop me the worse I would get. She stood by me for all these years and I do thank God for her.

In December 2000, on Christmas Eve, we got a call from our son in-law. They had just taken my stepdaughter, Barbie, to the hospital. A few days earlier at a doctor's exam they had sent her back home, thinking she just had a bad back. Two days later they rushed her to the hospital and found that her appendix had ruptured days before. Darcia and I drove two hours. I stayed with the two grandkids, Matt and Taylor. Darcia went to the hospital.

At the hospital where they sent Barbie there was no doctor who could help with her condition. She had so much poison in her they told Darcia that there was nothing they could do. They rushed her to the next hospital where there was a surgeon. He said there was nothing he could for her either. She told me to call the family and let them all know. I phoned Todd and he said he would pray, and told me I should do the same. "Todd I don't know how to pray." He said to just start, so I began to pray saying: "God, I ask you to save Barbie from death. If you do this I will seek and search for you." I prayed this over and over thinking, "Why am I wasting my time doing this?"

The doctors told us that her chances of living were 30 percent at best. "Don't keep your hopes up." Barbie went into a coma for two weeks. During that time I did as Todd asked, and kept praying the same prayer every day. On January 17, 2001 Barbie came home! That is a day I will always remember. Thank you Lord, what a great birthday present!

A month later Todd's mother passed away. Todd asked me to help him with the arrangements because he was out of the country. This would be the first time Todd and I would be together in a long time. A month after her death my own mother had passed away. This was a hectic six months that I wouldn't want to re-live.

A month later driving home one day I had the strangest thing happen. A voice out of nowhere spoke to me in the car. This was not at all what I was used to. "DO NOT FORGET YOUR PROMISES." I went home, lit a joint and opened a beer. When Darcia got home I told her what happened. She said I should follow what I felt. She was hoping that she would see the same change come over me that came over Todd and she was afraid, but also excited because

232

she knew I really needed a touch from God.

Todd called me and said he was coming to town for a couple days and wanted to get together. It turned out he had a position open in his ministry and wanted to know if I would work for him. I had been out of work since Barbie was in a coma. I had worked for this company 12 years and they let me go. After thinking about it for a while I said yes.

Driving to the airport the voice came to me, "DO NOT FORGET YOUR PROMISES." I called Darcia. "It happened again." (Later I realized that God was reminding me about my promise to seek Him out if Barbie lived.)

It was a new experience walking onto a job that I knew nothing about. Todd had me listening to all his teachings to find bad tapes and to fix them. I didn't realize I was being set up! I learned more about God every day. But this was Todd's plan from the beginning!

On September 28, 2001 Todd prayed for me to quit smoking, drinking and doing drugs. The next day God delivered me. No cravings; no withdrawals; all gone; thank you Jesus.

I traveled with Todd to a couple of conferences. I'll never forget my first experience, which was with a demon-possessed woman. She was screaming, rolling and biting at Todd. He asked me to help him with her. I was new at this and wondered, "Why not just knock her out and stop all this?" I held her down. Todd prayed and she calmed down some. But that wasn't the end of it—night after night the same thing would happen. The fourth night she came in and I thought she looked different. She was calm and happy. Then I knew what a difference God's power could make in the life of a person with a demon. She had been set free.

One night at a meeting in Ontario, Todd gave an altar call. Everything seemed normal when all of a sudden I was standing in the front of the church with a few other people. This was November 14, 2001. I gave my heart to the Lord that night. Still, I do not remember walking to the front. But I was there and have not regretted it since. The Lord has shown great mercy in my life and I am thankful for that day.

This was the beginning of a whole new life. The Lord was about to show me all I had been seeing in Todd's videos was true. I used to ask Todd, "How much do you pay those people to fall down?" My unbelief was about to change.

We were at a church in Toronto; Todd was calling people up for healing.

There was a young lady sitting about six rows back who kept waving at me to come to her. After awhile I asked Ivan, who was Todd's disciple at the time, what I should do. He told me to go to her. She said that God told her if I helped her to the front and prayed for her she would walk. She had been in a wheelchair for 10 years. I laughed and went back to my seat. I told Ivan I thought she was crazy. I stayed in my seat but she kept waving. I went back to her and tried to explain that she couldn't walk because she was in a wheelchair. She insisted on me taking her up front and praying for her.

I sat back down and Ivan told me to do what she wanted. With not one ounce of belief I gave her my arm and kind of dragged her up front. She went down on the floor and took me with her. It appeared to me that she had fallen asleep, but she said, "Pray for me." I still didn't know how to pray for someone so I said the same sort of prayer I used when Barbie was sick. The woman said she "felt something," so would I please help her up. I did and she went back down, holding on me even tighter then before.

After about 20 minutes she said she wanted to walk around the church. My thought was, "Yea, right. I bet you do." She asked if I would hold her hand, boyfriend and girlfriend style, and walk with her. We started to walk and WOW she was walking, slowly, but we actually walked around the church twice. Then she wanted to go up stairs. She did it! When we got to the top Todd and the whole congregation started to clap. This woman left the church walking and someone else was pushing her wheelchair. Praise the Lord! That was the first time the Lord used me.

The next night, at the same church, everyone was praying for people. Ivan told me to pray. I went to pray for a woman who had white blotches in both eyes. I watched every one else pray, they seemed to be touching the person they were praying for so I put my hands on her eyes. Then for some reason I thought I shouldn't do this. I took my hands away and looked at her. "Excuse me but did your contacts fall out?" The white was gone. She said she could see well. I thought she was joking but her friend said she had cataracts for 3 years and was almost totally blind. Well, I'll tell you, that experience sure helped boost my faith that God really does heal and that he can use anyone to do it.

I have been traveling with Todd for eight months now and have been saved for 18 months. Together we have been all over the world: India, Africa, South America, Mexico, Europe and many other places. I have seen all kinds of

234

healings and miracles, from headaches to limbs growing as well as the blind seeing, the deaf hearing, and the cripples walking. The only thing I haven't seen yet is the dead raised. But I know we will also soon see this because we ask people to bring the dead to our meetings.

If you're hungry for these experiences, come with Fresh Fire on an overseas crusade and you will see these things too. God bless you. I hope my testimony helps you to believe, even more, that God is the same today, and He does the same miracles as He did in the bible. Let's go out and obey Jesus command to His disciples: "Preach the Gospel, heal the sick, cleanse the lepers, raise the dead, cast out demons..." (Matthew 10:8). **Dave Bentley**

"These two pictures really represent God's grace in my life. My relationship with Todd while he was growing up was so broken—I was so broken, and unfortunately, so was he. But what the enemy meant for evil, God has used for good. He has truly done "exceedingly abundantly above all that we (could) ask or think" (Eph. 3:20).

Chapter 19

GET READY!

Let's talk about the incredible future that lies before us. God is getting ready to do amazing things. Get ready for supernatural visitation and open heavens—the supernatural is about to become natural. There's coming a release of an apostolic anointing, which I call the popcorn release into ministry, where men and women are going to be thrust into worldwide ministry overnight. Tomorrow you're going to go to work and the next day your city is going to be in revival. Can a nation be born in a day? "Can a country be born in a day or a nation be brought forth in a moment?" (Is. 66:8). Yes!

Get ready. There are things that are about to happen in the church that eye has not seen and ear has not heard and you can be part of it. Even if I told you, you wouldn't believe it. "For the earth will be filled with the knowledge of the glory of the Lord, as the waters cover the sea" (Hab. 2:14).

I want to share with you in more detail than I did in the opening chapter, the four aspects of what I believe will happen in our future and the future of the church.

1. Healing Revival

"And the inhabitant of the land shall not say I am sick" (Is. 33:24). I believe that this verse is speaking of a time in the church where there will be such a level of healing anointing that no sickness or disease will touch God's people, just like when Israel came up out of Egypt. "He also brought them out with silver and gold, and there was none feeble among His tribes" (Psalm 105:37). Not one feeble or weak? Think about that, more than three million people healed after 400 years in oppression and bondage!

Kathryn Kuhlman prophesied that there would be a day when the church would say, "I am not sick!" and in some meetings every single person would be healed. Many others have prophesied a great healing revival in the end times, including John G. Lake. There will be a renewed focus on the message of repentance. Sickness and disease started with sin. In the beginning the Garden of Eden was paradise without sickness, disease, poverty or death. That was always God's plan for us! When sin entered the world then came sickness, disease and death. "Therefore, just as through one man sin entered the world, and death through sin, and thus death spread to all men, because all sinned" (Rom. 5:12).

But with the resurrection of Jesus came a new law. Romans 8:1-2 states, "There is therefore now no condemnation to those who are in Christ Jesus, who do not walk according to the flesh, but according to the Spirit. For the law of the Spirit of life in Christ Jesus has made me free from the law of sin and death."

A new force is in motion today to empower us to live holy and be made righteousness. All the angels of Heaven are prepared to back up that law. "For the law of the Spirit of life in Christ Jesus has made me free from the law of sin and death" (Rom. 8:2).

We are redeemed from the curse of the law. "Christ has redeemed us from the curse of the law, having become a curse for us (for it is written, 'Cursed is everyone who hangs on a tree') that the blessing of Abraham might come upon the Gentiles in Christ Jesus, that we might receive the promise of the Spirit through faith" (Gal. 3:13-14).

Today God's will is 3 John 1:2, "Beloved, I pray that you may prosper in all things and be in health, just as your soul prospers."

Most of the world's sickness and disease stems from turning away from God to other idols and false religions. Whole nations are under curses (Deuteronomy 28) because they have turned to other gods. When we examine the beliefs of countries in Africa, India and South America, many are rooted in witchcraft or idol worship. In India alone, they worship over three million gods. I have been in many nations and have seen innocent children affected by poverty, famine, hunger, war, and sickness. I have grieved as I've driven down some streets and seen a temple on every corner. The innocent suffer because of the unrighteousness of governments and leaders.

In order for us to see a greater wave of healing in the church today there needs to be a renewed focus on repentance and personal holiness because many times our own sins of bitterness, envy, jealousy unforgiveness, sexual sins, etc. are not only the roots but the hindrances to healings. In the coming healing outpouring, as people repent of their willful sin and make a fresh commitment to holiness, then when healing is preached we will see more miracles.

James 5:15-16 says, "And the prayer of faith will save the sick, and the Lord will raise him up. And if he has committed sins, he will be forgiven. Confess your trespasses to one another, and pray for one another, that you may be healed."

The Lord has also showed me that as the church and as nations repent of corruption and worldly ways and turn back to God, He will bring a mighty healing revival. Hosea 6:1-2 implores: "Come, and let us return to the Lord; For He has torn, but He will heal us; He has stricken, but He will bind us up. After two days He will revive us; on the third day He will raise us up, that we may live in His sight."

As repentance and the revival of righteousness sweeps through the church, so will more healings and miracles. Healing will take place supernaturally without the laying on of hands. In Jesus' ministry He healed every sickness and disease among the people. (Matt. 8:16) "When evening had come, they brought to Him many who were demon-possessed. And He cast out the spirits with a word, and healed all who were sick."

2. Saint's Revival

Another thing we'll see in the future will be a saint's revival. God is going to do away with a clergy/layman mentality and raise up the saints— the body of Christ—to do the work of the ministry. I strongly believe in the local church and godly leaders, the fivefold ministry and apostolic relationships built on trust and friendship. But, it will not be just the pastors or evangelists, but the saints released by God who will begin to preach the gospel and heal the sick. It has always been God's plan that every believer gets involved in the ministry of Jesus. John 14:12 says, "He who believes in me, the works that I do he will do also; and greater works than these he will do, because I go to my Father."

I believe that when the early church was birthed, many ordinary people moved in signs and wonders. "The Apostles called out seven men full of good reputation and the Holy Spirit. They laid their hands on them... The number of the disciples increased greatly" (Acts 6:1-7). We all know Stephen, full of faith and power, was doing signs and wonders, but who were the rest in verse five? We never hear of them again or their works of power. But, I believe they flowed in an anointing just like Stephen. God is going to use the church deacons, businessmen, cashiers, housewives and children to work His great power—"nobodies," as it were, a nameless faceless generation. People we don't know, just like those chosen by the apostles, will flow in this anointing.

Through the church God will show signs and wonders in the heavens and the earth. The church will have the same power as Jesus over the natural elements—the winds and the sea obeyed Him. We will move into a ministry of wonders, fulfilling Joel 2:30-31. We will speak to limbs like Jesus did in Luke 6:10, when He said, "Stretch forth your hand...." and it will happen.

The wonders we will perform will be like in the day of Elijah or Moses. We will walk in authority like Joshua who spoke and the sun stood still. I don't just see healings and miracles, but signs and wonders of great proportion, which will jolt people from their busy lifestyles—the world will stop and see the glory cloud literally come down upon the church just like it did with Moses. In some cities we will witness signs of the Lord's glory for days that will even capture the media's attention.

"These have power to shut heaven, so that no rain falls in the days of their prophecy; and they have power over waters to turn them to blood, and to strike the earth with all plagues, as often as they desire" (Rev. 11:6). This scripture says, concerning the two witnesses, that they could do their signs as often as they desired. Now that's power! Pray it in. Let's believe God to confirm His word and trust us with the last-days anointing we'll need for the last-days harvest. The God of Abraham, Isaac, Jacob and Moses will once again begin to show up in the church just like He visited His people in Old Testament times.

3. Children's Ministry

I have seen a great move of healings and miracles by the hands of children. I had a vision of an eight-year-old boy with a bible in his hand preaching with fire and boldness to thousands. He preached the word of the Lord and the sick recovered in their seats. I see children being used to grow limbs working creative miracles by the spoken word and faith. Some children will become part of the prophetic Samuel generation as young as eleven or twelve years old.

We know that the kingdom isn't in word only but in power. Children are going to move in the power of the kingdom, drive out spirits and heal the sick because the kingdom is theirs. Jesus said in Matthew 19:14: "Let the little children come to me do not forbid them, for of such is the Kingdom of heaven."

4. Last Days Anointing of Power

I have seen a glimpse of the anointing that will be on the last days church. We think the book of Acts was glorious but the glory of the latter house will be greater than the former. We are going out with a bigger bang than we came in with.

The end time anointing is the Elijah anointing! The Elijah anointing turns the hearts of the nations to God like it did in I Kings 18, where Elijah called down fire on Mt. Carmel in a confrontation with the prophets of Baal. In these last days, it won't be Elijah as one man, but it will be the Spirit and anointing of Elijah working through the church that will get the job done. We'll do miracles and signs like Elijah did. Some thought John the Baptist was Elijah the man, but they were actually seeing the Elijah-anointing on his life.

In Matthew 17 on the Mount of Transfiguration, the Father sent Moses and Elijah as a prophetic fulfillment and to show that Jesus was who He said He was. I believe as we near the second coming of Christ, God will again confirm the church as His voice in the land. He will do this by bringing the spirit and power of Moses and Elijah upon His end-time army to release forerunners to prepare the way of the Lord and to prepare the

240

nations for God.

"Behold, I will send you Elijah the prophet before the coming of the great and dreadful day of the Lord. And he will turn the hearts of the fathers to the children, and the hearts of the children to their fathers, lest I come and strike the earth with a curse" (Mal. 4:5-6).

It will be a movement of the prophetic, power evangelism and healing that will turn nations to God—some in a day! I'll develop this is more detail in the next vision.

That hour is at hand and you need to reach out for this. The supernatural needs to be natural. It shouldn't be rare in the body of Christ. I believe that those who are hungry to have an encounter with the Holy Spirit will be filled.

It's not about who you are, or your righteousness, it's not about your ability, it's about your availability. It's about the time we live in and a mighty God who has chosen to work through weak human vessels. The Spirit and the anointing have the power and the wisdom. "Not by might, not by power, but by my Spirit says the Lord" (Zechariah 4:6).

Houses of Prayer Facilitate the Great Harvest

Recently I was in Latvia, a small Baltic state in Eastern Europe, formerly under Soviet rule. While traveling to an evening crusade I was caught up in an interactive vision. I saw the great harvest field already white. The angels were working in this field.

Then Jesus came to me. I knew in my spirit He was the Lord of the Harvest but He came to me dressed as the Good Shepherd (John 10) and holding a staff. I wondered why the Lord of Psalms 23 was the Lord of the Harvest. Then I understood – this is not just about winning souls but also about discipling these same souls. Jesus doesn't want to just be savior but He also wants to be the great overseer of their souls and He wants to lead them into the depth of Psalms 23. He desires to restore their souls and to lead them beside the still waters.

Immediately these scriptures came to my mind:

- Psalms 24:1, "The earth is the Lord's, and all its fullness, the world and those who dwell therein."
- Revelation 11:15, "The kingdoms of this world have become the kingdoms of our Lord and of His Christ, and He shall reign forever and ever!"
- Isaiah 40:15, "Behold, the nations are as a drop in a bucket, and are counted as the small dust on the scales; Look, He lifts up the isles as a very little thing."
- Psalm 2:8, "Ask of Me, and I will give you the nations for your inheritance, and the ends of the earth for Your possession."

This was a faith level where whole cities and nations can be saved in a day. The Lord said to me, "Todd, enter into My harvest power! It's the Harvest of Amos 9:13: "'Behold, the days are coming,' says the Lord, 'When the plowman shall overtake the reaper, and the treader of grapes him who sows seed; the mountains shall drip with sweet wine, and all the hills shall flow with it.'"

There is coming an acceleration of the laws of sowing and reaping. The seed will be planted and as soon as the seed is sown it will be reaped. There will be harvest until the days of sowing and sowing until the days of harvest—a holy overlapping of continual sowing and reaping. When this acceleration happens, men and women will cry out, "What must I do to be saved?"

As I continued to walk in the harvest I noticed a tent in the field and asked, "Lord, what is that tent doing in the harvest and why does it look so old and ragged? It's not as glorious and golden as these fields." The Lord responded, "Todd, this is the tabernacle of David and it looks that way because, for many, prayer is so uninviting. It is a matter of perspective and priority. To many prayer is tedious work but to others it is the glory. Most importantly the tabernacle releases the Amos 9:13 harvest."

In the book of Acts, Paul, Barnabas, Peter and their ministry teams are seeing tremendous harvest in cities. Churches are being planted and the Holy Ghost is falling on the Gentile believers as well as the Jews. In Acts 15 they meet for the Jerusalem council and give reports of the harvest and

242

discuss whether Gentile believers need to be circumcised. In the midst of this James quotes Amos 9:11-12:

> After this I will return And will rebuild the tabernacle of David, which has fallen down; I will rebuild its ruins, and I will set it up; so that the rest of mankind may seek the Lord, even all the Gentiles who are called by My name, says the Lord who does all these things (Acts 15:16-17).

I said, "God there it is again—the great harvest and the house of David."

Night and day prayer, 24 hours a day, seven days a week is already taking place in the church. These houses of prayer are essential to the releasing of an end-time signs and wonders movement, healing revival and the geographic healing centers.

The Healing Centers

I've already spoken about the many healing pools of Bethesda (like in John 5) that I've seen throughout North America and different countries. The grace of God will give us an outpouring of the rains of healing and miracles, until the power of God increases and we have a flood of miracle rain and many pools of healing. Once again great multitudes will come from all over the world to geographical healing centers just like God did in Spokane in the early 1900's with John Lake's ministry. This coming healing outpouring will be the forerunner to the great harvest.

Elijah Anointing

God has promised the spirit and power of Elijah in these last days. With the spirit and power of Elijah we also have a promised healing revival in Malachi 4:2. "But to you who fear My name The Son of Righteousness shall arise with healing in His wings; and you shall go out and grow fat like stall-fed calves."

The great prayer movement is the key to the release of the great healing revival that comes in the day of the Elijah spirit. But, before God releases the power to the church spoken of in Revelation 11:3, ("And I will give power to my two witnesses, and they will prophesy one thousand two hundred and sixty days, clothed in sackcloth.") the Lord conducts an evaluation of the church in Revelation 11:1: "Then I was given a reed like a measuring rod. And the angel stood, saying, 'Rise and measure the temple of God, the altar, and those who worship there.'" The angel was to measure three things: the temple of God, the altar, and those who worship there. The temple can represent the believers lives or the church, local, citywide or national. When the levels of worship, prayer and intercession are right in the church, God will release His end-time power and the promise of the spirit of Elijah. Only when the bowls of Revelation 8:3:5 are full will God release His power.

> Then another angel, having a golden censer, came and stood at the altar. He was given much incense, that he should offer it with the prayers of all the saints upon the golden altar which was before the throne. And the smoke of the incense, with the prayers of the saints, ascended before God from the angel's hand. Then the angel took the censer, filled it with fire from the altar, and threw it to the earth. And there were noises, thunderings, lightnings, and an earthquake.

God is checking the levels of intercession, worship and prayer in the believer's life, in churches, in cities and in nations. And when the levels are right then He will give power to the two witnesses. The House of David model (24 hours, seven days a week, day and night prayer, worship, intercession and intimacy with Jesus) are key to releasing power to prophesy and witness with signs following to the last day generation.

Now here is the part of the vision that should encourage us, but also make us tremble. When I asked the Lord which cities would have these healing centers He replied, "Which cities want them? I am checking the levels of worship, intercession and prayer. Their hunger will be the deciding factor. Every city has equal opportunity."

If there was ever a time to press in and go for it, now is that time.

I repeat the question I asked at the beginning of the book. If not now, when? If not you, who?

Be Encouraged

My life has been marked by the supernatural: my conversion; three-month visitation; move to Abbotsford; marriage; three months of soaking and God launching me into an international ministry with supernatural miracles, signs and wonders.

Maybe you are reading this and getting discouraged or feeling jealous. You're asking the Lord why things like this haven't happened to you. I want to say, I'm a sovereign vessel in a sovereign time. God will use and anoint anyone but He has a timetable and makes sovereign choices. God is God and we are not.

I encourage you who have been serving the Lord and waiting for the prophetic promises that haven't come true yet, to keep your eyes on Jesus and hold on to God's word. Jesus loves you as much as he loves me. I am only where I am because of faithful laborers who have come before me. Some of you were praying for this move of God while I was getting high on drugs! I'm the first-fruit of your labor. It's the time in which we live, certainly not because of my righteousness. I'm looking forward to the day when Jesus will do greater things than He's done with me. That's my prayer for faithful pioneers and intercessors.

Don't forget the parable of the laborers in the vineyard (Matt. 20:1-16) who worked for one hour and got paid the same as those who labored all day. It's not what track you run on it's that you finish the track the Lord put you on. Fight the good fight of faith.

Dare to Ask!

I wrote this book to help you understand what God is doing in our time and to encourage you to take steps of faith in areas where you may have been holding back. I want your heart to be inflamed with passion for Him and your vision to soar. I'm boasting in a big God. I'm excited about what He's done, but I'm more excited about what He's going to do.

He wants the supernatural to be natural. In Daniel 11:32 the Lord says, "...the people who know their God shall be strong, and carry out great exploits." That refers to you too, not just me.

I encourage you to believe in a big God and dare to ask Him to fulfill big dreams. This has become a key verse for me: "Ask of Me, and I will give You the nations for Your inheritance, and the ends of the earth for Your possession" (Psalm 2:8).

God will do amazing things with ordinary people who totally yield their lives to Him.

My Prayer for You

After receiving several e-mail requests asking for the transfer of the healing anointing through the internet, I felt God prompt me to also release that anointing through this book for those who would come into agreement with a prophetic proclamation calling for the release of God's miraculous power.

First, let's establish a biblical precedent for this. We know that Jesus didn't have a laptop and they weren't "on line" in Jerusalem. But consider the story of the centurion who said to Jesus, "Just say the word, and my servant will be healed" (Matt. 8:5-13, Luke 7:1-10). Jesus marveled at the centurion's faith, not because he believed Jesus could heal, but because he believed Jesus could heal even though He was far from the sick person physically. Jesus lavished praise on the centurion, saying he had more faith than anyone He had met in all of Israel! How would you like to have Jesus say that about you?

> When Jesus heard it, He marveled, and said to those who followed, "Assuredly, I say to you, I have not found such great faith, not even in Israel...Then Jesus said to the centurion, "Go your way; and as you have believed, so let it be done for you." And his servant was healed that same hour. (Matt. 8:10,13)

There are other New Testament examples of people getting healed

246

"from a distance." The use of prayer cloths is one example. "Now God worked unusual miracles by the hands of Paul, so that even handkerchiefs or aprons were brought from his body to the sick, and the diseases left them and the evil spirits went out of them" (Acts 19:11-12). It's funny that people think it's an awesome miracle when they read about Paul using prayer cloths, but when we try the same thing, or a variation of it today, the same people think it's weird or "New Age-y."

In my ministry I've seen the healing anointing transferred through prayer cloths and over cell phones. People are regularly healed, even of AIDS, when listening to my crusades over the radio. One of my favorite stories about this comes from Cal Pierce at the Spokane Healing rooms. He tells how a woman in Africa was healed when someone made a Xerox copy of a prayer cloth and faxed the copy of the cloth to Africa. What great faith! What great use of technology!

Can this transference really happen through a book? Well, if God can heal through cloths, over telephone lines and through radio waves, it's safe to assume He can also work through the printed page. In fact, He's done it before because people used to get healed when they would read John G. Lake's newsletters.

All these examples indicate what we really already know—God is not limited by time and space. If you believe that the anointing is transferable and you want to agree with me that a greater release of His healing virtue is going to come into your life, ministry and church, I want you to align yourself in simple faith with this prayer.

Here's the prayer I've prayed for you: "Father I ask You right now in the name of Jesus to begin to release Your transferable, tangible healing anointing for those asking for more of Your power on their life and ministry. I release healing virtue in Jesus' name! Let an explosion of miracles and healing come to them now. I pray that they would be forerunners; that they would lead the way into the coming healing revival. I pray that the spirit of Elijah would fall on them and that they would evangelize in the market place with signs and wonders confirming their message. Lord let them enter in to the night and day prayers of the tabernacle of David. Father, pour out Your power and grace, I ask, that those agreeing with this prayer will receive a fresh anointing now in Jesus' name."

Now, I want you to pray out loud:

Father, I want more of the anointing transferred into my life. I believe now for the healing power to fill me. Give me a greater release of miracles, signs and wonders from this day forward. Come now Holy Spirit – I receive. I exercise my faith and declare that, "The same spirit that raised Jesus from the dead lives in me." I will take this healing gift to the sick in Jesus' name.

From this day forward, I want you to believe God, to preach the gospel and to heal the sick! Go lay hands on them and see them recover. Start where you live, one person at a time. Now if you need a healing miracle get ready! If you are believing God for a healing right now I want you to put your hand on the part of your body that needs to be healed. Or, if there is someone in your house that needs a healing, lay hands on them and pray this prayer of faith with me: "Come Holy Spirit; heal me now in Jesus' name. Father I command this sickness to go; I command my infirmity to go. Satan loose me now in Jesus name. Touch me Jesus. I receive my healing!"

I stand in agreement with your prayer, "Lord, I pray that you would let Your healing touch every infirmity of those reading this book, right now." Rise up in Jesus' name and do something you couldn't do before. Move your body; thank God now for healing you.

Let's not stop. He's got an unlimited storehouse and He loves you—continue asking for more: "Father, I want to cooperate with what You are doing in heaven, so I pray for the Spirit of wisdom, revelation, council and might. Please give me eyes to see and ears to hear so that I can understand eternal things. I earnestly desire spiritual gifts, especially that I would prophesy. Let it come right now Lord—let the Holy Spirit fall with that prophetic mantle. Holy Spirit come! I want a download of the Spirit of prophecy.

"Lord give me the word of knowledge for my workplace and for my school. Let me go into the marketplace with Your anointing, authority and mantle. Let me hear Your word, wherever I am, whenever the lost and hurting need Your loving touch. Oh God, let your mantle fall on me for healing and for prophetic evangelism.

"Lord, thank you for the coming power, miracles, healings, signs and wonders. According to Your word Father, as I speak words of faith, I can see supernatural manifestations. Let the authority and spirit of Elijah come again—let it come into my life. Surprise me Lord, it's not by my might or power but it's through Your Spirit.

"Let me produce 100-fold fruit that remains for your kingdom. Help me to do exceedingly, abundantly above all I can ask or think for Your glory. Lord, draw me into night and day intercession too. I want to help fill those golden bowls to hasten Your coming. Let me not grow weary; open my eyes to see the power and impact of my simple prayers on the lives of others.

"Thank you, Father for answering this cry of my heart."

Now here's a tear-out sheet of the previous prayers. Put it on your mirror, refrigerator, or any place you will see it regularly. Pray these prayers every day and see what the Lord does in your life over the next year.

"I want more of the anointing transferred into my life. Father, I believe now for the healing power to fill me. Give me a greater release of miracles, signs and wonders from this day forward. Come now Holy Spirit, I receive. I exercise my faith and declare that, 'The same spirit that raised Jesus from the dead lives in me.' I will take this healing gift to the sick in Jesus' name. Thank you Lord."

"Come Holy Spirit; heal me now in Jesus' name. Father I command this sickness to go; I command my infirmity to go. Satan loose me now in Jesus name. Touch me Jesus. I receive my healing!"

"Father, I want to cooperate with what You are doing in heaven, so I pray for the Spirit of wisdom, revelation, council and might. Please give me eyes to see and ears to hear so that I can understand eternal things. I earnestly desire spiritual gifts, especially that I would prophesy.

Let it come right now Lord — let the Holy Spirit fall with that prophetic mantle. Holy Spirit come! I want a download of the Spirit of prophecy.

"Lord give me the word of knowledge for my workplace and for my school. Let me go into the marketplace with Your anointing, authority and mantle. Let me hear Your word, wherever I am, whenever the lost and hurting need Your loving touch. Oh God, let your mantle fall on me for healing and for prophetic evangelism.

"Lord, thank you for the coming power, miracles, healings, signs and wonders. According to Your word Father, as I speak words of faith, I can see supernatural manifestations. Let the authority and spirit of Elijah come again — let it come into my life. Surprise me Lord, it's not by my might or power but it's through Your Spirit.

"Let me produce 100 fold fruit that remains for your kingdom. Help me to do exceedingly, abundantly above all I can ask or think for Your glory.

"Draw me into night and day intercession. I want to help fill those golden bowls to hasten Your coming. Let me not grow weary, open my eyes to see the power and impact of my simple prayers on the lives of others.

My wonderful family. What a gift from God!
November 2002

COME SEE THE WORLD WITH US!

Fresh Fire Ministries is an international ministry called to global harvest. Todd Bentley and his team take God's saving, healing, delivering power to the nations. Todd and his team conduct healing crusades throughout Africa, India, South America, Europe and beyond. Thousands have been saved, healed and delivered.

Todd preaches the word of God with the power and demonstration of the Spirit—God confirms His word with signs and wonders following. God has released an increase of the healing anointing into Todd's life and the blind see, the deaf hear and growths dissolve as Jesus heals sickness and disease.

The harvest has never been so ripe, and we are praying for laborers to go on these crusades to help bring in souls for the kingdom of God. Literally, dozens of nations have been calling us, and urging us to come and hold pastors' and leaders' conferences (in the mornings), and crusades in the evenings.

Whether you're a housewife, student or pastor, there's room for everyone. It seems wherever Fresh Fire Ministries goes, and whatever nation we are in, Matt. 10:7-8 is fulfilled. The sick are healed, the spiritually dead are raised, (and we are believing for the physically dead to be raised as well!), devils are cast out, the lame are walking and the blind are seeing. Without a doubt, we are fulfilling Acts chapter 29, experiencing the very same miracles as the early disciples did!

We have great anticipation, believing the Holy Spirit is going to double our efforts in the area of miracles, signs and wonders, and in the giving of prayer and financial partners.

Todd has been impressed by the Holy Spirit to include humanitarian aid in many of their overseas crusades. We believe it is important to minister to the whole man - spirit, soul and body.

The many partners and friends of FFM are shaking the kingdoms of darkness because of their passionate praying and giving. I guarantee your spiritual life will never be the same after coming on a crusade with Todd and the FFM staff. Your life will be absolutely "wrecked" for Jesus! We trust that you'll impart that fire and passion back to your local churches.

We at FFM desire to work in close association with the pastors and their local congregations. If you have any questions about us, or are considering on sending those from your church, (i.e.-Youth groups, college and career groups etc.), please don't hesitate to contact us. If we can be of any service to you, it would be an honor and a privilege. Together, let's reap a worldwide harvest for the King of Kings and the Lord of Lords!

Pastor Ken Greter
Missions Director-FFM

If God is touching your heart to be a part a FFM crusade You can call for information at our US office, 816-761-0033 or Canadians call 604-853-9041. E-mail missions@freshfire.ca or ken@freshfire.ca.

INDIVIDUAL TESTIMONIES

Here are more testimonies from people of all ages that have been on a Fresh Fire Mission's trip. The first testimony is from a self- proclaimed, "grandma type" and the next is from one of the youth on the Mexico trip. There's a place for everyone in the harvest!

Patricia Mason (Spring Hill, Kansas)

I am a woman who is a grandma type. But I told God I wanted to refire and not retire and He met me at that season of my life. It was totally awesome what I saw in Malawi and South Africa. God used just little nobody people like me to open blind eyes and bring deliverance to people who had been deep into witchcraft. I was used a lot in ministering deliverance especially to young people and children, just pouring out motherly love to them and seeing them change in the spirit. Mothers lined up for me to just bless their infants and I believe the Lord released destiny to them as we laid hands on the future of Africa these young ones represented. I will never be the same seeing God perform miracles of all

254

kinds through Todd, his family and us, his team—it was amazing and over the top. I think I was one of the oldest ones on the team and I loved every minute of it. No one discriminated against me because I was a senior citizen—they just loved me.

Lindsay Larson (Portland, Oregon)

Hey, I went to Mexico with Todd and a bunch of other youth in July. That mission trip changed my life. Before I went I never felt comfortable worshipping God or talking about God around my parents even though they were Christians themselves. After I got back from Mexico I realized I was totally free. I worship God in church, at home, and I talk about him with my parents all the time. I even spend more time praying and seeking God. I love it. I would go on another mission trip with Todd in a heartbeat. God bless you to the fullest!

Kevin Basconi (Infirmity Prayer Service, Bluefield, WV)

I could write a book about how Todd's ministry changed my life! However, I will put together a couple of short paragraphs. I first met Todd Bentley in a very small church in Newfoundland, Canada, November 2001. During those meetings I was healed of near deafness, a ruptured disc in my spine and heart and lung disease. Today I have perfect hearing, (had it tested), and have not suffered any back pain for nearly 3 years. On the night of November 26th, 2001, at 10:37 pm, after Todd prayed for me and released the healing anointing, I received a visitation of the Lord Jesus which lasted for nearly 5 hours. Since that night I have walked in "the book of Acts" on a daily basis and been released into ministry. I see Jesus heal all types of infirmity in my ministry including around 22 people healed of total blindness, cataracts dissolved, several deaf ears opened, mutes speak, and documented cases of AIDS and cancer healed. I have seen Jesus touch paralytics and raise them up, I have witnessed legs grow more than two inches in length, spines straighten, fingers and toes grow, withered hands restored, and, recently, I saw a blind man, who had no orb, grow an eyeball and have his vision restored. However, the greatest miracle of all is that the Lord has allowed me to lead about 1,380 to Him.

The only Miracle I have not witnessed is the dead raised, and I believe God for that this year. The Lord has supernaturally opened doors for me to minister all over North America, and beyond, confirming his word with signs

255

following. Todd imparted the word of knowledge and I receive detailed downloads from the Holy Spirit on a daily basis including types of illness, how injuries occurred, many times with dates and names, as well as accurate prophetic words of encouragement. I have never had someone who responded to a word of knowledge that Jesus did not touch and heal. I give God all glory for these things. I believe that Todd is a forerunner of the coming move of God in the younger generation. He is called to release this generation into such miracles, signs and wonders that the four walls of our churches will not be able to contain them! I consider Todd to be my mentor and spiritual father even though I am 44 years old.

Jim Drown (Atlanta, Georgia)

I was at Todd's meeting in Atlanta, Georgia about 3 1/2 years ago. I had a growth on my inner thigh that really hurt badly, especially when I walked. I didn't get specific prayer from Todd, just the general prayer for everyone. When I woke up the next morning the growth was gone.

I'd been reading books about John G. Lake and had been asking for a powerful experience with the Holy Spirit, wanting that healing anointing. Todd was the closest thing I'd seen. I started listening to all his tapes and going to more of his meetings and he's right, the anointing is transferable and tangible.

Now I have confidence to do what God has called me to do. We've been doing crusades or meetings about once a month either on our own or with Fresh Fire. We've done several crusades in South America this year and have seen miraculous healings with thousands coming to the Lord.

Ardena Shipp (Canada)

I had been really seeking God's direction in my life. God directed me to take this trip. He provided finances for me that I didn't have which was a miracle. I went on the trip thinking, I know that this is a God-directed thing because I would not just decide to go to Mexico without my friends and I would not just decide to go on a trip like that out of the blue. I am not that adventurous and I am not usually a risk taker. But God is changing me. I prayed that God would teach me about healing and that He would use me to bless others. Praying for others on my own was an easy thing for me but when I would go to pray in groups I would feel bound up. The first night we were in Mexico Todd

256

called us to go and pray with the sick. I remember praying - God help I can't do this without you. We went and prayed for a young girl with a lump in her breast. The lump got smaller as we prayed. We kept praying for her and I felt like I should pray for emotional healing. I was like, "God I don't even know this girl, if this is You, You have to confirm it." The translator suddenly says, "She needs emotional healing." It was so cool—that was all that it took to release me to trust that what I was hearing was the direction of the Holy Spirit. It gave me a confidence to pray with boldness for people all week and it has continued since I returned home. I am walking in an incredible knowledge that my God is a God who heals and one that I can place my hope in. We will see the captives set free and people healed.

Jessica Maldonado *(Gardena, California)*

I've traveled with FFM to Tanzania, Malawi, and South Africa in the summer of 2002 and 2003. Traveling with Todd Bentley has changed my life drastically. The spiritual covering that we ministered under allowed me to move in supernatural ways I had never experienced before. I prayed for the blind, deaf, and crippled and they were healed. My faith grew by leaps and bounds in a matter of seconds and increased rapidly over the following two weeks that we ministered together. It was out of this world!

I always believed that we served the God of the impossible. However, I had never seen Him do the impossible through me. I was blown away and loved every minute of it. I preached at a church of approximately sixty members on a Sunday morning. The Lord used me to prophesy over people. It was like a chain reaction, one after the other non-stop. I didn't know what hit! It had to have been the Holy Spirit because it certainly wasn't me.

Traveling with Todd and the Fresh Fire team has changed my life, expanded my faith and build life-long relationships. I've enjoyed being part of a ministry that truly moves in the full gospel of Jesus Christ and I can't wait to do it again.

Judy Desjardins *(Springfield, Massachusetts)*

I went to Goma, DRC, Africa with Fresh Fire in March 2003. Afterward, I wrote a 16 page report. I was so moved I spent months weeping over Africa, trying to understand all I experienced. I hear the children's voices in my mind's ear still. I see their eyes looking at me. I have never seen such desperation and at the same time so much faith as I saw in those eyes.

The anointing that is on Todd is transferable. My husband and I prayed and God moved with power, healing blind eyes, tumors, fevers, and every sort of sickness. I have faith I never knew I had. We prayed for rain to stop and it did, convincing many that the witch doctors were not as powerful as our God. Many miracles happened.

The last person I prayed for was a believer in Rwanda named Peter. He asked us to pray for his daughter, Glory. This man spoke perfect English. He said a man with AIDS had raped his daughter and his wife was fasting and praying for the test results to come out negative. When I asked how old his daughter was, he said, 2 years old.

This wrecked me. I knew that I could never go back to life as usual. The call of God on my life compelled me to change. I am planning another trip to Africa now. I am going on missions trips until Jesus comes. It was the best choice I made in my life. My husband agrees.

Cliff Pash (Lawrence, Kansas)

When I traveled with Todd Bentley, I saw God work in the same way that He did in the bible. I believe that every believer should accompany somebody such as Todd on a ministry trip. Being a part of a large Crusade is exciting enough, but to see the miracles, the healings and the manifestations of the Power of God as He moves through a crowd is an experience that every Christian must experience. Then, to pray for people under the anointing that God has put upon Todd Bentley, and see our God move and break into lives and change them causes the whole bible to come alive in ways my 30 years of being a Christian never really prepared me for.

For the most part, we are a people who are filled with such doubt and fear and unbelief. While we believe that God exists and that He has the power, most of us have never experienced that power, nor do we believe God would ever manifest Himself through us. To watch tumors disappear, to pray for a woman who was blind for 30 years and see her receive her sight back and to watch as a whole deaf school receives prayer and 28 out of 32 get healed. Well, all doubt, fear and unbelief have just melted away and I am now filled with an awe of God that just continues to grow.

My wife and I have been in business for ourselves for over 20 years.

Our world is being rapidly changed as we find God working through us in ways we had only talked about or dreamed about before. We are being called to ministry work in Uganda and Kenya—that could have never happened years ago. The purpose for which we were created and the works we have been called to are finally being fulfilled.

Debbie Lenz *(Columbia, Missouri)*

Thirty-three years ago I took three years of high school Spanish hoping to travel to Mexico on a mission trip. My 12 year old daughter and I both saw the "Youth Outreach to Mexico" on Todd's website and God quickened it in our hearts. Although I was no longer a youth at 50 years old, and my daughter was only 12, we began to pray about it.

Neither one of us will ever be the same again! Todd has an amazing heart for God and freely imparts everything that God has given him—so we got to do "the stuff!" We saw miracles, healings, deliverances, and salvations as we watched deaf ears open, tumors leave, lung conditions healed, cancer healed, gang members saved, people receive the Baptism of the Holy Spirit, and demons cast out!

While we were in Reynosa, I realized I did not really have a heart for the lost, but I wanted one. The Holy Spirit did that for me. I began to weep uncontrollably as I looked over the homes in the village and realized there were precious people that did not know the saving power of Jesus Christ. I have an intense longing to return and minister in the streets of Reynosa, but now I also have a longing to go into the streets of my own city and see the same things!

I came away with a larger vision of the IMMENSITY and the POWER of God's love. God's heart is that the Holy Spirit would be released in power, that Jesus would be exalted in the earth and that all people would come to know the Father's love. Todd asked me if the trip had met my expectations, and I had to be truthful and tell him, "No, it did not." Then I continued, "It so far exceeded anything I could have ever imagined, or hoped for, or even dreamed about that I can hardly contain what He has done in me!" Would I do it again? Absolutely! In fact, we are already praying about when the Lord will have us return to Mexico with Todd.

Fresh Fire Ministries

Is an international ministry called to global harvest. Todd Bentley and his team take God's saving, healing, delivering power to the nations. Throughout North America sparking revival fire and equipping the body in power evangelism and healing Ministry. As well Todd and his team conduct many healing crusades throughout Africa, India, South America, Europe and beyond. **Thousands have been saved, healed and delivered.** Fresh Fire Ministries Vision is to see people revived in a new passion for Jesus, burning with the fire of evangelism to reach the lost. Todd believes the kingdom of God has come in power and through crusades and healing meetings he reaches out to the lost giving them **more than just words.** Todd believes that in order to have maximum impact he needs to stir the church through revival meetings and ministry resources like tapes and books. Canada will be used of God to send healing to the nations of the world. In (Rev 22:2) it declares that the leaves of the trees were for the healing of the nations. Todd's vision is to see Canada fulfill her destiny and to **GO INTO ALL THE WORLD** and preach the Gospel. Todd has already established contacts in other nations like Africa, New Zealand, England, Russia, India and more. **He has a vision** and is taking healing teams into these nations to bless them with the power of God to save, **heal and deliver.** Fresh Fire is looking for those who will partner with Todd and help him begin to double the impact in every area of ministry. We can only do more with you and your financial gifts and prayers. We at **Fresh Fire Ministries** want to give you the opportunity to give to this ministry and partner with Evangelist Todd Bentley. Not because we need your gifts, but as Paul said, **"I seek the fruit that abounds to your account."** We know that God shall supply all your needs according to His riches in glory by Christ Jesus. One thing that we have noticed over the years is the fact that **God always uses people.** Whenever there is a need God always finds someone with a heart like the Philippians to give.

*If you would like to have Healing Revivalist Todd Bentley speak at your Conference or Church meetings please invite Todd in writing with details of your engagement. You may mail, phone, email, or fax your ministry request to Fresh Fire Ministries head office to the attention of: **FFM Conference & Scheduling Coordinator.***

FRESH FIRE MINISTRIES
PO Box 2525, Abbotsford, BC, Canada V2T 6R3

TEL: 604.853.9041 · FAX: 604.853.5077
EMAIL: Invites@freshfire.ca · WEBSITE: www.freshfire.ca

Journey Into The Miraculous
Todd Bentley: An Ordinary Man Touched By A Supernatural GOD

Todd Bentley's life story will do more than merely entertain you; it will inspire you to believe in a bigger God than you've ever known. You'll read how this supernatural God can take an ordinary man and do extraordinary works through him. Todd's life is truly a miracle! His story testifies to the Father's grace, love and transforming power; it demonstrates that God is truly looking for ordinary people with a "yes" in their spirit to do the "greater works than these" that Jesus prophesied. If you've ever felt disqualified or inadequate to do big things for God then this book will revolutionize your thinking.

The passion of Todd's life and ministry to the nations is to see others come into the reality of intimate relationship with Jesus and to experience the transferable, tangible anointing of the Holy Spirit. Today God is releasing His presence and power through Todd's life to the point where the blind see, the deaf hear and the lame walk, confirming that Jesus still heals every sickness and disease. This anointing is available to enable all believers to fulfill the great commission with miracles, signs and wonders following the message.

Journey Into The Miraculous will give you a greater passion for intimacy with God and convince you that Jesus' words are really true for you, yes; even you…and they're for today. "Preach the Gospel, heal the sick, cleanse the lepers, raise the dead, cast out demons... (Matt. 10:8)" *What are you waiting for?*

For order information contact: Sound of Fire Productions Ltd.
Box 1163, Ladysmith, BC, Canada, Soundoffire@shaw.ca, Tel: 250-245-7003

The Voice Of Healing ... CD

This CD takes prophetic declarations of the coming healing revival, healing prayers from the bible and sets them to original music. It is similar to the "Praying the Bible" series with Wes and Stacey Campbell of Revival Now Ministries.

"The Voice of Healing" is a spontaneous project that will bring the transferable, tangible healing anointing and atmosphere to your home, hospital room or healing service. This is not just a healing prayer CD but a healing experience. This CD will bring you into a healing commission and release faith for the coming healing revival. Experience through healing prayers and music, the healing word that you may be delivered from your destruction.

Soaking In The Secret Place
Prayers for the manifest presence ... CD

Healing Revivalist Todd Bentley's brand new CD on Soaking and Intimacy is finally available after 4 years of Ministry. People have asked all over the world, Todd do you have a music CD we can use when we want to SOAK and wait on the Lord? If you have ever heard Todd's teaching on the Secret Place (Soaking), or as he puts it, pickling in the presence, then this new prayer CD will help you come into the Father's House and sit at the feet of Jesus.

Join Todd on a journey into the Presence of God using prayers from the bible and prayers that come from a deep passion and longing for Him. Prayers for the Manifest Presence is a meditative, contemplative CD with music, combining piano style music, and numerous sounds such as: rain, flute, trumpet, shofar, and more for a deep prayer experience. *ALSO AVAILABLE - INSTRUMENTAL ONLY VERSION!*

FRESH FIRE MINISTRIES
Toll Free: 1.866.853.9041 · Fax: 604.853.5077 · Secure Online Bookstore: www.FreshFire.ca